'Beautifully written . . . I love this book.' India Knight

'Heart-wrenching and beautifully written.' Polly Samson

'Fearless, frank and so beautifully told, *The Wild Other* is a defiant story of love and motherhood in the face of loss. One of those books that makes you resolve to wring every last exhilarating drop from life while you can.' Gaby Hinsliff

'So haunting and brave and beautiful.' Polly Williams

'A dazzling, searingly honest book. Love. Sex. Grief. The Wild West. I couldn't put it down.' Esther Freud

'An extraordinary memoir . . . Stroud writes with moving, eloquent honesty.' Elizabeth Day, *The Pool*

'Life-affirming, whip-smart, gripping, this book crackles with vitality and joy. From tragedy Clover Stroud has conjured sheer brilliance - what a story, what a woman, what a book.' Decca Aitkenhead

'An astonishing book about loss, love, darkness, pain, sex and adventure. I adore it.' Dolly Alderton

'This redemptive memoir will steal your heart; it will return it bruised but emboldened.' *Mail on Sunday*

'Some books have the power to make you reconsider certainties, to reflect, alter and transform previous assumptions about love, sex, freedom, friendship, courage and death. Clover Stroud's memoir, *The Wild Other*, is such a book.' *Telegraph*

'I have huge admiration for the spirit of this memoir, and its author: full of heart, bravery and adventure. A moving, gripping read.' Amy Liptrot, author of *The Outrun*

'A survivor's tale that is both redemptive and cathartic.' *Observer*

'A moving account of the tragic consequences of a horse-riding accident on a loving daughter.' *Sunday Times*

'An uplifting and achingly honest personal story about loss, trauma and grief.' *Woman and Home*

'A startling and raw memoir, which has drawn comparisons to Cheryl Strayed's *Wild* . . . Brave, beautiful writing, which can't help but inspire us to find our own "wild others".' *Red magazine*

'An astonishing piece of work that at times made my heart burst. All of human life is contained in this book. Clover Stroud is a remarkable woman, and an incredible writer.' Bryony Gordon

'Compelling and candid, deftly weaving together past and present . . . a heart-wrenching story told in haunting, lyrical prose.' *Tatler*

'Some events can't be mitigated; they can only be endured with grace and style, something Stroud certainly achieves, to judge from this marvellous book.' *The Spectator*

'Stroud writes with considerable power, resonance and brutal honesty. *The Wild Other* will enthral anyone with wanderlust.' *Sunday Express*

'This heartfelt account begins with a young girl lost in the hinterlands of grief, and ends with a woman coming to terms with the wildness within herself.' *Financial Times*

'There is so much richly evoked life here . . . beautifully written.' Cathy Rentzenbrink, *The Times*

'Enthralling' *Country Life*

'I loved this beautiful, passionate, troubled book, which gallops courageously over difficult terrain. At once a wrenching account of a tragedy and a love letter to the solace provided by horses, Stroud's clear-eyed look at how wildness and domesticity have entwined in her life is both heartening and inspiring.' Olivia Laing, author of *The Lonely City*

'Clover Stroud is a born writer: honest, tender, moving and true. A beautiful book.' Cressida Connolly

'A stunning story of courage in the face of fortune's cruellest blows, Clover Stroud's extraordinary memoir charts her journey from child to adult, from daughter to mother, proving that bravery - and love - will triumph even in the darkest situations.' Rosie Boycott

'Beautifully written and so moving . . . a gritty, passionate, searingly honest meditation on grief, love and motherhood.' Katie Hickman

THE
WILD OTHER

A Memoir
CLOVER STROUD

HODDER

First published in Great Britain in 2017 by Hodder & Stoughton
An Hachette UK company

This paperback edition published in 2018

1

Paperback ISBN 9781473630246
eBook ISBN 9781473630222

Typeset in Bembo Std by Palimpsest Book Production Limited,
Falkirk, Stirlingshire

Printed and bound in Great Britain by Clays Ltd, St Ives plc

Hodder & Stoughton policy is to use papers that are natural,
renewable and recyclable products and made from wood grown in
sustainable forests. The logging and manufacturing processes are expected
to conform to the environmental regulations of the country of origin.

Hodder & Stoughton Ltd
Carmelite House
50 Victoria Embankment
London EC4Y 0DZ

www.hodder.co.uk

For Pete, forever.

CHAPTER 1

I spent the hottest summer of my life shut behind glass. By mid-June my fourth child – a second son, called Dashiell or Dash – was two months old, and I felt completely enclosed. I was here with Dash, and everyone else was over there, in the sun, rainbow prisms of light shimmering around them as they ran through a hose sprinkling cold water onto the lawn, pink mouths open with laughter.

I felt like a fist. Dash was always naked, plastered bare to my breast, sucking from me as my body dripped milk and tears. Here, beside him, was the only space I belonged, even if I could barely breathe. I kept myself pressed to him, limiting the time I had to look away from his tiny face and up out at the world, which had spun right away from me in the weeks since he'd arrived in my arms.

The sitting room and kitchen where I spent most of that summer were on the first floor of our 1960s townhouse. Getting downstairs and out with a new baby and a toddler was a performance, so our home changed from the place where I'd felt most happy to my own private prison. Dash was born when his sister Evangeline was not yet two. She had to be watched, lifted, bathed, fed and cared for all the time as well. We had no garden, except for a communal, unfenced space running onto a road in front of the house. Jimmy and Dolly, my elder children who were then fourteen and eleven, seemed far away from the babies and me all through that summer holiday. Sometimes they ran in and out of view, ice creams running onto wrists and wet hair plastered to their necks, dripping water from the paddling pool on the strip of shared lawn. I sat on the sofa upstairs, feeding Dash, but the toddler Evangeline had to be locked in upstairs too, since she ran into the road if someone didn't watch her all the time.

'Outside,' Evangeline would sigh, climbing onto the back of the sofa, reaching sticky hands up to the big glass windows. She pressed so hard on the glass I was afraid she'd fall through, so a carpenter put wooden bars across the panes. Then the sitting room felt even hotter and the world outdoors even further from reach.

In the late evenings, after it was dark, the elder children would pad around me like leopards, mewing and hissing when I turned around to them on the stairs. In the daytime they ignored me and ran away when I asked them what they wanted for lunch, but when the darkness of night came and Dash and Evangeline slept, they needed me so much. Motherhood was suffocating me.

When Jimmy and Dolly had been born I'd felt like a warrior, but becoming a mother a third and fourth time had undone me. When I looked at Evangeline's tiny hands – curled tight, urgent with need – or the gently closed lids on Dash's tiny face, I became overwhelmed with fear that I'd fail them. I was terrified I'd spent all the mothering I had first time around with my older children.

Depression had first slid inside me when Evangeline was two or three months old. It slunk around after me, following to the shops, waiting at the school gates, sitting beside me in the car, however much I blinked and told myself: 'I'm alright. I'm alright. Am I alright? I'm alright.'

I still felt for my new children every ounce of the painful and ferocious love I'd had for Jimmy and Dolly, the sort of love that made me want to consume my babies, but that love was now undercut by a brand-new sense of panic. It echoed far away, beyond me, but right inside me too, like a quiet, persistent noise in a distant room in my head. That panic switched itself on as soon as I opened my eyes in the morning and rang all day; an inner alarm that stopped me thinking, stopped me being, sometimes stopped me breathing. Several times a day I'd catch myself holding a breath for seconds at a time. I was very far away from everything close to me.

When Evangeline was still a baby, I would take her into bed with me, pretending to sleep. The covers felt like a hide in the forest into which I could crawl to bury myself among the worms, while beetles scurried over me and the wet earth oozed inside my clothes. Sticky with guilt, when sleep finally came it wasn't comfortable, but it silenced the alarm for a bit.

My family and friends came to see my third baby and some of them said to me, 'You must be so happy now,' and I would nod, gulping back at them, 'Yes, I must be so happy.' What they meant was: you must be so happy since for a while back there, Clover, it really looked like you'd fucked up! How you were living back there, with different men in your life, made us uncomfortable.

And they were right because when I lay in silence with my baby, I was happy. But there was also something nameless and murky, imprecise in shape yet as hard as flint inside me. I was living a version of me but it felt like the real me was watching, judging, from a distance. I was beside myself.

In the kitchen I'd turn my back on the sharp silver knife lying beside the onion I'd been slicing, afraid that my hand might quietly run it into my baby's skull. I'd imagine the knife slicing the skull as neatly as a melon and calmly wonder if a baby's head would make that same, soft, wet, *thunk* noise fruit makes when split open. A high window or bridge made me giddy with longing to gently drop my baby over the edge, so I'd tuck my hands under my armpits to make sure I didn't do it. Once, beside the tall stairwell of a friend's house, I'd had to sit on the floor to resist my desire to throw the baby down it. Walking along the river with the baby in a sling, I imagined filling my coat with rocks and wading in because then we could be cosy and go together. I loved them deeply and completely but with a consuming passion that scared me.

More than anything, I was filled with a sense of homesickness for a mother and a home I hadn't known for over twenty years. Being homesick felt like it might kill me.

'Do you imagine harming yourself?'

The health visitor dropped the question into our conversation like an egg yolk falling silently into a bowl of flour, as I poured steaming water over tea bags in my kitchen.

'Of course I do,' I replied, putting the kettle carefully back onto its stand to avoid her eyes. 'I imagine doing the very worst thing I can possibly think of to my baby. And then I imagine killing myself. But isn't that normal?'

I had told her my thoughts, but I imagined it was as obvious to her as day is light that I wasn't going to act on them. She kept telling me about mindfulness so I thought she'd understand. They were just thoughts, taking me to the darkest place they could to teach me how to get back into the light. They weren't real.

She sent me to talk to a perinatal psychiatrist, who filmed me playing with a toy tea set with Evangeline. For the first minute I felt embarrassed by the sound of my own voice, which for the past few weeks had sounded quite alien to me, as if someone else's voice box – lower, sterner than mine – had taken over my throat. I leant forward towards my daughter, holding out a plastic cup while trying to imagine what a good mother might say and how she would sound.

'Evangeline, where is your cup of tea? Is this the teacup?'

Evangeline's cobalt blue eyes fixed on me, as if I really had become the mad woman I felt was living inside me. She grabbed the cup, banging it against a pile of coloured saucers, sending them flying across the mat as her face creased into a pink grin. I clapped, then pretended to drink from it and she laughed again so that I forgot the camera and for a few moments could play with my daughter as if I wasn't being watched and my ability as a mother wasn't being scrutinised.

A week later, in our next session, the psychiatrist played the film back to me. In those few moments of footage, I didn't see myself. Instead I watched a different woman smiling at Evangeline, gently stroking her hair flat, then leaning in to kiss her, and in that moment I felt a thread that had been tugging and tangled inside me suddenly dragged tight. The past was pulled into focus shrill and sharp, delightful and terrible at the same time, and there was my mother in my place. As I watched myself in that footage kissing Evangeline, I understood that that was how she had kissed me, that was how she had cared for me and talked to me. I saw that that was how she had loved me.

Of course it was my mother. My mother, who was alive and dead at the same time.

'Your mum, is she nearby? Could she pop over to give you a bit of a break?' the health visitor asked innocently as we stood in my kitchen again. She had red hair as thick as her Irish accent. It hung in a heavy fringe over her eyes, and she wore leather lace-up boots with flat soles that reminded me of a pair Mum had worn when I was a child: they were green leather with hooks and eyes that she'd tied with black laces.

I paused, pushing the spoon I was using to squeeze water from the tea bags so hard against the edge of the cup that the tea bag ripped, sending black dots of leaves swirling across the water. And then I spoke.

'I do have a mother but she's not here. I mean, she lives quite near here in a nursing home near Swindon, but she's not really around, or here, or anywhere. She's got brain damage from a riding accident on her horse a long time ago and she doesn't know anyone and she can't do anything. She can't talk or feed herself or walk and she's incontinent and has epileptic fits and she doesn't have any teeth any more because she got ulcers so they all had to be taken out and—' I took a gulp of tea, galloping on before she could say anything. I wanted to get it out there quickly, like a road map smoothed open on the steering wheel when you're lost. 'She doesn't know who I am or who anyone is and it's been like that since I was sixteen. She hasn't been able to talk or communicate in any way since then, although she did try to kill herself when I was at university, by taking an overdose of anticonvulsants, and then she was in a coma again for a few days and a bit worse when she woke up. She's lived in hospitals or nursing homes for twenty years now but it's fine. It's really fine. I mean, she's not fine but I'm fine because it's been like that for a long time. So. Well, you know, she's not dead but she's not exactly here either. It was just an accident. A very bad riding accident.'

I smiled at her, to prove I really was OK with it. I'd spoken those words so many times in my life and I always felt I had to reassure the person who had asked, so that they didn't need to be embarrassed by the answer.

The health visitor hugged her hands around her cup, glancing briefly at a recent photograph stuck on the fridge of Jimmy leading a pony along a road. She tipped her head to one side, looking even more concerned than she had a few minutes before.

'And you . . . you still ride, do you?'

I don't know what our childhood would have been like if Mum hadn't left the city and taken us to the country. I cannot conceive of my life now without the influence that ponies and then horses have had on it and the thread they've woven through every single part of my life, even when I didn't know it. We moved from Oxford to a village in Wiltshire when I was seven and when I allow my mind to spool around the maze of other avenues I might have taken, the thing I find hardest to imagine is life without horses.

My life with no horses would have been very different, because if we hadn't moved to the country there would never have been an accident. Or, at least, not a riding accident. There might have been other horrors, because most people have something, but I don't think there would have been an accident quite like that one, which has changed the colour of every single day since then. And although I know my life without the accident would have followed a completely different course, the only one I want is this one, with the accident right in the middle, running through everything I do. The day of the accident wrote *trauma* inside me and I've never rubbed that out because it's part of me and it's mine.

Sometimes my sense of Mum is bound so closely with the accident that I see them both as one word: mumsaccident. Mumsaccident was a single domino that tipped over on 25 November 1991 and sent a trail of little black squares tumbling forward, their onward force unstoppable through time.

The funny thing is that hurting us was the last thing my mother wanted to do. She wasn't barbed and she didn't criticise. 'My mum's a bitch,' my friend Sarah told me on the bus to school, but I didn't understand what she was talking about. Mum was never one of those mothers their daughters complain about. I never wished she'd just leave me alone. I never wanted her to mind her own business; I always wanted her there.

Mum loved expansively. Her love was huge and generous and everywhere, so that just existing a single day as her daughter felt like standing under the bright spotlight of a force that only ever protected. From the day I was born, on 16 April 1975, I had 6,067 days like that before the accident turned the spotlight off; the flick of a switch plunging a bright room into black. That number of days is the same as 866 and a half weeks, or 145,608 hours, or 8,736,480 minutes, or 524,188,800 seconds. It can never have been enough.

Very occasionally, I dream about Mum, but time in my dreams is indeterminate so when I wake up I feel as if she's always been there with me in the thick syrup of sleep, but just a few moments later she's gone again forever. Maybe my sleeping self knows this because when I wake up dreaming of Mum, my face is always wet with silent tears. Give me back just five of those 8,736,480 minutes with her and I promise I'll never complain again.

I don't know if Mum set out purposefully to create a kind of enchantment in our childhood, but it is what she achieved.

'Housewife' isn't the right word to describe Mum, as it makes me think of dusty brushes left too long in a cupboard under the stairs, and she would certainly have resisted the more lyrical, American 'home-maker' too, although that's what she was.

When we were small, Mum occasionally did some very part-time work as a secretary in the psychology department in Oxford. Once, when I was five and Mrs Sandles, the lady who came to clean the house and look after my sister Nell and me when Mum was out, was ill, Mum took me with her. Nell went to play with a friend, but Mum put me into the seat on the back of her bike and cycled to the office.

I sat under her desk and drew a picture of a house on a piece of lined paper, using a ruler and a pencil. The house looked pointy and not like somewhere anyone would want to spend time, so Mum pulled me up onto her lap, tearing a clean piece of paper from her pad.

'Look, what about nice big lines like this?' she said, holding my wrist and sketching the shape of a house across the sheet. I'd tried to draw a tree using the ruler, but Mum created a whole garden and a house with a chimneypot and big windows and an open front door in a few generous strokes. 'You need a garden and lots of rooms for your children and smoke coming out of the chimney so it's cosy like this.' Her long, brown, curly hair brushed against my face as she drew, her hand carefully holding mine. When she hugged me, she smelt of Chanel No. 5 and something else which was only hers that made me feel everything would always be good.

After the accident, when she was in a coma, I went to the cupboard in her room to press my face into the tangle of her scarves – to try and smell her again. The pink silk scarf she wore with a tweed coat swirled away, dizzying me, as the silence of her room enclosed me. I pressed my face hard into that scarf, but it didn't smell like her any more.

The day Mum drew the house with me at the psychology department was not the first time I'd been there. When I was one, Mum volunteered for some research into maternal bonding that was part of a university study. Afterwards, she kept a black-and-white photograph of me by her bed, which was taken as part of the study. Printed from a video still, it had a number on the bottom of it. In it, I'm staring wide-eyed with attention into the camera.

'We had to do little tests, like to see if you would follow my eyes when I was looking in a certain direction, or whether you would look at my hand when I was pointing at pictures,' Mum told me later. 'They looked at lots of mothers and babies, but you and I had the highest score.' She made me feel as though, together, we'd won a big, important competition, and I imagined a whole line of mothers pointing at things to make their babies prove how much they loved them. I'd tell other people about this study: 'Did you know that when I was one I was more closely bonded with my mum than any other baby?'

Mum said we were telepathic too. When I was seven she ran a stall for 'guess the number of sweets in a jar' at the school fete. The jar was a glass spaghetti jar that an actress had given my father after he'd directed her in a film.

'I mean, who on earth bothers to put spaghetti in a jar? Spaghetti gets eaten, not displayed,' Mum had said, stuffing the pale-green glass jar with flumps, white mice and tutti frutti we'd bought in white paper bags from the shop. She wouldn't tell my sister Nell or me how many sweets she'd bought; 'And anyway, you're not going to enter as the last thing I want is this awful jar back in the kitchen,' she said, although I'm not sure it really was the jar that had offended her. My father also had a framed photograph on the mantelpiece in his study of a woman's suntanned, slender feet, with a label attached in elegant handwriting that read, 'It *was* a photograph of my feet you wanted, wasn't it, Rick?' He'd been given the picture by another actress he was working with, and Mum didn't like that photo much either.

We took the spaghetti jar to the school fete and after I'd spent my pocket money on a doll in a knitted dress from the bric-a-brac stall and Nell had won a bottle of Lambrini and a fondue set on the tombola, I persuaded Mum, yawning at her stand, to let me have a guess. I knew I'd guessed just right when I saw a certain look of surprise and irritation pass across Mum's face, although she didn't tell me until later, when I was old enough to understand what telepathic meant. She sent the spaghetti jar off to a child whose father had died falling off a roof fixing some gutters, but she stopped at the shop to buy sherbet lemons for Nell and me on the way home.

It's perhaps misleading that one of my earliest memories of Mum was of her doing the drawings with me in the psychology department, because I don't really remember her sitting down to draw, or sitting down to do anything very much. She was always standing: in the garden to dead-head roses; or at the kitchen table to pound dough for the bread she baked most days – thick brown loaves with crunchy crusts that she'd slice for us while they were still hot, spread with cold yellow butter in pats so thick they looked like chunks of Cheddar. She also stood at the stove to make hot milk with honey for us at bed time, or in the tack room, to clean a bridle, and she stood at the gate too, to watch us on our ponies as Nell and I cantered around the field beyond the house after the hay had been cut.

She was not a mother who did crafting, or who would sit down on the carpet to play with dolls. I don't think I ever once remember her playing a game like that, although when we were teenagers we forced her to play Monopoly when she'd much rather have been watching *Dallas*, because she really liked JR. So Mum didn't really play, but what she was, was always there.

'Isn't it wonderful how they can stick egg boxes together without their hands shaking?' she'd comment, standing behind the sofa after she'd come in from the garden, dogs trailing her, and found Nell and me, legs draped over the edge of armchairs in front of *Blue Peter*. The presenters in primary-coloured jerseys with big hair were making a model village out of cardboard boxes, green felt and poster paint. Mum shifted from one foot to the other, and I felt guilty she'd found us in front of the television when I knew she wished we were out riding before it got dark. 'Wonderful, actually, how they can stick cardboard together in all that fiddly detail without going off their heads,' she said, and then was gone, headed into the kitchen to cut up boiled mutton bones for the dogs.

When I want to find Mum, the place I go in my mind is to Minety, the village we moved to in Wiltshire on my seventh birthday. Nell and I were given kittens called Tibs and Tats, and ponies too, Marble and Pudding. It was a bit like being children in storybooks, the old-fashioned ones that Mum read aloud to us when we were still living in Oxford, and only thinking about ponies rather than living with them, like *The Black Riders* or *Jill's Gymkhana*. Of course she sat down then to read to us, her voice as constant and low as the oily paraffin night flame that she'd sometimes light in our bedroom as a treat, and not just when we were ill.

When I need the deep comfort that really going home feels like Minety is the place I take my mind to. Minety, or Myntey, from the word 'minty', because wild mint grew in the ditches and water meadows around the village where Mum taught me to recognise kingcups, campion, dog roses and harebells. We lived at Hovington House, but Mum hated the name because it sounded grand, so in my mind it's always Minty, Myntey, Minety: the lyrical word from childhood that's also haunted me because of what happened there.

But Minety didn't start until I was seven, so until then the place I remember spending most of my time was on Mum's lap, with my arms around her neck, although the place we actually lived was Oxford. That's a different world altogether, of flagged pavements, towering libraries and redbrick houses with a single light bulb left on in a top-floor window. Wildness as a child in Oxford was confined to the walls of our back garden, and it's not as vivid a place in my mind, nor does it have that pull on my heart that physically hurts me in the way Minety does. I was there but I remember only ever existing in my sister Nell's shadow. People called Nell a tomboy because she wore a blue Aertex shirt and navy cotton shorts and had bare feet all summer. Her short, dark-blonde hair made her look like a boy, and when she was really concentrating, like when we were building a den or cutting an arrow from a stick or tying our Collie dog to the sledge to make a cart, she would bite her tongue between her teeth.

'Me and Nell, we have the same thinks,' I told Mum when I was five or six, but there was a tough physicality to our sisterhood too. When we were very young we'd stick our fingers down our throats, shoulders convulsing as our eyes ran tears of discomfort and also excitement at the strange things we could make our bodies do. Nell would time how long I could hold a fizz bomb sweet in my cheek even when the acid burn hurt my face, and she'd dare me to jump from higher and higher branches of the trees in the garden. I'd always do what she said, gasping at the shooting pain rushing through my heels when the branch was too high.

We loved and fought equally so that the slap of a palm against a cheek, the breathless dig of nails into arms and thighs, and the bee-sting anger of pulled hair was there in our sisterhood too.

'Don't fight, be kind to each other. Be kind,' Mum said as we lay on a scratchy woollen rug on the floor beside her feet, scribbling on the radiator in the kitchen to make wax crayons melt. Nell gave me my first understanding that pleasure and love could hurt. We fought hard but I loved her harder than anything too and I knew she'd die for me.

'Let's make a den,' Nell would say every day, every weekend; we had an obsession to create nests we could call our own around the house and garden. My hands would feel hot and unusually close to my face as we crawled through tunnels we'd made from eiderdowns draped over our beds in our shared bedroom, our teddies and books suddenly looming large in the confines of the den, rather than on high shelves in the playroom downstairs, where everything was a tangle and always a mess.

Mum made us run outside in the early mornings in our pyjamas, out onto the wet dew of late winter, so we could feel greenness beneath our feet. By spring we'd drag eiderdowns shedding feathers or sleeping bags with crinkled orange centres into the garden to zip ourselves into them in the sun, sweating as we lay on our

stomachs and imagined what we'd be when we grew up. I wanted
to be a cowgirl, but Nell's ambition was to be a monkey trainer
and she slept with toy monkeys clustered around her head.

'Tell me when you're going to shut your eyes and I'll shut mine
at the same time,' I'd whisper to her as we lay in the dark of our
bedroom. But that was only at night. Nell is two years older than
me so she started school before I did, and Mum believed in putting
me to bed for an afternoon rest even when I was four. Then, I'd
lie alone. Sometimes I'd hear a clop on the pavement outside, and
would creep from my bed so Mum couldn't hear to sit on the wide
window ledge and watch the street outside. I'd always think the
sound might be a pony walking down the road; I'd feel only disappointment when all I could see was a woman in high heels, smoking
as she passed.

The landmarks of our life in Oxford were the place at the end
of the garden where my dad had a bonfire, the redbrick garden
walls that enclosed us, and the grey pavement outside the front of
the house. If we were being adventurous, there was the post box
at the end of the road, but that was a no man's land that Mum
didn't really let us visit on our own.

By moving to the country, Mum threw the boundaries of our
world wide open. The pavements became fields around the house;
our enclosed garden transformed into a tangled wilderness with a
stable block with a tack room that smelt of leather, and a pond
where muddy ducks splashed through shallow water. The post box
was replaced by the village shop where we bought cola bottles and
prawn cocktail crisps. And Nell was still barefoot all the time, even
when we were riding our ponies.

What happened to Mum in the accident on 25 November 1991,
and then for a long time afterwards, was as violent as flames licking
through a house, burning everything that's there and leaving the
heart black like charcoal. But in all the days which made up sixteen
years of my life before that happened, she was just love.

'Do you love me more than a thousand monkeys?' Nell would ask her, standing barefoot on the tiled kitchen floor as Mum stirred handfuls of cheese into sauce for fish pie.

'More than all the jewels in all the world,' Mum would reply, beating melting cheese into the yellow sauce.

'More than a million pounds?' I'd say, pushing in front of Nell, hungry to be part of their exchange.

'It doesn't even compare,' Mum laughed as the sauce thickened and she pulled it from the cooker. 'You can't think about love like money. I love you more than you can imagine, more than any number your mind can think of,' she said, pouring the sauce over a dish of cooked fish coloured with pink prawns, then opening the back door so that sunshine spilt onto the kitchen floor and we blinked in the sudden warm light.

Hovington House wasn't grand but it was big, with a swarm of rooms, some with two or three doors so that 'Shut the door, it's freezing out there!' was shouted to anyone who went into the playroom. There were two staircases – games of hide and seek could last for hours – and enough bedrooms that when our elder brother and sisters, Tom, Emma and Sophy, came home at the weekends, there was always somewhere for them to sleep, even when Mum's Citroen picking up from the Friday night train from London was full of visiting friends.

The house breathed with new people on Fridays. My father Rick worked in London all week but caught the train home at the end of the week, when the kitchen table would be crammed with people and Mum would ladle out soup bowls of beef stew and the bottles of red wine would sink fast, as candles overflowed with yellow wax into the grooves in the table.

Mum and Rick laid that beautiful life out for us like cakes with shiny coloured icing on a tartan rug. Mum let the grass on the lawn around the house grow very long, then mowed paths through it, leading out to the stables, where horses stamped in the shade, and beyond to the pond and herb garden, past a tangle of Virginia creeper which smothered the base of the big yew tree whose blood-red berries I'd split between my fingers and thumbs because I liked seeing the poison on my skin.

There was no uniformity at Minety. The rooms that slid into cold tiled corridors and then twisting stairways without any order were covered with walls of books and a patchwork of watercolour paintings beside Lyons coffee adverts and pop-art posters my father Rick drew in his study. There, three walls were covered with video tapes marked with strips of white gaffer tape with their titles written in felt tip in my father's strong writing: *The Dam Busters*, *Paris Texas*, *A Bridge Too Far*, *The Rocky Horror Picture Show*, *Once Upon a Time in the West*, *Nashville*. I didn't like going into Rick's study in the week when he was away and the curtains were drawn, but at the weekend it became an exciting place to be, especially as I got older and was allowed to stay up after supper to watch films with Rick, Mum and Nell. There was a hand grenade on his desk, and a glass bottle with three painted cigarettes in it that Rick's sister had given him when he stopped smoking the 100 a day he smoked when he met Mum. He was an undergraduate of twenty-one back then, and she was thirty-two, with three children – my siblings Emma, Sophy and Tom – and a divorce behind her.

Nell and I always called him Rick, not Dad, since that's what Emma, Tom and Sophy called him, as he was their stepfather. He often didn't feel like a 'dad', either. If I went to play with a friend after school, the sunny afternoon their mother had set up in the back garden might be darkened by the arrival of 'Dad', who was usually cross and tired and didn't want to find screaming children in the back garden. Those children's dads came back from work in a suit, carrying a briefcase, and Rick never had those. He usually wore a leather jacket and was the first person I knew to buy Timberland boots.

If Mum was all-embracing love, Rick brought glamour and excitement home to Minety. He smelt of London and although he was a television director for a while he also had an advertising agency in Soho with an office with a glass desk and very shiny wooden floor. He talked about actors and shoot schedules, and when I watched a film with him he made me feel part of it by telling me about the continuity or lighting of each shot, and how the casting agent had got the characters just right. When he was away on shoots he'd send me postcards with the cartoon characters he created but I liked it better when he came home. Then Mum was always laughing.

In the summer after we moved from Oxford to Minety, a lot of my parents' friends came to stay, bringing children they'd unpack from their cars. Those children would blink and yawn before vanishing into the depths of the garden with Nell and me to make dens. Mum's friend Candida also came to stay. She and her daughter Lucy drove her horse and cart over, pulled by her skewbald mare, all the way from her house near the Ridgeway.

I knew Candida well because Mum and Rick often took us to her house for lunch with her husband Rupert. They lived in a huge house with their five children, who felt like versions of my brother and sisters. It was an intimidating, beautiful place, with rooms painted in jewel colours and a wide river running through the bottom of the garden. After lunch Candida would usually take us out for a drive along the Ridgeway on one of her carts. She had an elegant dog cart with vast wheels, and a covered wagon painted with all her children's names, but I liked the governess trap best. It had a neat door with a brass handle, through which you would let yourself into the back of the cart, and padded leather seats. Candida let Mum drive me in that cart, and I felt excited by the way the cart bounced along as Candida's pony cantered across one of the fields by her house, although it was scary too, and made me grip harder onto the sides of the cart.

When Candida arrived at Minety on her cart that summer, I watched her in the stable yard as she fetched buckets and sponges so she could wash the sweaty pony down. My jodhpur boots were grubby and my jeans grimy with grease from my pony's saddle, so I was envious of the way Candida managed to deal with the sweat of her horse but still look beautiful. She wore brown cowboy boots and a long red skirt with a thick leather belt with a gold buckle, which matched the tiny gold heart she wore on a chain around her neck and the gold heart studs in her ears. When she smiled I could see all her teeth and she called me darling, even when she was talking to her horse at the same time.

Rick had made a table using breeze blocks and a trestle top, setting it up under a hazel tree in the garden. Mum and Candida sat in the shade under the light-green leaves of the tree and Mum smoked Silk Cut from a packet my brother had left at the weekend. Candida shook her head when Mum offered her one, saying she thought she'd start again after her dad died, but she hadn't. Mum broke off crumbs from a loaf on the table, waving her hand across the dish of macaroni cheese where flies were buzzing, and threw the crumbs to the chickens scratching nearby. The dogs stretched under the tree, panting in the heavy, late summer heat. Mum and Candida talked about the names of the roses and what herbs Mum might grow and where in the garden would be the best place for a party.

'It's heaven here,' said Candida, stretching her neck backwards so that her blonde hair fell down her back like a silk curtain. 'Complete heaven. I don't want to go anywhere else ever again.'

After Evangeline and then Dash were born, a sense of our home at Minety came rushing back to me with a force that hit me so hard it felt like repeated physical blows. The house came alive again in my mind, even though I hadn't been there since I was eighteen, twenty years before, when the events of the accident were only two years old. I'd shut it away for two decades, but becoming a mother for a third and fourth time magnified it terribly, so that I felt the past and present were competing as places I wanted to be, and the past was always winning. Trying to find Minety in my head turned into postnatal depression, although my friend Virgil has a theory that women succumb to postnatal depression after childbirth because in labour they touch the gaps between life and death.

I am not scared of labour. I love every part of it and, if I could, I'd do it this evening as I'd certainly far rather give birth than have to cook supper. I love the pain, and the exhilaration of holding a slippery new life in my arms, and I even love the feeling of the battering my body's been given in the days afterwards. When I'm giving birth, I feel my role in this life is at its most vivid and precisely defined. There's no smudginess but instead just ecstasy. The slump of postnatal depression was the diametric opposite of this emotional clarity. It was far, far more painful than childbirth, and unlike labour went on for weeks and months, not hours.

When Dash was born, those gaps in between were so vivid that for a moment my mother was in the labour room with me. It was at the moment when my body was resisting the test lying before it. My labours have been successful when I've moved right into them, rather than retreating, but at that moment I was overwhelmed as contractions hit me every few seconds. Clear fluid laced with blood and strings of gunk ran down my thighs as I gripped the edge of the bed. I was scared and crying, my courage deserting me, but in a few empty moments I looked up across the room and suddenly she was there.

'Come across to me,' she said. 'Come across. Come to me.'

She was there in the room, smiling and talking to me as I'd last seen her twenty-two years ago before the accident. I went towards her in my labour and then, with a rush, Dash was arriving, and Mum had gone.

The one thing that did make me feel better, as my life, pixelated with depression, started coming back into focus as Evangeline approached one, was a small white pony called Bliss. We kept her in a segment of damp fields on a farm between the edge of Oxford and the ring road, where buses rushed past beyond a thick black-thorn hedge and fallen-down stables held together with tarpaulin and string. The land was on the green belt, a bucolic echo of a bigger farm long since swallowed up by houses and dual carriageway.

The same family had owned it since the war, running it as a dairy and piggery, but most recently a livery yard where ponies grazed in the fields running down to the Thames with the spikes and spires of Oxford behind them. As a livery yard it struggled, as most people with horses want a floodlit indoor arena for show jumping and proper hacking, neither of which it had, but as a result the grass rent was very cheap.

All summer, my daughter Dolly and I biked through the housing estate with Evangeline in a bike seat, to this haven on the edge of Oxford where I'd teach Dolly how to pick out Bliss's hooves or tie her lead rope into a slip-knot. The ring road rushed past on the far side of the field from the yard, but I found it calming: the tangle of jangled nerves in my head smoothed themselves when I was with my daughters and the ponies. It was familiar, like being at Minety.

Dolly and I found unexpected bridle paths running round the edge of Oxford. I'd lead Dolly around those paths, past hedgerows laden with early green blackberries, and then out into an underpass coloured with graffiti and into the housing estate where we lived, ready to buy sweets at the corner shop.

Once, after Dash had been born, I rode Bliss alone through the fields that bordered the city, even though my legs dangled below her girth. It rained hard: hot, fat drops of English summer drenching my T-shirt as we trotted through a dripping, green landscape north of the city but still within the ring road. Flashes of river appeared behind the bank of nettles running alongside the hawthorn hedges dividing the fields.

I jumped off to drag open a rusting gate, which led to a field of shoulder-high reeds. On the far side of the river I could hear the pulse of urban life, and behind me a police siren tore along the ring road, but the fields were a pocket of wilderness I'd found in the gaps in between. I rode on around the edge of the field, skirting the hedge where fat bumblebees hummed over dog roses, and under the spreading canopy of an oak tree, where four deer sprang out of the rushes, startling their heads to stare at us, making Bliss snort and prance like a thoroughbred. The deer fled, bouncing away through the reeds, towards the city, so I kicked my pony onwards to canter to the top of the field. There was nowhere else to go. We'd ridden to the edge of the city and the fields had ended at the metal crash of the ring road, where cars sat bumper to bumper in teatime traffic. I'd felt as if I could ride for ever.

But I couldn't ride for ever, because I had to go back home to look after the babies. As I sat feeding Dash with the blinds pulled down against the intense summer heat in our upstairs sitting room, all I could think about was escaping to a place where the ponies and the outside world could be part of our lives all the time, not just something we visited.

Outside, the sound of Jimmy and Dolly's laughter carried up to the sitting room above, but I didn't hear it. All I heard was the muted suckling of my child. All I saw were the walls shutting me in. I couldn't breathe.

Before that summer was over, we went to Wales. Oxford was dull with heat as life flattened into the shapeless morph of August. In the suburbs, boys, stripped to their shorts, sat on garden walls drinking Lucozade and smoking in the shade. The glass separating me from my children and from my life was now so familiar I couldn't even remember what it felt like to be present. In the back of the car, Jimmy and Dolly argued over my iPhone, as Dash mewed in his car seat. I switched on the radio to cover the sound of the children, pulling dark glasses over my eyes that were fixed on the road.

Three hours later, the diamond brilliance of rain on bright emerald hills greeted us. I opened the window, cold air rushing into the hot cocoon, and I felt a throb of unfamiliar energy – enthusiasm, even – dart through me, like the hills before us had sprung open, showing me their elemental heart.

We stayed in a slate-grey cottage surrounded by green. At night it was deep dark: Jimmy and Dolly slept together in a single bed, and the skylight above them was a square of silver stars pricking holes in an onyx sky. We had a picnic at Raglan Castle and, on the advice of a guidebook, one rainy day we went to Brecon to go to the local butcher. The shop had a door made of strips of striped plastic and displayed green pieces of plastic parsley between the mincemeat and rows of sausages. There was a corkboard on one wall, covered with photographs of local events: a man doing a thumbs-up to the camera at a classic-car display sat beside images of a school fete and a handful of pictures of a local gymkhana; children beaming into the camera, rosettes tucked into the sides of their ponies' bridles as parents looked on.

I studied the pictures as the butcher made a joke about the weather. Dash struggled in his sling on my front, and I kissed his soft head, catching sight of the butcher's blade as it flashed through slabs of red meat. I watched, but looked away quickly as the butcher wiped his hands in red streaks on the front of his white overalls.

'Well, you know what they say about the weather in Wales?' the man asked, in an accent that took his voice in surprising directions. 'If you don't like it, wait a bit, then see what happens.'

He smiled, handing me the change, as if it was all so obvious.

We cooked the lamb steaks on a disposable barbeque beside a stretch of river near Brecon. We'd waited long enough and the butcher was right: the rain stopped, revealing a wet landscape, which blinked as if astonished to find itself bathed in clear afternoon light. The grass was drenched – too wet to sit on – but Jimmy and Dolly happily played tag in the field as Evangeline crouched down to watch me light the barbeque, the coals turning white as Dash slept in his buggy.

Jimmy and Dolly's voices bounced back to me across the field as they climbed on a gate where some ponies were grazing. The steaks fizzed on the flames; when I lifted them from the metal grill, they were criss-crossed with black marks. As Evangeline played with some buttercups in the grass, Dash woke up, gnawing on his wrists, oblivious to anything but the moment. I pulled my denim jacket off to use as a blanket to sit on as I watched the steaks colouring and then sliced the white loaf and cucumber we'd bought in Brecon. On the far side of the field, my elder children moved around in my vision, laughing as they leant over the gate to look at the ponies, and sunlight dazzled. And, for the first time in months, the glassy sadness trapping me was gone and a stillness sat in my head instead.

The butcher had been right. The field, the fire, the ponies and the glassy brilliance of the wet landscape. I needed the children to live like this, not just for a few days on holiday, but for their whole childhoods. It all seemed so clear now.

I lifted the steaks off the flames, setting them aside on the cardboard wrapping of the barbeque. Jimmy and Dolly had moved on around the edge of the field, ignoring my calls to come back to eat. Taking Evangeline's hand, I left Dash staring into the grass in his buggy to walk with my youngest daughter through the long, thick, wet grass to where the three ponies grazed.

The grey pony lifted its head, mid-chew, a thick fringe of mane obscuring its eyes. It watched Evangeline and me for a moment, then went back to the grass. Along the hedge line, Jimmy waved to us, so that Evangeline disentangled her hand from mine and ran away from me towards her elder brother and sister.

I rested my forearms across the top of the gate, laying my head sideways on my arms, and closed my eyes. There was no sound, no birdsong: nothing except the rushing of blood in my head and the silent pressure of the ponies, heads down, working their way through their grazing. The top of the metal gate felt cool against my palms and the warm air made my breathing deepen. The deep green of the landscape enveloped me, so that time moved backwards and instead of my own children on the far side of the field, I saw myself, in a flash, as a child, walking beside Mum on a green hill with a white chalk track running ahead of us.

I opened my eyes, turning my face to the sky and the red kite, which wheeled around, an endless spin of energy way up there beyond my reach, like a thread of life looping me out of this present moment from my children and back to Mum; and back further beyond her too, into a past I didn't know and yet was so strongly a part of that it was within me all the time.

Five months later, we left the city and I moved back to the country. We found a green hill, just outside Oxford in a village called Baulking, beneath the shadow of the Ridgeway near Uffington, where an ancient chalk horse galloped across the hill beyond the bedroom window.

CHAPTER 2

A white, hard day in early February, six weeks after moving to Baulking, and the belly of sky isn't blue today. It's white in the best patches, but mostly grey like dirty iron. Specks of black crow wheel above, keeping track, as there's no one here but Dash and Evangeline and me. It's as cold as glass on White Horse Hill, and my hands in purple woollen gloves grip the handles of the double buggy like they're separate from my body. I'm rushing, breathless, because the sound of the children whining makes me keep on moving very fast. I shush them, ignoring their demands to stop. If I lose momentum, it will only result in pointless clambering in and out of the buggy and dropped gloves from tiny, icy hands.

'Look, look, what are we going to find up here? Are we going to find something wonderful, Evangeline? What will there be at the top of this hill? Dash, can you imagine what will be here? Will we find a dragon? Or a white horse?'

Their small red faces implore me to take me somewhere different, inside, but I march on. I'm impatient with the children, irritated I can't see the white chalk horse I've promised Evangeline. I really wish I could escape the cold and the whining, until I force the buggy up the final slope of the hill fort on top of the hill, then turn around.

Everything is suddenly silenced. The dark winter world in the valley below throws itself open and beneath me is the horse, because we're standing right on top of it. I exhale, feeling the jagged irritations that have been scraping inside me smooth out. I feel part of the land and sky, but separate too, like I'm watching myself standing on the hill where it's silently starting to snow, even though the villages below look wrapped up and warm. Beside me, Evangeline has unclipped herself from the seat and is scrambling from her buggy like she's climbing from a great height.

'Cooooooowwwwwld,' she says, screwing up her face as she tugs at my legs, so I lift her into my warm arms. 'Cowld, cowld Mumma.'

The air has anaesthetised Dash, who is now sleeping under his blanket in the buggy. I lift Evangeline's face to mine, our cheeks touching.

'Come on, let's run while Dashy sleeps,' I whisper. Barrelling through the flecks of snow, we run around the White Horse, which stretches out over an acre of the hillside like a Mensa mathematics puzzle. 'Hold on tight, Evangeline, we're going to fly!' I laugh as I leap, as if stepping off the world, into the chalk circle forming the eye of the White Horse. 'Wish, Evangeline. Make a wish with me. Make a wish.'

★

I was nine when I first walked on the White Horse and since then it's held some of my most powerful secrets and longings; there's a local superstition that a wish made standing in the horse's eye will come true. 'Please respect this ancient monument and refrain from walking on the horse,' instruct the National Trust signs on the hillside, and I do, of course I do, but sometimes the urge to get right inside the horse and feel its chalky whiteness beneath my boots is too great to resist.

'Clover, is it? Three leaves or four, darlin'?' is a line I've often heard from men who think they're being original while pressing themselves against me. Those men were not magic, but magpies, black cats and salt thrown into the eye of the devil have a power I do believe in, and standing in the eye of the White Horse is a place where I can believe in luck and the force of time and landscape as much as fortune.

Uffington White Horse lies on the Ridgeway, which gets its name from '*hrycg*', an Anglo-Saxon word meaning 'ridge'. Crossing time and space, this prehistoric route runs from the ancient stone circle at Avebury across the North Wessex Downs and up to Streatley, where it crosses the Thames and continues into the Chilterns, touching the furthest suburban fringes of London to become the Icknield Way. It has been many things, but was certainly a route across country from the Channel to the North Sea, and while the Romans ignored the Ridgeway, since it was too high and dry to be that useful, they used parts of the Icknield Way for their road system. The sprawling mass of Swindon lies below, but the height and loneliness of the Ridgeway means it feels like a wilderness, even with the main railway line from Paddington and the M4 trundling along in the distance.

When I was younger, Swindon was the stop before Kemble where my father got off the Friday night train back home from London. There are daffodils painted onto the posts of the station at Kemble, and hanging baskets of coloured flowers, which mean it's always in the running as the prettiest station in Britain, but I can't drive past a sign to it without a spasm in my body: muscle memory responding to a blow. Kemble was where Mum had her accident on the disused airfield, where the overgrown grass hid strips of old concrete, which her horse fell on that day.

Swindon has nothing on me, though. Sometimes I take a deep breath before plunging into the retail parks there to buy new school shoes for the children. Swindon really does sprawl, and the shops lie beside housing estates called 'The Orchard' or 'Meadow View', because Swindon swallowed whole villages which lay between it and Minety when we were children.

'Swindon's the fastest-growing town in Europe,' Mum told me as we drove home from Cirencester, where we'd been food shopping before the weekend. In the back seat of the car was a bridle she'd had re-stitched at the saddler and beside it was the wicker basket she used as a handbag. Propped up inside were large blue legal notepads, so I knew she'd spent the day volunteering at the local court as a JP, or justice of the peace. When we moved to Minety, she threw herself into village life, volunteering on the parish council and playing a visible role on the church flower rota. Our garden was separated from the church by a high limestone wall and Mum went to church at least once a day on a Sunday, sometimes twice if there was evensong as well as a morning service. When I was too small to see over the pew, I liked kneeling by Mum, trying to picture Magnificat as a huge black panther, and then later, as a teenager, making the achingly long sermon pass faster by flicking through the prayer book and mentally inserting the names of boys from Pony Club that I hoped I might marry in the order of marriage service.

Mum had got bored of the academics and claustrophobia of Oxford, and she enjoyed village life. She certainly would never have been organised enough to wield a clipboard, or manage the village hall accounts, but her father had been a vicar and she loved the church. Her church flowers were like those she picked for the kitchen table or to go on the mantelpiece in the playroom: big, wild arrangements of cow parsley, horse chestnut and daisies in the early summer, or bay, ivy and hellebore when it was cold.

Mum didn't work in the sense of having a career or doing a job, but as we grew out of babyhood she was driven to be something beyond just our mum. She sat as a JP in Malmesbury, overseeing petty cases in the local courts, and became increasingly interested in penal reform. When I asked her why Swindon was growing so fast, she said it was because of computers.

'IT, and I think that stands for information technology,' she said smartly. That morning in court, she'd heard a case of a man who was being charged with possession of stolen goods, specifically a computer mouse. 'I felt sorry for him because it wasn't worth very much so he must have been absolutely desperate to steal it. Although what a computer mouse actually is . . . Well, I really can't tell you that, Clover,' she said, raising her eyebrows to mock her own ignorance as she reached for one of the buns we'd bought in the bakery in Cirencester.

The bakery was called Anne's Pantry and sold sugar cakes called honey buns, which had a thick crust of melted sugar on their base, a sweet, doughy centre and a dusting of sugar on top. I've never eaten buns as sweet or strangely delicious as those anywhere else, and since Anne's Pantry is now an antique shop, I probably never will again. Mum had bought two bags of buns because we had friends coming for tea. We never ate the buns that day, though, because just before Minety we saw a wide verge where two horse-drawn wagons with lurchers chained under them were parked up in the grass. Four heavy black-and-white gypsy ponies grazed on tethers in the cow parsley while smoke from a campfire floated under a line of washing slung between the wagons. Mum darted out of the car, grabbing the buns from my lap and leaving the engine running as she handed them over to the family who stood in the waist-high cow parsley.

When she got back in the car, her face was bright, like that glitter of raindrops when they're just caught in the grass.

'I can't resist them. The washing and the ponies and the camp-fire. There are always more honey buns but the gypsies . . .' Her voice sounded distant as she glanced sideways at me, observing me sulking about my lost buns. 'They're just so beguiling, with their black-and-white ponies, aren't they, Clover, darling?'

After that, Mum took our grey riding pony, Annie, to be broken in to pull a cart by her friend, Mark Palmer, who lived near Cirencester. Mark was a horse dealer who had travelled with horses and wagons in the 1960s and still trailed an intoxicating sense of everything illicit.

'He's the original New Age traveller,' Mum told us, sounding almost breathless as we took Annie over to his yard. Black-and-white horses bobbed their heads in and out of his stables, and some fat brood mares grazed comfortably in the paddock above the house. Mark was younger than Mum but didn't look like a lot of the people I'd met around horses since we'd moved to Minety. He wore a red satin bomber jacket rather than tweeds or a waxed jacket, and his grey spiked hair was shaved into a Mohican. Mum had told me she loved his deep, almost lyrical voice because it made her feel more confident when she was around horses. He leant up against his car as he told Mum about the work he would do with Annie, and in the back I could see leopardskin seat covers slung with a saddle. When Mark smiled at Mum, gold teeth glinted in his mouth.

Annie stayed with Mark for a few weeks while he taught her how to wear a thick leather collar to pull the weight of a cart from behind her, rather than just support a rider on her back. He harnessed her to a tyre first to drag around his yard, then yoked her up to one of his green-and-yellow flat carts. Annie was broad-shouldered, a Welsh mountain cross with kind eyes and pointed ears who took easily to driving. After Mark had taught her about carts, Nell and I drove her all summer, and she became a form of transport we could use to move between neighbouring villages with our friends to swim in gravel pits when the nights were hot.

Mark came to stay at Minety too. He was travelling to a horse fair in Somerset with his painted wagon. Nell and I helped wash his horse down in the yard, then hammer a tethering stake into the lawn so it could graze. Although Mark ate the lasagne Mum had cooked in the kitchen with us that evening, when it got dark he lit a campfire on the lawn, the flames making the shadows of the fruit trees move like small spectres on the grass.

'You could join me on the road, girls,' he said, his golden teeth shining through the darkness.

The next morning, both of us screamed at Mum and Rick when we were posted off to school on the bus. I didn't understand how they could be so completely unreasonable. I thought I'd never see another wagon again, let alone have the chance to travel in one. On the school bus I hated my tight nylon blazer and the morning

sunshine beating through the coach window. I felt furious, longing
for some of the wildness Mark had showed us, for the timeless clop
of horses' hooves on the road as wagon wheels rolled behind.

A weakness for a black-and-white pony is what makes me, thirty-
one years later, drive three hours from Baulking to Leominster
on a hot Saturday afternoon to look at a miniature skewbald
Shetland pony called Holly. She's no bigger than a large Labrador
with a shaggy brown-and-white mane and I watch Evangeline
falling for her with all the same fervour Mum would have done.
Evangeline is small for her age but has a reckless energy, like
Jimmy when he was very little. When she was seven months old
she climbed out of her high chair and she hasn't stopped jumping
since. The house in Baulking has a very small paddock that's just
big enough for an equally tiny pony. I buy Evangeline a cub
saddle, which has a high pommel to hold her snug and a handle
at the front, so Evangeline doesn't have to struggle with the
complexities of reins.

Holly's arrival also means I can avoid those hours in a park spent
standing behind a swing or waiting at the bottom of a slide. Instead,
there's a pony to play with. Evangeline and Dolly pull bits of old
tack from a cardboard box in the barn, leather browbands and
mismatched stirrups scattering around the garden as they buckle
up the cheek piece to the smallest snaffle bit I can find.

Outside our house in Baulking is a village green of 17 acres
stretching a mile along a track, which leads into open countryside.
There are a dozen houses around the green and a lake on one side
through a field of reeds used for thatching, and in late May cows
are put out to graze on the green. In the distance, to the south, is
the crooked horizon of the Ridgeway, and stuck onto that the
outline of the White Horse.

Dolly runs up and down the green with Holly on a leading rein,
Evangeline riding in a red tutu over jodhpurs and a crash hat
covered in purple-and-pink racing silk. Trotting makes Evangeline

bounce up and down in the saddle, her crash hat bobbing on her head as she squeals at the speedy feeling of being on a pony.

'And her smell,' says Dolly, leaning down to stroke Holly's tiny ginger muzzle. 'I don't want to wash my hands but always have the smell of pony on my hand.' Dolly cups her hand over my face so I can smell Holly too, and for a moment I'm back with Candy, the pony who really taught me to ride. He was the colour of mushrooms left a little too long in damp grass, with black eyes and a thick mane falling on either side of his neck.

'Hold on to his mane if you think you're going to fall,' my aunt, Theresa or Teesa, used to tell me, when we stayed with her in Northumberland in the school holidays. My earliest pony experiences took place in those school holidays. Candy was her pony, along with a hillside of heavy cobs, hysterical racehorses, sleek hunting horses and a scrappy selection of ponies for her two sons; my cousins, Sam and James. Teesa can make anyone sit on a horse, even the boyfriend who's never been outside London and feels concerned about his suede shoes and leather jacket. She's the sort of woman who hoots with laughter and strips off to nothing to swim naked through a lake in midwinter. 'Like Rambo,' said one friend, breathless after I introduced him to Teesa. We didn't move to Minety until I was seven years old, so earliest pony life was in the school holidays staying with Teesa and Mum.

Rick was often working when we were children, directing *Coronation Street* straight out of university, or living Monday to Friday in Manchester or Glasgow when he was working for Granada, or then, later, in London during the week, or shooting abroad. He was there for my early childhood, but because work took him away, Mum's the continuous note, at least until I was a teenager. After Mum's accident, Rick's figure comes into bright, vivid focus and stays there, always walking beside me when I need him, his hand on my shoulder when I falter, his presence beside me only increasing with the passing of time.

Even though he didn't like the mucking out that went with our ponies and mostly left it to Mum, Rick really liked coming to Pony

Club events and horse trials to watch Nell and me compete. Then he would pretend to be fiercely competitive, shouting instructions at us as we approached the water jump, when he couldn't really identify the difference between either of the grey ponies Nell and I were riding.

Almost all of the time Rick let us do exactly what we wanted and he didn't often tell Nell and me off for anything, except when he thought we weren't trying hard enough at school. Then he'd make it clear how disappointed he felt and that he didn't want to talk to us until we were doing better.

Because he worked so hard to support Mum and her five children, Rick didn't often come on holiday with us, avoiding the long drives to stay with our cousins in Scotland, Norfolk, Northumberland or Cornwall, and instead catching a train to meet Mum for a weekend at either end of our break. It was Mum who would pack every inch of her burgundy Citroen with luggage, squashing Wellington boots, suitcases and dog beds onto the back seat while Nell and I made nests in sleeping bags in the back, our bodies pressed against the boot door. I loved the feeling of being cocooned in the hot car with just Mum and Nell, especially when it was raining and I'd watch the drops of water jumping along the top of the window. Nothing felt safer.

Holidays with Teesa were never like the deep relief I felt when school was over for weeks and I could just be with Mum and Nell, since the sort of mothering she provided was sharper and louder than my mother's, but it was daring and made my palms prickle with adrenalin.

'Faster, go faster, kick on, let him go, kick on' was Teesa's refrain if we trotted rather than cantered. She wanted us to gallop and jump, and fall off and then get straight back on again. 'Treat the ponies like motorbikes,' she instructed us.

She knew how to make ponies as desirable for her sons as the motorbike her husband Derwy kept in the garage. James was constantly being shouted at, usually when he was found leaning over the petrol tank, inhaling fumes, and we were all told off when I burned my leg on the exhaust pipe after Derwy had put the bike away. We weren't supposed to be sitting on it and the burn felt like a wasp sting.

With Sam and James, Nell and I spent days on ponies on the fell behind their house, taking a picnic and a watch so we knew when to come home. We rode through mossy forestry the colour of dark-green wine bottles, stopping to poke sticks into the heaps of ant hills that lined the shaded tracks, then kicking our ponies on to jump over trees fallen across the way. The forestry felt cloyingly artificial compared to the wide open fell above the house, where we'd pick handfuls of yellow gorse flowers, cupped in our hands like sweets because they smelt of peaches when we pressed them to our faces. Teesa taught us how to tie our reins to our stirrups so the ponies could graze free beside us. Then we would lie on the grass shorn short by the fell sheep to picnic on egg sandwiches and Penguin biscuits, sharing a plastic tonic bottle filled with lemon barley water.

On the fell the domesticated dens of our Oxford back garden became much bigger camps that we'd build around the grey, flat stones dotting the landscape. We were children, so hierarchy mattered. Nell would always be leader, with Sam her attendant, even though he was a few months younger than me. James, a year younger than him, was my natural twin.

'We're fledglings together, Clo,' he'd say, and I'd take his hot, pudgy hand in mine to go and look for the rotted dry logs that Nell had sent us off for. Back at camp, we'd break the logs open to reveal white, flaky wood which would become the most vivid roast chicken for Nell's pretend campfire kitchen.

We spent two weeks every summer with Sam and James in our early childhood, and sometimes we'd do Pony Club rallies, learning how to rise to the trot and lean forward as Candy moved over coloured poles on the ground. It meant that, by the time we moved from Oxford to Minety, Nell and I knew how to sit on a pony with heels down, holding the reins so they slipped through ring finger and little finger, and how to kick a pony on over a jump and not be scared to be bucked off.

On my seventh birthday Minety became home and Pudding, a bay-coloured half Arab with a soft yellow muzzle, became my pony. My granny knitted me a brown jersey, which I wore with a red metal badge on it saying 'I AM 7' while feeling so grown-up wearing my new black velvet riding hat.

Pudding was fat and pretty with long lashes, but she was also lazy and basically a bitch. She was terrible at show jumping, grinding to a halt in front of jumps as coloured poles clattered out of metal cups, or ducking out the side of the fence as she bucked me off. Mum bought me a whip with a metal top and a loop to put around my wrist so I wouldn't lose it even when I fell off, and I learned to turn Pudding into every jump with my legs flapping, whip whirring. At Pony Club, I never won rosettes for best dressage test or fastest clear round, but always was awarded the prize for most determined rider.

I didn't want to be the most determined rider. I wanted to be like Georgie, who'd arrive at rallies in a lorry with her own girl groom. Georgie would lead her pony, glossy as a conker with tight balls of plait running down his neck, from the lorry as the groom ran around, unwrapping the pony's bandages, pulling strands of bright-yellow straw from his tail. After Georgie had been legged up, the groom would kneel down to paint oil on the pony's hooves. Her pony was clipped out and looked racy, like a mini thorough-bred; different from the hairy ponies Nell and I rode, who lived out in muddy fields, hock deep in clay all winter, so had shaggy coats and mud stains on their sides.

I hated the times we parked beside Georgie because Pudding would squeal and whinny, making the cattle trailer Mum drove shake and rattle. Georgie never had to be a determined rider and always won the clear rounds that were well beyond my grasp as Pudding bucked me off again. She lived an hour from us, on the other side of Cirencester high in the Cotswolds, where Range Rovers purred past limestone houses and where there were none of the water meadows or ditches full of frogspawn like there were in Minety. I heard Mum telling Rick that Georgie's father worked in security in South Africa, but he never seemed to be at the house. Georgie had a magenta-coloured swimming pool with steam rising from it, and thick carpets soft like cashmere lying wall to wall in every room, so that her mother walked barefoot through the house, even in winter, her toenails as bright pink as the geraniums growing in their hothouse. I pretended to Georgie this was normal to me, and didn't tell her about the Indian rugs eaten by moths and the frayed rush matting that Mum sewed back together with a really thick needle in the playroom at Minety, where the kitchen was the only really warm room. Mum switched the heating off when Rick went back to London at the end of every weekend, and if we complained about being cold she'd always say, 'Well, be sensible then and put some shoes on, darling!'

Georgie had a big bedroom with rosettes above her bed and a glass-topped dressing table with a taffeta skirt. I'd sometimes break off from our games playing with her Barbie mansion to go to the loo at the far end of the corridor simply because it gave me the chance to walk silently through her house and pretend I lived there. I saw a rugby shirt pinned to the wall in her brother's room, and on the marble worktop in the kitchen was a television her mother watched, unblinking, as she warmed a quiche for supper which had been made by their Australian nanny.

A few months after we moved from Oxford to Minety, Nell's pony Marble bolted across the paddock behind the house and Nell fell off, breaking her arm. Nell was brave on her ponies and for the next few years broke almost every single limb in her body. She was always the one getting a new cast signed on the school bus or hobbling into assembly on crutches having smashed her kneecap. I felt fiercely jealous of those crutches, and the drama Nell wore around her, but she chose to reach for it and spent less time on Mum's lap than I did. She kept a magpie chick that had lost its mother in a wicker basket in her bedroom, taking it into school to keep it in the science lab all day so she could feed it with a

pipette at break. She fashioned bridles out of our rocking-horse
harness for Mum's sheep, and wherever Nell went a menagerie of
smaller lives followed. Even with her arm in a cast, she never stopped
riding, but after she fell off Marble, Mum sent Pudding off on loan
and into my life trotted a succession of three small white ponies:
Henry, Twiglet and Dapple.

I found my first sense of being and doing something separate
from my mother riding these three ponies. I could control them
to make them trot or canter, or jump on my own, not just on the
lead rope with Emma running beside me. On the back of my pony
I could ride away from Mum and from Nell and have a relationship
with an animal that was completely exclusive. At school I was just
Nell's younger sister: less clever; less popular than her. I didn't take
magpies to school, or know how to marshal a group of other children as she did. On a pony I was at least somebody separate. And
I was good at riding. It felt natural to sit deep and still into the
saddle so that my hips and waist became part of the movement of
my pony. I liked jumping and galloping, and learned to ride side-
saddle.

'You have very good hands,' said my instructor at Pony Club
when she chose me above everyone else to ride a champion dressage
horse, which had been brought to camp by a woman called Pammy.
Pammy wore a headscarf and looked a bit like one of the royal
family, and Mum nudged me and whispered, 'Do look . . . she won
an Olympic gold medal riding for England,' as we stood watching
her horse being led like a celebrity from a lorry the size of a house.
It was my first experience of riding a serious horse. He responded
to the faintest pressure I applied with my calves, while I kept close
contact, using my reins on his mouth that felt soft as butter.

Sometimes my siblings Emma, Sophy and Tom would come to
watch us riding when they came back to Minety. When they were
children, Mum had split up with her first husband and moved with
them to Oxford, where she later met Rick and had Nell and me.
By the time we moved to Minety, a decade and a half later, Emma,
Sophy and Tom had all left home, although they returned, often,

at the weekends or for holidays and Christmas. They came to watch us at competitions where Nell and I won walls of rosettes for the fastest pair across country. We still had a cattle trailer, but our ponies were quick and accurate.

Mum made all of this happen, getting up early to help us plait and clean tack, driving miles to Pony Club trials or one-day events. Rick recorded it all. He always had a camera slung around his neck, and would make Mum laugh, her head thrown back at something he'd said as he passed her a hip flask of whisky or ate all the sausages she'd cooked for our picnic.

My sister Sophy lived in Yorkshire so she came home less, but the weekends when Emma and Tom arrived, trailing friends, were always the best, even if they didn't arrive until very late on a Friday evening, after Rick was already back, bringing with him unusual treats like pesto, parmesan and olive oil that he'd bought from an Italian deli in Soho.

Emma came most often. She had brown curly hair and drove a bright-red Metro, into which she would have folded a tall boyfriend. I might have had to go to bed before Emma arrived, but there was nothing in the world more exciting than her arrival in my bedroom, bringing with her a sense of London and a world very far away from the ponies at Minety. She'd kneel by my bed, telling me about a party she'd been to, the thick gold-link chain bracelet she wore jangling in animation.

'Stay, please stay, just for one more story,' I'd plead, wrapping my arms around her neck and breathing in the excitement of just being near Emma, who was, and still is, the sweetest combination of sister and best friend. She'd laugh and kiss me, telling me about all the fun we'd have in the morning, then vanish downstairs into the kitchen world that sounded adult, with scraped chairs on the stone floor and the glassy chink of bottles and glasses.

When I was ten, my brother Tom went to live in Australia for a year and Mum helped Nell and me make cassettes of conversations as a way of keeping in touch with him. Telephoning was out of the question, and Mum anyway rationed the amount of time any of us spent on the phone. She, though, would sit for an hour, laughing down the line with Teesa, in the alcove where the phone was kept. I'd watch her from the kitchen where I was doing my homework, and imagine what it would feel like to be a grown-up. I could see Nell and me in the future, smoking as we laughed into cupped telephones like adults always did.

When Tom came back from Australia, he had a pierced ear and his hair was so blond Mum said it looked like he'd dyed it white. 'Not white, Mum, peroxide,' he laughed as Mum hugged him. It felt very glamorous to have a brother with hair like Billy Idol who had travelled around Australia and returned with a different accent. He didn't come to Minety quite as often as Emma, but when he did Mum always made sure there was cream in the fridge because it was what Tom really liked on his cornflakes, with table-spoons full of brown sugar.

Emma and Tom had grown up in Oxford, but Teesa had taught Emma to ride when she was a child too, and so Emma would occasionally ride with us on one of Mum's horses. Tom didn't like to as it would have ruined his black suede shoes, but he did like going racing to the local point-to-point where there was a beer tent and bookmaker stands, and he could smoke joints and Mum wouldn't mind.

Mum made Minety into a place no one wanted to leave. I felt any absence keenly. School was to be endured, a brief blotch on the day, something I had to check in to before I could go home and start living again. Today I'm good at spotting when Jimmy and Dolly are faking sickness for a day on the sofa, but Nell and I didn't even have to bother pretending. Mum didn't need an excuse to keep us off school.

'You're having a day of nature studies and something like, oh I don't know, geography, perhaps?' she'd say as she loaded the ponies into the trailer to take us riding on the Ridgeway. She'd ride her big grey gelding, Joe, who had blotches of black dapples across his back and a thick white tail that flicked up and down as he trotted. She didn't have Teesa's iron nerve on a horse, but she'd ridden as a child and returned to horses in her forties after two decades of bringing up us five children.

Even when we lived in Oxford, she rode. She and Rick kept a bay horse called Bandit at a farm in Gloucestershire. Mum would leave Nell and me with Mrs Sandles and drive out on a Wednesday to ride him. She spent less time in the kitchen cooking moussaka and cheesecake then, and more time polishing her long black boots or brushing flecks of dirt from her blue riding coat. I'd watch, sitting on the edge of her bed before school, as she tied the tight white knots of a tie called a stock, securing it neatly across her neck with a thick gold pin.

I can see now that Bandit woke her up from the haze of mother-hood. At the time there was something almost estranging about her riding trips. They took her away from early morning until after dark, and when she'd return, flushed, her coat spattered with mud, she'd be humming with a vital new energy, which made her impatient when I asked her to sing me to sleep.

People who do not really know horses might raise their eyebrows, possibly even smirk, when they see a little girl lavishing devotion on her pony. The idea that a pony is an early experience of sex in the pre-adolescent girl is a cliché, because what a girl is getting from her pony has absolutely nothing to do with sex. That connection definitely did come later, but before my body started changing in adolescence, my ponies gave me a sense of being able to do something powerful and independent when I was essentially power-less. This is the gift of a pony to a child, as the animal gives the child a strong sense of how their life can be away from the control of their parents. The wild other of an animal is something strange and thrilling when a child is no longer an animated Thelwell cartoon on the leading rein but can escape altogether into a landscape that child and pony create together.

In the life before the accident, when our world was still a familiar shape, our ponies were our transport into this world away from our parents. After school Nell and I would tack up to ride to the wood called Flisteridge, which was two miles from Minety, to canter along the paths and make jumps from fallen branches. There was a sign saying 'Beware Adders' nailed to an oak tree on the road beside the wood, and in winter the tracks where too clogged with mud to ride there, but in the spring it would turn electric blue with a carpet of bluebells forcing its way up through leaf mould and bracken.

By the time I was nine, Mum and Rick would take Nell and me onto the Ridgeway at the weekends with our ponies, dropping us by the Devil's Punchbowl above Childrey and arranging to meet us later at a point ten miles on.

'This is Lambourne, and this is Ashbury, and we're going to meet you on this track just above Bishopstone,' Mum would say, tracing the route with her strong fingers on an OS map. 'If we're late there's a pub here and there'll be a phone box in the village. And if you get lost just ask someone.' Nell would be in charge of the ten-pence pieces we could use to ring Minety to pick up a message from Tom, who would have stayed at home to watch the football.

It made us feel brave to ride up there on our own on the Ridgeway, with the corn shivering in the wind as we raced along beside it, like the whole world was breathing. An hour might pass between us in silence broken only by the dry clop of a pony's hoof on the track, and then we'd talk without stopping for an hour about the teachers we didn't like at school, or whether we'd ever move from Minety, something that seemed as impossible as Mum having another baby, the only thing I really wanted from her that she denied me.

'I can't imagine that at all. Mum's really old. Forty or something,' Nell would say, kicking her pony into a gallop as she twisted round to face me in her saddle, mouthing, as a challenge, 'Catch me.'

We practised jokes for the school bus and sang the country-and-western songs Rick listened to on a record player in his study. My favourite was a song called 'Georgia', by Willie Nelson, but even we could hear it didn't sound right in a child's voice, so instead we belted out an Emmylou Harris song called 'Tonight the Bottle Let Me Down'. I didn't understand the words, but they possessed an adult sense of longing, which felt familiar and alien at the same time. 'Tonight the bottle let me down, and let your memory come around.'

Looking back on that time now, it doesn't just feel like a different decade, but a whole different dimension.

The five years of the end of my childhood slid past, infinitely valuable. But our worlds were changing anyway in the year and a half before the accident. Nell moved to London for her A levels, living with Emma and her husband Matthew during the week. She had new friends and new clothes, and suddenly knew about nightclubs on Kensington High Street and how to get around London on her own. She was always leaving me and it felt like a very special sort of betrayal. I see it now when Jimmy walks away from Dolly to catch a bus into Oxford to meet his friends, leaving her speechless with loss and longing for that tangled feeling of being siblings together with absolutely nothing and no one between you.

I'd started growing away from the scruffy ponies who'd taught me to ride, onto bigger horses, but none of this took me away from Mum. I only ever wanted to be with her, and she held me close to her, sometimes too close without realising it, so that at early teenage parties I felt clumsy in my knee-length kilt while Georgie and her friends wore black tights and tight denim skirts with ballet pumps. They could talk about skiing holidays and knew how to dance so the boys wanted to win them when it was time for spin the bottle. I'd lock myself in the loo and will the time to pass, yearning for the moment when Emma would arrive to pick me up and take me back to Minety, where her friends, sat at the kitchen table, would let me fall asleep on their laps.

If being at a teenage party was bad, school without Nell was even worse, and I started to dread the end of the hour-long bus journey from Minety to Cheltenham, when I'd have to face the classroom. Maths and chemistry tied me up in knots, but I loved

English lessons, when reading poetry from the Second World War or a passage from Hardy or a sonnet would make the teenage noise of the classroom vanish.

At breaktime, though, that noise would flare up and I'd feel completely alone. I never got used to the sniggers that came when another girl asked me what music I liked and I said Loretta Lynne and Tammy Wynette. I hated the taunts when I wore a second-hand uniform, and the giggles every time I put my hand up to answer a question in English. At breaktime I'd walk out of school to go and sit in a park alone. School made me feel completely left out of a group I'd never belong to.

But school was like a foreign land that I could forget existed when I got home. Flinging my schoolbag onto my bed I'd peel off my nylon blue-and-yellow uniform, pushing my legs into jeans and stuffing my feet into jodhpur boots to run outside to Ginger, the rangy, 16-hands-high chestnut gelding who'd replaced Claude, the small bay pony who looked like a racehorse that I'd started eventing on. I didn't want to be Georgie any more after Claude became my pony, even though the cattle trailer still rattled and Minety was still draughty. In the saddle, facing Claude into a hedge and ditch, or over a set of show jumps, all the fear in my life vanished. Ginger was a step up again from Claude, with a gallop that ate up the grass and a jump that made me feel I was flying.

Mum bought me some dressage lessons at an equestrian centre outside Cirencester. Most of our riding as children had been through muddy fields on ponies, so trotting around a floodlit arena was something new of my very own. Under the peaked brim of my black riding hat I'd feel sweat pouring down my face as the trainer taught me that if I sat hard enough into the saddle and applied the correct pressure between my thighs and calves, the tiniest movements would make Ginger respond in a more subtle and powerful way. It was like speaking to Ginger in his own language.

But it was distracting too. Trotting across the arena with my hips pressed down into the saddle, I felt myself come. It wasn't a new feeling, but something I'd been doing to myself alone in my room since I was much younger, but it was the first time it had happened in the saddle. Trotting across the ring, I didn't reveal on my face what was happening inside me as the instructor shouted out commands. Later, I found blood in my pants where my clitoris had been rubbed raw by the pressure of the saddle. I didn't mind, but I wanted to know what to do in the next lesson if it happened again. Mum spoke with the trainer, who said that kind of bleeding was normal when there was such an intense connection between rider and saddle. 'It might help if she wears tights under her jodhpurs, to reduce the friction.'

Our ponies had become horses and our games had grown up. When Nell came home at the weekends now she still made dens of a sort, but they were grown-up versions. Rather than piles of eiderdowns and pallets tied together in the garden, she moved around the house, changing bedroom every few months. Minety had enough rooms to accommodate her changing tastes, so that when she left our shared room with its twin beds and stuffed toys, she moved into the rooms in the attic. She cut stencils to decorate the walls, fashioning curtains out of scarves or lengths of Indian fabric from the dressing-up box. Incense burned on the window ledge and sometimes she'd go to parties with her friends Jackie and Emma. They'd arrive home at breakfast time and sleep until supper, emerging looking battered, their faces changed by the night-time.

'She's just tired, that's all,' said Jackie, hunched under a duvet beside Nell as I nagged them to get up before it got dark again. 'She's just really tired. We stayed up all night.'

However often Nell moved bedrooms, there were still extra rooms to fill. Emma, Tom and Sophy came home less frequently as the years passed, until Emma got married. I cried hysterically at their wedding, but Matthew became my friend, and he and Emma created a home with their children first in London, then later in Norfolk, before they moved to Oxfordshire. Tom got married to Mils, who was beautiful and kind, and they later had two sons. Sophy, still, was almost always in Yorkshire.

Siblings splintering away made spare bedrooms which Mum filled with lodgers: boys from the agricultural college in Cirencester with loud laughs and Golf GTIs. She cooked spaghetti bolognese or roast chicken for them in the evenings, and they would exercise her horses or help with the mowing. She liked the energy they brought to the house, especially after Nell had moved to London, when during the week it was just Mum and me at home. Sometimes she'd drink glasses of whisky with them by the fire in the playroom if she'd come in late from riding, while I did my homework at the table in the bay window. They brought a generational blur into the house too, which she found familiar. Emma is fourteen years older than me, and Mum is over a decade older than my father, so generations have always slid into one another, blurring the fringes of what was going on upstairs.

Until I was fourteen, all the clothes I'd ever worn had once belonged to someone older than me. Although Nell's move to London had brought a higher quality of cast-off, they still weren't my clothes. But when I was fifteen I spent some birthday money on an extremely tight pair of white jeans, which I wore with brown leather cowboy boots from the dressing-up box and a red vest with spaghetti straps that had once belonged to Emma. I started going to parties with the boys from the college and swam naked at midnight in a lake near Minety with a boy who was the first one to say, 'Three leaf or four?' when I told him my name. Once, at a party, I got into a car with one of the older boys who put his hand into my pants and jabbed inside me as he opened his flies. Outside the misted windows I heard Nell shouting my name to go home, so I scrambled out of the car, apologising to his angry erection as he shouted, 'What the fuck? Stupid little bitch!' into the dark.

Not long after that, I slept with Alex, one of the boys living with us. He was twenty-four, a student at the college in Cirencester whose progress from the kitchen table to my bed seemed completely natural after I started wearing those white jeans. Mum hadn't been shocked, or even surprised, when she came into my room before school and found him in my bed.

Alex wasn't actually the first person I'd slept with, but I let her believe he was. Once, on a summer evening so hot I could feel sweat in the small of my back even after dark, I'd knelt down on a concrete track behind a friend's house while her brother unzipped his trousers and pushed himself into my face. Inside, my friend was watching *Dirty Dancing* with another two girls from school. I'd told them I needed to go to the loo. Having a boy's cock in my throat wasn't as nice as the feelings I'd been giving myself alone in my room since I was seven or eight. When I went back into the house there was blood on my knees, but I preferred that feeling to the unfamiliar salt in my throat which made me rub my lips and look away from my friend when she asked me why I'd taken so long.

I had sex for the first time with another older brother at a house in London. Mum knew him, vaguely, as a friend of a friend's son, and didn't blink when I'd asked if I could go out with him in London.

'Of course, darling, of course you can go, but just make sure you don't use the Tube alone,' she'd said. 'And please don't smoke cigarettes. They're so boring.'

I'd expected sex to hurt and for there to be blood, but I liked it; a milky feeling of the loss of myself, despite his face being pressed so close to mine. He gave me a lift to the Tube the next morning, and all seemed easy and free, but on the train back to Kemble a galloping anxiety convinced me I'd definitely got AIDS and was clearly pregnant. In my bedroom I swallowed five contraceptive pills I'd found in a sponge bag that one of Emma's friends had left at the weekend. I'd read that the morning-after pill was the equivalent of several of these pills and I wasn't ready to ask Mum what to do. At fifteen, pregnancy seemed like the most horrific future possible. Later that evening, I was sick on the rush-matting beside my bed, so Mum brought a dishcloth and washing-up bowl from the kitchen to clear it up.

'Are you sure you weren't drinking last night?' she said, her voice sketched with uncharacteristic anxiety, as I hunched over the kitchen table in my pyjamas. 'Or did you smoke a joint?'

'No, Mum, please, of course I didn't . . . I'm just tired,' I mumbled, pressing my forehead into my palm until she leant over and pushed my hair back across my face to look right at me.

'It's fine. I love you whatever you were doing. You know that? Don't ever forget how much I love you.'

Sex was much easier to arrange when I was at Minety. Mum was vague about where the lodger was sleeping because she trusted him. In the week he'd sleep in my room overlooking the paddock behind the house, with my school uniform scattered across the floor, and the sex we had was electric but it was also familiar and safe because I was at home.

Without many questions, Mum took me to the GP in Purton, the shabby town on the outskirts of Swindon, to get a prescription for the Pill. She knew the GP as I'd been in the same class as her daughter at the village school.

'So maybe it's best if you go in and explain on your own. It'll be fine, just explain you want the Pill. It's very sensible,' said Mum.

Afterwards, we went next door to the newsagent and Mum paid for two Orange Maid ice lollies and a packet of Jaffa cakes from the last bit of change in her purse.

'You don't need to tell Rick until you're sixteen,' she said, dropping her lolly stick on the floor of the car. 'And anyway, he might be a student but he's so lovely and handsome and I know you're safe, not in some strange place or being driven by someone I don't know. It doesn't matter what anyone says. I know you're safe.'

I cannot look back at my life without seeing a jagged dark scar through the moment that separates the time immediately before the accident from the time after. Even the year before the accident is smudgy in my head, like someone has loaded a gun and there's a timer counting down to the really terrible thing that none of us can stop happening.

I was a child, and then I was an adolescent, and then there was the accident. If I want to make myself dizzy, I take my mind on a trip where the accident didn't happen. It makes me spin: with melancholy and also with desire, to look at an alternative life where I can pick up my mobile phone right now and call the number I have stored there under a contact called Mum. Where I can walk into her kitchen and resume a conversation like it never ended, or sit on the edge of the bed while she gets dressed to talk to her about what's happening for Christmas.

I imagine driving my children over to her house to spend the weekend with her, but when I bring the children into it the vertigo really gets me. If the accident hadn't happened, would those children be Jimmy and Dolly? Would Dash and Evangeline exist if Mum hadn't fallen from her horse? Would this life be mine if there had been no accident? And then I don't know which future I want to protect: the one in which the accident never happened, or the one in which it did, but all the other stuff is mine too.

When I force myself to remember it's like watching a car swerving all over a road and knowing it's going to crash and kill everyone inside. I play and replay the moments before school, when Mum was making breakfast in her riding clothes, and I want to stop those moments and reset the day: the conversation we had about how she might still be riding after I got home, and the macaroni cheese she'd already cooked for supper; the space in the car as she drove me to school where I felt irritable, since she was dropping me off early to get out on her horse; the way she engaged me by talking about a history project I was doing; how the scent of Chanel No. 5 filled the car as we sat by the school gates, engine running, watching other pupils stream into the building; how I'd said 'I love you', slightly begrudgingly, as I was still sulking as I got out of the car; how she'd replied, 'I love you more' after me, before the door slammed between us. I want to catch that last glimpse of smile she gave me before the windows of the car separated us, and turn it into just one more of hundreds of thousands of smiles I could have had with her since. But I can't, and instead I vanish into school, enveloped into assembly while Mum moves completely out of reach.

On that day there were also hours spent outside intensive care with Rick and Nell, the displaced feeling of sitting on plastic chairs in a special waiting room, separate from the main room, which meant we were going to be told something no one else should hear, and then the unreality of standing beside Mum's bed, looking at her head, as big as a balloon, bloody-bandaged with closed eyes like purple plums, and the sound of the rise and fall of a plastic tube in her mouth, hooked up to machines that were making her breathe.

I know there were all those things but what I remember most vividly about that day is a pile of ash. Cigarette ash, late that night, made by everyone smoking under the lamplight around the kitchen table. Until then, I wouldn't have called myself a smoker. There had been the occasional stolen cigarette around a bonfire in a field at Minety and once I'd smoked with the lodger after we'd had sex in a wood. But after we got back from hospital I started smoking because it was a way of focusing on something other than what I'd just seen.

I was at school when I found out there had been a bad accident. It was double history, and the head teacher interrupted the lesson to speak quietly in the corner to our teacher, who glanced up at the classroom halfway through the brief conversation, anxious-eyed. Simon, who sat in front of me, flicked a ball of paper across the room while Neil, who sat beside him, jeered quietly.

'Woah, sir's here. Someone's in trouble if sir's here,' Neil said, motioning to the head, and the class swayed into nervous laughter. Someone was in trouble, and sideways glances were exchanged, checking whose turn it was for a detention for skiving, or having been seen smoking in town in school uniform. I carried on reading a comprehension about the Suez crisis, since none of the above would have been me.

'Clover, would you mind stepping outside?' My name was plucked out of the classroom air and my pencil made a hollow sound as it dropped onto the table then clattered to the floor. Stuffing books into my bag, I dragged my coat from the back of the chair as it scraped across the silence of the classroom. Everyone else leant back in their seats and stared as I made my way out. The corridor was dark with the muffled sounds of teachers in further classrooms, pupils laughing, chairs moving, a raised voice.

'Your mother,' the head said, reaching for a light on the wall that didn't work, then putting his hand forward to motion me through the gloom. 'Your mother . . . I believe your mother has . . . There has been an incident. But your sister is here.'

At the far end of the corridor was Nell, her strong face crumpled, pulling at the sleeve of her jersey. I fell on her and the head vanished, muttering there was no need to sign myself out, he'd see to it.

'Mum's alright? What sort of accident? Has she broken her leg?'

'I don't know, I don't know. She's had an accident, on Quince, a riding accident. She fell off and I don't know what's happened.'

Nell didn't tell me that she had already seen Mum, unconscious in the cottage hospital in Cirencester as she was stretchered into an ambulance. Afterwards, much later, Nell said there were sirens and lights and many people moving around Mum, who was in her riding clothes with blood on her face and an oxygen mask strapped to her. Nell has since said she didn't know what was going on because there was so much noise, but she felt like she'd been hit in the back with a sledgehammer. Nell is brave in everything she does, but I badly want to be able to reach into the past and lift her out of that hospital courtyard to take her away from the sirens and paramedics and Mum's blood and unconscious body.

Time heals so much of what goes wrong in life but, twenty-five years later, the memory of what happened to Mum on that day still makes my body react. I feel a straightening in my wrists and a silent pressure descending. My breath lightens, my mind flickering to find a concentration that won't stick, and I'm suddenly irritated by everything in my immediate environment. My mind is a pony spooked by a shadow in the hedge. It doesn't want to move forward but shies away, determined to return to the safer place it's come from.

Nell took me to the car and then we went home. Rick had left Kemble on the early train for London that morning, but he came home wearing London clothes. Mum's closest friend in the village,

Dawn, drove Rick, Nell and me to hospital in Bristol. We sat for several hours in the white waiting room designated for intensive care – it had boxes of tissues on the table and no magazines – until a big man with huge hands like a butcher came in and told us he was Mum's surgeon.

'The prognosis is very grave,' he said. On either side of Rick, Nell and I shook from the inside out. 'Here we have a fifty-two-year-old woman who has suffered a catastrophic blow to the head and during surgery we have found areas of damage on both temporal lobes of her brain and several blood clots. Her brain is very swollen.'

Would she die? Would this fifty-two-year-old woman with a catastrophic blow to the head die? How many blood clots? How swollen was her brain? How much damage on the temporal lobes? Would she die? Would Mum die? Would Mum die? Would Mum die?

He didn't have any answers, but when Rick asked, 'This is a two-year recovery process?' the surgeon hesitated for a moment, as something untold registered on his face.

CHAPTER 3

'Is the White Horse real?' Dolly turns to me in her seat, switching off the radio and dusting sugar from the doughnut she's been eating from her palms. She is twelve now, and looks grown up in her new uniform for secondary school. The wet verges rush by outside the car window, but as we turn off the main road from Faringdon, Uffington lies ahead of us, and suddenly the chalk horse is visible on the hill ahead. 'I mean, do you think it really can walk off the hill?'

Dolly is profoundly dyslexic, and while her upside-down mind means learning to read has been much harder for her than it was for Jimmy, hers is also a mind not bound by the limits of rationality. Much is possible in Dolly's world that others could never imagine.

'And if it did come down from the hill, would it be bigger than the biggest horse possible, or even bigger than that?'

I pull over, into a track just before the village, where the long-distant view of the White Horse is best. It's the view that unfolds every time I drive home from Faringdon, from the supermarket or after collecting Dolly from homework club, but no matter how mundane the chores I'm running, the view of the horse is always arresting. It has an almost kinetic quality, with a vivid life of its own, depending on the quality of the light at that point in the day. Now, sitting in the car with rain blurring the windscreen, I explain to Dolly that the horse is not real in the sense that Holly, the miniature Shetland we bought together, is real.

'But it's a real part of the landscape, so it depends what you think landscape really is,' I tell her, and after staring out to the horse for a bit longer, she turns to me, her eyes clear and unblinking beneath her thick brown fringe.

'Well, the landscape is part of the world, which is a living thing, so I think that means the horse is alive like any other animal, or alive as humans definitely,' she says simply.

Inside the car, our breath is contained, but in the soft, early spring rain outside, the horse gallops on, endlessly, over the hill above Uffington, as it has done for the past three or maybe four millennia.

Dolly sighs, frowning at the horse, then turns back to me.

'Shall we go up there, just you and me?'

The sky is huge and blue up at the horse, punctuated only by the briefest comma of a cloud as Dolly and I run around its outline. Dolly's questions about the horse aren't so wild, since a local legend says that for one night of the year, it will come down off the hill to feed in the Manger, the local name for the steep green glacial folds of the hill that rolls beneath it. While there are other white horses nearby, all created during the eighteenth and nineteenth centuries – at Alton Barnes and Cherhill, and chalk giants and crowns in Sussex and Kent – Uffington White Horse is by far the oldest and strangest of them all.

There has been speculation that it was commissioned by King Alfred in 871 to celebrate his victory over the Danes at Ashdown. Alfred was born in Wantage, a few miles across the Downs from Uffington, so this is a neat theory, but archaeological excavations and carbon dating have pointed to the idea that it is much older, and was probably created between 1400 and 600 BC by Bronze Age man.

Dolly was just four or five when she first saw the White Horse, but as a very small girl she struggled to identify its shape as a horse. This isn't surprising, as this shape created by humans thousands of years ago across time often doesn't look like a horse at all. Depending on your mood when you first see it, it can look more like a white gash, or a comical squiggle. Neck, body and tail are represented in a single line, with two legs attached to the body, and two detached. The horse's head is stranger still, with a deep V shape between the ears, a high brow and beak-like jaw. It's an energetic image, the long lean white lines of the animal creating a sense of crescendo, and as Dolly and I stand facing the horse, the curves of landscape before us feel like the hills themselves are moving with the galloping pace of the horse.

The horse itself is magnificent, but one of the strangest things about Uffington White Horse is that it's seen best not from the rolling hills around it, but from the sky, as if ancient man had flown up into the heavens and thrown the horse back down onto the hill below.

Horses are the source of powerful magic that's changed my life, so to me the shape will always be a horse, but some people think it's a unicorn, or that it may have had a foal beside it that's now lost in the grass. I was once berated by a man with tattoos on his neck in the Fox and Hounds pub in Uffington when he heard me referring to it as a horse.

'No fool could think that's a horse,' he growled over a yellowing pint. 'That so-called horse is a dragon.'

Dragon or horse, the creature's whiteness, and the energy of its etched movements, give it bold presence and are what pull Dolly and me from the car and out into the rain to walk around it, as we try to imagine the sea that once covered this part of England.

There's a relief being up there alone with Dolly. It's cold, but the sun's been out in patches all day; one of those sharp, bright afternoons where flashes of sunlight collide with the wind and wet.

The grass is too damp to sit on but we crouch down on top of the hill, sharing a finger of Twix I've found in my coat pocket.

I rake my hands through the wet grass as Dolly tells me about her afternoon, about her lost PE kit and a test she had in science. A friend had seen her copying and now she doesn't want to be friends any more. The everyday cruelty of schoolchildren pinches me from a distance as I listen to Dolly, resisting the urge to swamp her with how much I hated school, or how much I longed for every single second of it to be over, and instead I stand back, allowing this experience to be hers completely. I'll never stop worrying about any of my children because I am their mother, but in the clear, white afternoon sun I think not of the meandering friendships of Dolly's schooldays, but of the water that flowed across frozen chalk, two and a half million years ago, and, before that, of the billions of tiny, crushed sea creatures floating in the seas which created the chalk itself. Broken like a jigsaw, even the white chalk in the grass beneath my hands reassures.

*

The first day after Mum's accident, I woke in bed with Nell and Emma. We lay in a line, our outlines still, like three spoons in a drawer.

It was November, so the early-morning house was chilly enough to make me pull the duvet closer to me as I yawned, blinking, the confusion of why I should be in bed with my sisters not really registering yet. For a minute the room was frozen in a few seconds of time that weren't real, and when that quick moment had passed, my delight at having woken with them was replaced by a cold fear about what the day ahead would hold.

The days after that were filled with crying and driving. Mum was in hospital in Bristol, which was an hour and a half from Minety down the M4. It was the route Mum used to drive when we were going to Cornwall to stay with her brother and our cousins, but until then I'd never paid attention to roads. I'd just been a passenger.

Now there was a constant stream of cars moving between Minety and Bristol as we travelled to see Mum in intensive care. Somebody was always at the hospital, or leaving the kitchen to make the journey, or arriving back looking broken. The second time I saw Mum in her coma, I stood beside her bed with Nell and my brother Tom as the extremities of what had happened crackled around us. Her head was even bigger that second morning and her puffball eyes were turning from bright purple to dark blue. I tried not to look at her forehead, where her hair had been shaved off and a deep jagged scar with fresh stitches in it ran from one ear over the crown of her head to the other ear. Her skin had been peeled back, like the oranges she used to arrange in segments for us on a plate with brown sugar in the middle to dip into.

There were two deep, round indentations in the top of her skull, in line with each of her eyes at the place where her hairline started. Her head was swollen and huge but in these two areas the skin sagged inwards, where circles of her skull had been cut out to relieve the swelling on her brain.

The tube in her mouth breathed for her, a machine above the bed occasionally making an alarming bleeping noise that would send a nurse running to change switches and check pressures. All her nails were stained a dark-blue colour and there were clips on the ends of her fingers. I could see blood swelling up under her nails but, if I didn't look at her hands, her forearms speckled with liver spots were the same strong, brown arms that had wrapped themselves around me so often.

Tom held her hand, telling her he loved her, that she was going to be alright, that we all loved her and that we were always there, that she didn't need to be afraid, that she was going to be just fine, just fine. Then his voice became very distant and I was aware of gripping hard onto the rails around Mum's bed as the floor suddenly rushed up and a nurse ran forward, thrusting a plastic chair under me.

In the car on the way back Tom, Nell and I started talking about what would happen when Mum got better. She would wake up and she would recover and life would go back to how it had been before. We prayed and begged and prayed that she would survive and prayed again that she would not die. We did not imagine that there would be a future for Mum that was worse than death.

She was operated on three more times within the first week and each time her surgeon, that butcher with big hands who'd talked to us on the first night, warned us the chances of her surviving another twenty-four hours were slim. He was a huge figure in those first few weeks, blustering into the ward, trailing stunned-looking junior doctors as he made a flying visit to each terrible casualty on the beds around Mum.

When he came to her, he'd sometimes shake her or squeeze her hands, thundering, 'Good morning, Char, time for you to wake up, come along now,' in a voice that boomed confidently through the otherwise hushed sobs that are the more normal sounds of visiting hours in an intensive care ward. Once, he arrived wearing a greasy pinstriped suit straining across his vast stomach, as if he'd come from a club lunch.

To start with, I found his visits exciting because he was the man who was keeping Mum alive. Because I was only sixteen I didn't have long conversations with the surgeon about Mum's prognosis, but he talked a lot with Rick and Emma about the extent of the swelling on Mum's brain, and the number of blood clots and the severity of the damage he'd found there when he went back into her head for further operations. Now, it's very obvious to me that he knew with absolute clarity what lay ahead for Mum, if she ever did wake up. She had acute damage on areas of her brain which controlled speech and memory. He would have known that the age of her brain and her body, and the extremity of the damage to that poor brain, would mean recovery would be very difficult. But he never told us this. Instead, he continued operating on her, and he ignored what Rick said: that if the extent of her brain damage meant she'd never recover, he should let God's will play its course.

Later, many years later, I dreamt about him. It was a time when I'd spent months fighting with the NHS about the provision of

Mum's care, and had driven her across London, during which she'd had an epileptic fit in the car as I drove her through Fulham. When she had stopped convulsing, I'd changed her incontinence pads in a petrol station, ignoring that wide-eyed look you get from other adults when you're with someone whose disability is shocking, while you pretend this is all normal. And that evening I dreamt quickly about a man gouging into Mum's eyes with a blunt scalpel, as I stood and watched from a house with no furniture and all the doors and windows wide open to a howling, screaming gale.

I didn't go to school for a few weeks after the accident. Mum was on a precipice between life and death every day, so getting to double history on time wasn't important. I spent all my time with my siblings and Rick but otherwise everything familiar had become alien. No routine, no normal mealtimes, no school, no early nights, no homework.

A perpetual stream of people arrived at Minety. That bit was quite exciting. At the house, a hysterical gothic party was forming. This was one of the very strangest things about the weeks immediately after the accident. The very, very worst thing I could imagine in the whole world was happening, live, constant and in vivid wraparound technicolour, but with it came all the people I loved most in the world; except for Mum, of course, who was sleeping on in her deep dark coma in Bristol. But Emma, Tom and Nell were at the house the entire time. Sophy visited. Rick didn't leave.

Mum's closest friends Dawn, Felicity, Candida and Ken arrived midweek to cook supper, and neighbours arrived with casseroles, chocolate cakes, plates of flapjacks and so many flowers we ran out of jugs and glasses in the kitchen to hold them all. The flowers were there for the moment Mum was to come home: artificially grown pink roses, a bright bunch of orange-and-gold chrysanthemums, a chorus of sunflowers with heads the size of dinner plates, whose yellow petals unfurled in the warmth of the kitchen as they turned to look at the lamp hanging over the table. Mum's dog,

Piper, a big white lurcher with a brown-and-black brindle patch on his back, would stand shivering beside the Aga, and when I came down in the mornings he'd blink his round saucer eyes at me, waiting, as we all were, as the sunflowers dropped their heads, shedding petals onto the cold stone floor.

Time changed when Mum was in peril; it slowed and yet became at once more immediate too, so that I lived fully in each moment, wondering if this second would be the one in which she would blink her eyes and wake, or this one, or this one . . . I found myself living painfully in the present tense.

The person you know as Mum remains unconscious. You spend a big part of each day making plea bargains with God. *If you make her wake up, I'll go to church with her every single Sunday, not just at Christmas and when she forces me to. If you make her better, I'll never swear again and I'll always be really helpful around the house. If life can go back to how it was before, I won't be rude to Mum and Rick ever again or answer them back.*

When God ignores everything you ask Him, you find objects and elements to plea with all around you. *Let us get through that green light before it changes and Mum will have woken up by the time we get to the hospital. If it goes on raining this hard for another ten minutes it means she's going to be home by Christmas. If I can stay underwater in the bath for thirty seconds, she'll survive the operation tonight.*

Constantly, you think about what it will be like when she opens her eyes. You understand that it will be difficult and recovery will be slow. She'll be confused and probably won't recognise you for a bit. She might find it hard to speak for a few days or even a few weeks. She might even have to have speech therapy. You think about rehab a lot, imagining the weeks of physical and mental rehabilitation she'll probably go through to learn basic things again, like walking or getting dressed. She might find running difficult, although the X-rays show her spine and vertebrae are not damaged at all, so you're pretty sure she'll be able to learn to walk again.

You try to imagine how your life together will be once she comes home. Perhaps her voice will be slurred; you get your head around the idea she might always talk rather slowly, be a bit more forgetful or need extra help with things like cooking. She may not even be able to drive any more, but that's OK because you'll be seventeen next year and can take your driving test. And then you consider the very worst possibility: that she might not be able to ride a horse again, either. That makes you feel so sad you decide not to think about it, and anyway all those other things really will be OK, because you love her so much, so that even if she's a slightly more confused, forgetful or eccentric version of Mum, it will all be alright.

When she wakes up, everything will be alright again.

In between imagining those things you cry. You sound like an animal caught in a trap and when you lie in bed your body shakes uncontrollably. The skin on your face feels permanently cracked as though a clay mask has dried on it, and after a while this feeling becomes normal.

Mum had always said she would never leave us. The idea of her not being there was the worst thing I could imagine, and sometimes when we were children Nell and I would wrap ourselves around her and wail about how terrible life would be if she died.

'You can't ever, ever, ever die, Mum,' I gulped. 'And if you did die then I would die too. I know I would die if you weren't here. I promise I would die.'

She'd say to Nell and me, 'I love you so much, I'll never leave you, I promise, even when I die, I'll always be watching for you and I'll be with you. I'll be like the wind all around you, holding you close. But I'll never leave you.'

But now she was in a coma, and trying to comprehend where, exactly, she had gone was terrifying. I imagined her soul swirling around, trapped in her skull as it dived deeper and deeper downwards, and at other times I imagined it shooting up into the night sky, or whistling along beside the car, all blurry and close while trapped on the other side of the window.

If she had died, there would have been no hope or optimism in those first few weeks. There would have been no conversations about what we would do when she got better and how we would look after her, dominating everything we talked about. There would have been grief, and mourning, and trying to understand the terrible tragedy of a mother who had died at fifty-two.

But if she had died, there would also have been the rituals of bereavement to step into: a funeral to organise, hymns to choose, readings to find, conventions to follow. Instead, with no death, but no real life either, there was an endless sense of waiting and missing and hoping and waiting and missing.

Some days after the accident, after visiting the hospital, I retreated to the stables at home. I wanted to bury my face in Joe's white mane. He was Mum's horse, a big grey gelding, but he wasn't the horse she'd been riding on the day of her accident. That was one she hadn't had for long: Quince, a small bay, thoroughbred mare. She hadn't been hurt in the accident and I didn't know what had happened to her, but she wasn't in the stables when I went there to seek comfort from Joe.

He stood gently in the stable with me, hot breath steaming from his nostrils, almost as though he knew he had to stand very still. I wanted to be close to him, to feel his warmth and smell, that sweetness on his nose that belongs only to horses.

Mum's accident was on a Monday, and on the Wednesday I went to the stables in my jeans and riding boots. Joe opened his mouth without resisting as I slipped the cold metal bit into his mouth, pulling up the girth and adjusting Mum's stirrups to my length. Living through the hours since the accident had felt like being held underwater, and I needed the absolute reassurance and shared energy of breathing with a horse.

It was November, and in a wet month the ground would have been sodden, but the days and weeks after Mum's accident were cold and sharp. Mist blanketed the early mornings and frost spiked the grass, so Joe's hooves made a soft thud as we trotted across the fields away from the house, rather than squelching through the quagmire of mud that the fields around Minety could become in autumn.

I knitted my hands into Joe's white mane and felt the power of his strong shoulder moving beneath the saddle, reassured by just being close to him. I wasn't scared of the horse or the speed of the ground rushing past me below. I did not imagine that anything about being close to this animal would hurt me but instead it made me feel brave when I was very afraid. And I remembered a passage from one of the books Mum had read us aloud, *The Black Riders* by Violet Needham, where a mysterious group of soldiers riding through an unnamed mountain range would repeat a special phrase to any stranger they met, to test if they were fighting on the same side. That phrase was 'It takes fortitude to ride tonight', and I said it to myself as Joe galloped across the field, because even then I knew I was reaching for fortitude, and that if I could find it anywhere, I'd find it with my horse.

At the far side of the field, I pulled harder on the reins, so that Joe slowed to a trot, and we were both panting.

When I looked back at the house, the windows of my bedroom were like eyes staring back at me.

The house looked exactly as it had three days before, but there was something different about it too. Without Mum in it, the house seemed to know it was emptier, holding its breath, waiting.

I wanted Mum to come back so badly it felt like I was walking around with a big gash cut through my body. We would all visit her every day in hospital, but as days moved into weeks moved into months, we developed a rhythm. One of us would always be there, driving early from Minety, sitting with Mum and talking to her, until another one of us took over. The grown-ups, Rick, Tom and Emma, handled the conversations with the doctors, and although we all wanted answers, it started to become clear to us just how mysterious the brain really is. Mum's surgeon couldn't really give us any clarity. He didn't know whether Mum would wake up, and if she did, what her recovery would look like. And as the weeks passed, his interest in her seemed to fade. She lay in a coma, unresponsive, replaced by newer, fresher patients. It was like she had been his experiment that he had moved on from. We were brimming with questions, day after day, and there was a sense, as time passed, that he was avoiding those questions, or that they were unanswerable.

I talked to Mum a lot in my head and sometimes out loud if I was on my own. In my bedroom I'd look out to the fields and imagine what it would feel like to see her walking back towards me. In between loving her with my whole being, I felt flashes of rage with her too. Once, I sat on my bed in the half darkness of my room and I challenged her to show me she hadn't been lying when she said she'd never leave me.

'Do something to prove it, Mum. Do something to show me you're here,' I whispered. The room was silent, but from the kitchen came the muffled sound of Rick and Emma talking as they got ready to leave for the hospital. 'Go on. Please, Mum. Show me you're here.'

I stared around the room, willing a picture to fall from the wall, the curtains to billow, the door to gently close. On my lap, my hands were shaking, nails bitten to red, raw cuticles. As I spoke to Mum my voice rose then fell then rose again, so I was almost screaming.

'Show me that you love me, if you're not gone, show me, show me! Mum . . . Show me you're here. Mum?'

But there was only a deafening silence, as a deep, deep longing for home with Mum in it enveloped me.

I'd seen someone in a coma before, although not in real life, but quite vividly on television, as there was an elaborate plotline in *Dallas* involving one of the stars being unconscious for months. He woke up very suddenly, just as his life support was about to be turned off, with all his family gathered around his bed, silently crying. It was dramatic. His life was saved and he was back from the dead! But seeing someone waking up from a coma is really nothing like that.

First of all, Sue Ellen and Lucy and all the women in *Dallas* looked wonderful and very glamorous with tear-stained faces. Their eyes glistened and their beautiful features appeared gorgeously enlarged by grief. On screen, trauma was flattering to those living it. In real life, trauma made us look punched out and shocked, as if our eyes and mouths had been stretched in different directions.

Also, when people wake up from a coma on screen, it happens very quickly. An actor will simulate a moment of confusion about where he is, before there's an audible gasp of relief he's alive and awake and obviously going to get better. But the process of someone waking up from a coma doesn't work like that at all. It's slow and laborious and goes on for a long time so that sometimes you don't know if the person you're looking at is awake or unconscious or dead.

For the first weeks after the accident, Mum barely moved at all, even when they stuck needles down her nails to try and wake her up. I couldn't understand why her nails were blood coloured and sometimes got redder and more angry, even when the bruising across her face calmed from red to purple to green and yellow.

'It's an attempt to stimulate her, to bring her into consciousness,' a nurse explained, glancing down at her clipboard then shifting to the next bed, where the family of an unconscious teenage boy, who'd arrived fresh from a motorbike accident the night before, were wailing around his hooked-up body.

The nurses told us to talk to Mum about everything she loved and to remind her of her childhood, as it was possible her long-term memory might be quite sharp if she could hear us.

'Or just tell her what you have been up to, what you're making for tea and what's been going on at home,' one told me, chirpily, as she checked the tubes running out of Mum's body. I wasn't at all sure that Mum would want to know anything about home, since everything there was going wrong. Mum might never have had a career, but looking after everyone and running the house was a full-time job we'd all underestimated until she wasn't there to do it.

So, instead, I talked to her about the horses and about her dog Piper and the chickens and the cold winter garden, which all needed her back.

We all believed at that time that we might be able to say something that would spark some memory or play a powerful role in bringing her back into being. We only ever wanted Mum to get better, so the thought that one of us might hold the key to bringing her round into stronger consciousness meant we all poured our energies into her. We tried talking about the things she loved most, like the horses or the garden, and we even took Piper into the hospital. We hoped that if she put her hand on his head, or heard us singing a carol she had especially loved, or registered the sound of her sister's voice, she might be woken from this endless stillness. The monologue was exhausting, all the more so given Mum's motionless response.

After a few weeks, Mum's head lost its melon swell, and her body did too. She started to look thinner, her cheeks hollowing slightly and her skin crepey around her upper arms. Four weeks after the accident she was moved out of the wraparound horror show of the main intensive care ward, where terribly damaged bodies were wheeled in day and night, into her own room that looked out onto a garden with pots of rosemary and lavender lining a courtyard.

When she started breathing on her own we celebrated because it meant she was getting better. The ventilator making her chest rise and fall was taken away and there were fewer wires coming from her body. Gradually, she started to move. To start with, this was just a little movement in her finger or a shift of her arm, barely slight enough to notice, but seized upon by all of us as dazzling proof she was getting better. We celebrated together, spirits more boisterous than normal as we sat around the kitchen table, trading extraordinary stories of neurological recovery which just proved it was possible.

Then Mum started opening her left eye. She'd stare glassily at us as we sat beside her bed talking to her about everything we could rip out of ourselves to give to her. By Christmas, her right eye had half opened too. She started moving as well, but there was no intention in her movements and instead when her hand pulled at the edge of a sheet, or her body lurched slightly sideways on her pillow, it was as if an automatic impulse was moving her forward. Mum's eyes were open now, but she was entirely absent.

It wasn't like a film at all. The only remote similarity between seeing someone in a coma on screen and watching it happen in real life is that for a short time you are like a celebrity. A mother in a coma brings about a special status. Your presence can instantly silence a room.

Just before Christmas, I'd started doing the occasional day in school again. Looking back I really don't blame the other students who thought I was weird, because by then I was very weird and very strange, all the time. In the school canteen I avoided eye contact, convincing myself if I did not catch anyone's eye my swollen, red face would be invisible. I couldn't stop the tears flooding down my face, and would walk into an English lesson through a mist of salt water. Simon and Neil messed around less during history on the rare occasions I was there. Maybe it seemed disrespectful to flick paper across the room when someone else in the room was crying into their textbook.

In between hospital visits and time spent in the kitchen with my brother and sisters and with Rick, imagining how we would manage our lives when Mum returned, a strange version of life went on. By mid-December, tinsel and a Christmas tree covered in smudgy baubles decorated the entrance to the hospital. Some of the nurses wore Santa hats and once I arrived with Rick to find a brass band singing carols outside, collection boxes rattling as we skidded over frozen ground.

We limped through Christmas, but eventually Rick had to start working again, and so did Emma and Tom, so the shrill hysteria of fresh trauma at Minety dulled, and it was just Nell and me and the lodgers at the house during the week, with a full house of siblings at the weekend.

Rick employed an Australian girl called Ali to help run the house and cook meals. The lodgers liked her brassy accent and the kitchen chat when she cooked stir-fry and banoffee pie. Later, I'd stand in the kitchen, eating straight out of the fridge. The achingly sweet pie tasted so good, but it wasn't what Mum would have made. Her idea of pudding was stewed apple with top of the milk from a glass bottle as cream. I ate straight from the fridge until the pie made me sick and I had to kneel down to stomach the pain, cold from the stone floor shooting up my ankles and the room quiet apart from the thrum from the fridge beside me.

The centre was breaking apart but amid the emerging horror that was Mum's awakening, my schoolwork became a benign sort of consolation. Poetry I'd never understood and might have thought dull started to make sense. We were studying Keats at school, and I returned to his Odes almost obsessively as if they were clues to the puzzle that getting through every day had become. There was a consolation in 'the sad heart of Ruth, when, sick for home,/She stood in tears among the alien corn' and in the fleeting nature of happiness he told me were part of being human in 'Ode on Melancholy'.

Better even than Keats was the way Emily Brontë's *Wuthering Heights* made powerful and familiar a violent world where home and family were lost and broken. When the childish ghost of Cathy had her thin wrists rubbed into the jagged broken glass of the window frame as she mourned her lost home, my own pain felt less strange and ugly. It made pain feel beautiful.

There was also sex. A grown man's clothes were flung across the floor when I was doing my homework, because I clung to the man who was the lodger who had become my boyfriend. Emily Brontë had shown me the way out of my head, but sex was a way out of my body. I started having sex with him again two weeks after the day of the accident. It felt disgusting to be reaching for that kind of ecstasy when Mum's head was blown up and nurses were sticking pins inside her nails, but it was also a way of surviving the night. Countenancing what had happened to Mum was like trying to stand still and calm while someone screamed into my ear, but being a physical part of another person felt like protection. I had someone else not just beside me, but inside me too. Sex and darkness wound themselves together like a viper coiling around a silk scarf tied at my throat. It hurt so badly but the pain also felt good, flooding clear white light into the black space in my head.

Mum started being moved from her bed into a chair by the window, where she viewed the room cautiously, always looking at it as if seeing it for the first time, every day. Her shaven hair at the top of her head was growing back into thick stubble, but her scar from ear to ear was still vivid and angry. She was thin but strong, the hands that had kneaded bread on the kitchen table and rubbed soap into saddles or held me when I was a baby now grasping the edges of her hospital chair, squeezing it so that her knuckles went red. Mum had never spent any money on clothes and most of what she wore, apart from riding clothes, seemed to be garments she'd had since the 1970s: long circular skirts, chequered shirts and striped jerseys. Emma brought her clothes into hospital and the nurses dressed her in them, but I found that frightening, to see such a very unfamiliar body wearing clothes I knew so well.

But we were excited, because her physical recovery moved forwards quickly, so that in late January she started walking; hesitant steps at first but then, within days, strong strides along the hospital corridors. Her strength surprised and delighted everyone, as it suggested her mind would soon heal too. The nurses talked to her in loud voices, instructing her to *stand up, Charlotte*; *walk towards your daughter, Charlotte*; *now sit down, dear* and she did it all, but afterwards she hissed sounds at them as she reached for words that didn't form.

We took her for walks around the hospital, down to the café and out around the car park, with her arm linked in ours. Her grasp was very tight and sometimes she'd hang onto my arm with such force it felt as if she might pull me over. But I cried a bit less when I was alone now, because Mum was strong and could move her body which meant that, one day, she might be able to wrap her arms around me and embrace me again.

In the hospital café, she could reach forward and pour a cup of tea from the metal teapot, then follow it with milk. There was so much she knew how to do; it seemed like a miracle. It might have been a bit strange that after drinking one cup of tea she'd reach for the teapot and drink every drop in the pot, then lift the milk to her mouth to drain the jug before trying to eat all the sugar lumps on the tray as well, but we overlooked this because in some senses she was starting to behave like a normal person. When we took her to the car she opened the door, climbed in and belted herself in, like she was waiting to be driven home.

But although she was physically deft, she could not speak. Instead, she made noises at us, as if trying to find a language that had gone. Sign language could not replace it either. When we asked her to signal what she wanted, or to point to a picture of a cup of tea, for example, she looked anxious but also blank at the same time. She'd turn away, putting the picture cards down, muttering and rubbing her forehead with both hands.

We thought she might be able to write, and I felt thrilled and delighted when she signed her name on a piece of paper. Her handwriting was the same as it had been before the accident, curly and almost illegible, but she held the pen perfectly, writing her name again and again, then following it with swirls of ink that looked like writing, but spelt nothing. It didn't matter, we told each other, because she'd learn in time. We promised one another she'd learn. Very occasionally, words appeared in her scribbles but they never made sense, apart from her own signature. Once, she wrote 'jewels for divers' and later 'Basingstoke'. These words didn't mean anything but we used them as props for our optimism. I told Mark Palmer, her horse dealer friend who'd taught Annie to pull a cart, about 'jewels for divers' and he said that was a wonderful sign, because it might mean she'd discovered something beautiful when she'd been diving down deep into her coma.

We sat with her and talked and talked, pushing her to communicate in any way at all, or just to nod if she was hungry, and then she'd stare at us, eyes as unreadable as her swirling writing.

The only word she could say was yes, and it was suddenly extraordinary to ask her questions she seemed to understand.

'Mum, are you hungry?'

'Yes.'

'Would you like a cup of tea, Mum?'

'Yes.'

'Shall we go to the café and have some tea?'

'Yes.'

'Do you want milk in your tea?'

'Yes.'

'Do you want sugar in your tea?'

'Yes.'

'Do you want salt in your tea?'

'Yes.'

'Do you want washing-up liquid in your tea?'

'Yes.'

'Do you want to go to the moon, Mum?'

'Yes.'

Her surgeon didn't visit her again after she'd woken up because as far as he saw it, his cutting in her brain had been successful. She had regained consciousness. She could walk. She could even pour a cup of tea. She was beginning to speak because she could say yes. Apart from incontinence pads and a cocktail of medication, she didn't need medical equipment.

And she confused us all so much because recovery seemed quite close. She wasn't locked in, or vegetative, and very occasionally, standing in the hospital garden in her long denim skirt and red checked shirt, from behind, she almost looked like Mum. But she could also say nothing, and do nothing, and knew nothing, either.

But because she was awake and moving, it was time for her to leave the care of the NHS and come home. Our prayers had been answered. Mum had survived.

A trinity of three broad flat stones, twice as tall as me, stand at the entrance to Wayland's Smithy, the Neolithic long barrow just over a mile west of the White Horse. Excavations in 1963 suggested the timber chambered oval barrow that exists today covers an even older one lying on the same site. A cathedral of beech trees surround it, the crows a congregation who soar starkly overhead, because even on the hottest summer day with walkers and dogs around there's something remote about this place. I like the walk down from the White Horse, along a distant track sheltered from the wind by bundles of blackthorn hedge.

'This dates from 3590 BC,' I tell Jimmy and Dolly and the babies as I drag them, protesting, through the mud to Wayland's Smithy on a dark March afternoon when I need to smooth out the cracks that hours spent at screens have carved into them. 'That's three thousand five hundred and ninety years *before* Mary had Jesus. Can you imagine that?'

They stare at me blankly, and Jimmy throws a flint at a crow who's landed on the barbed wire fence beside the barrow. I try to engage them by talking about Wayland, the ancient smith god, but the children have already vanished like marbles among the beech trees, leaving me to trudge around the edge of the stones three times, a pointless personal ritual I feel unnerved to neglect.

Wayland comes from the Proto-German '*wela-nandaz*' meaning 'battle brave', and some of the stories in Rudyard Kipling's *Puck of Pooks Hill* are set near the Smithy. Mum read them aloud to Nell and me when we still lived in Oxford, before I'd ever heard of the Ridgeway, but I don't remember anything of them, apart from the children in the opening chapter having a picnic of boiled eggs with salt in a twist of paper, and the fact they weren't surprised when Puck stepped out of the hill and started talking to them.

Wayland is a magical blacksmith from Norse mythology said to own a white horse. I can see him clearly in my mind because the blacksmith's visits at Minety were really important. Every two months, Robert shod the horses and ponies, and I remember vividly my delight at the way he could bend black iron into a C shape to hammer onto their hooves. He had a mobile furnace he'd fire up in the yard, in which he'd heat the iron until it was red hot. I never minded when Mum asked me to take him a cup of tea and a digestive biscuit, since I loved the precision of the way he cut the ponies' hooves back, trimming them as neatly as if he were cutting their nails. I was horrified and fascinated by the way Mum's dog Piper would eat the shavings of hoof, and the hiss of black water as Robert plunged the red-hot iron of the new shoes straight from the furnace into a bucket of water.

It's not unusual to see a smith competition at an agricultural show too, where young blacksmiths create a linked chain or set of horseshoes against the clock. You can see them sweating as they work beside their furnaces, and they usually wear T-shirts with the sleeves cut off, so that the taut contours of their biceps are shown off best, shiny with heat. These competitions are a bit like displays of manhood, and I'm pretty sure this is how Wayland would have looked, his excellent male body made for working with horses.

Of course there's magic around Wayland too, and if you believe in the legends of the White Horse, and in Dolly's conviction that it can come down from its hill, you might believe the legend that says it sometimes gallops from the hill to be shod in silver by Wayland. More prosaic, but still as fantastical, is another local legend that says the traveller who needs a horse shod can leave it at Wayland's Smithy with a coin, and on returning the horse will have new shoes and the coin will have vanished.

Wayland's Smithy isn't a place I'd want to hang around on my own,

but on my eighteenth birthday, Nell and Emma and I camped here
with some friends. It was mid-April, a year and a half after Mum's
accident. Emma came down from London, and we drove in a convoy
to the Ridgeway. Back then there was no sign at the entrance
instructing, 'No fires, no camping', so we built a shelter using a tarpaulin
tied to the edge of the long barrow and made a fire to cook sausages,
drinking red wine from Mum's enamel picnic cups as we did. There
was a birthday cake bought from the village shop and when it got
really cold we drank a bottle of tequila so that the stars above the
beech trees spun. Emma had brought a plastic champagne bottle with
an exploding lid which emptied coloured confetti all over the grass.

I'm eighteen and now I'm an adult, I thought, as Wayland's beeches
whispered above me. And that night I dreamt of Jimmy and Dolly.
They were there in my dream as vividly as they are now when they
bang through the front door at 4 p.m., dropping schoolbags in the
hall and popping bagels out of the toaster to spread with Nutella. At
Wayland's Smithy, I saw them in my dream before I ever knew them.

I feel this deep magic everywhere on the Ridgeway, from the more
obvious stone mysticism at Avebury, to the haunted high elevations
of Segsbury Camp above Letcombe Regis, to the hill fort, Barbury
Castle, soaring above Swindon. The reassurance of standing on this
old road is profound and archaic, which is perhaps why it became
one of the places I'd go to most regularly in the first two years after
the accident, when Mum had left hospital and was living at home.

'Home' is probably the wrong word for what Minety had become,
since the house was more like a hospital with Mum there, and an
asylum for the rest of us. We tried to look after Mum ourselves, as
we thought her recovery might be quicker with us caring for her.
We all learned how to change incontinence pads, wash her and
dress her, but none of us are nurses and it was obvious Mum needed
a carer with her the whole time. Managing her incontinence was
really difficult and she also needed watching constantly, since her
automatic impulse to go on acting out the tasks of running the

house was strong. It was like looking after a deranged but capable toddler, as her actions were as chaotic and destructive as my son Dash's would later be when he went on the rampage. She'd take pans out of the cupboard and put them into the cooker with the gas turned on full or leave taps running in upstairs basins. Outside, she'd walk to the stables then lead Joe out to the field still wearing his saddle and bridle, or empty whole sacks of meal out for the chickens, who normally had only a handful. Most frighteningly, she'd sometimes try and get into the car to drive away, so we became vigilant about hiding the keys of anyone who'd arrived in a car.

Mum was a very fit and apparently physically able madwoman, reliving the rituals of a broken life. She could do a lot of things, but also nothing at all. She still couldn't speak or even communicate her most basic needs, like hunger or cold, but because she had come home, we had our collective vision firmly set on a future in which her recovery would continue. We had to believe there would be a future other than the present we existed in, since stopping our attempt to recreate what we had lost was too difficult a decision to consider.

Those days were wild too. Rick was away all week, and although Emma and Tom came back at the weekends as much as possible, apart from the lodgers the only other real grown-ups in the house now were Ali, the Australian girl, and the carers looking after Mum. They had a madwoman to care for so they really didn't know or probably care what Nell and I were doing. No one knew if I left the house in the morning or not, although I always went to school because in a terrible exchange it, rather than home, had become the place I wanted to be. I didn't want to rush down from my room to share breakfast with Mum, or sit with her and her carer at the kitchen table as she choked over a bowl of soup and I talked at her, pretending this was normal life. I didn't want to have to change her pads, or wash her, or find a clean skirt for her. I wanted Mum more than anything in the world, but I didn't want to do any of these other things.

Instead, my tight white trousers were still working well and sex was now joined by drugs in a combination too powerful to resist. There was the lodger, but there were also boys from the neighbouring villages to go to at night-time. It's never boring being a teenager in the English countryside as long as you have a car and the kind of mentality that likes taking drugs. We smoked cigarettes and then joints, and soon it became essential for whichever boy I was with to have a car with a dashboard big enough to slice up lines of speed on and a stereo loud enough to turn the bass right up. Acid was a psychedelic trip into an imaginary world where the accident had never happened. And sex outside at night with grass under my hips, or pressed up against the cold metal bonnet of a car, or with the branches of an oak tree chequering the sky above me, was always a better way of doing it than at home, where Mum now crept along the corridors, trailed by a nurse.

As time passed, it became clear that Mum might need much more sophisticated nursing help to recover than that which we could provide by simply being in a familiar environment, surrounded by her previous life. Rick and Emma organised therapy for her and she started to be sent off, usually for two or three weeks at a time, to residential rehab centres. The other patients were almost always young men, three decades younger than her, their brains and bodies smashed up in motorbike accidents. The nurses and social workers tried to teach her to express herself through painting or sign language, but were always frustrated by the brittle shell of complete mental incapacity surrounding her. She didn't understand anything and couldn't communicate in any way whatsoever, but she would still try to escape the building and find a way home. Once, she was caught walking along an A road, trying to hitch-hike out of there. All she knew was that home was a place she wanted to get back to. The next time I went to visit, her wrists and ankles were tied to a chair to keep her safe and a young man was screaming in the next room.

It hurts to send my mind back. I don't want to go there and I cannot linger to look around, but I know that shortly after I turned eighteen

I was suddenly in the final months of my A levels. My brilliant English teachers Mrs Withers and Mrs Robbins gave me some extra lessons to help me catch up on those I'd missed because of the accident, so I did well in my exams, but then there was the question of, what next? Rick had always made it clear that Oxford University was the place he expected us to go, and a year after the accident Nell took up a place that she'd been offered before it had happened.

I couldn't imagine leaving Minety, but I couldn't imagine what was going to happen if I stayed, either. I drove myself to school on the morning of my final A level exam and that afternoon I took Joe out to the fields near the house and jumped him over some of the wooden post-and-rail fences separating the fields from a neighbouring farm. It made me forget everything terrible for a few moments, and afterwards I leant forward and hugged him around the neck, adrenalin coursing through my body as my heart thumped against his side. Then I rode slowly back across the paddock to the house, where Mum was sitting inside with a nurse, daytime TV flickering in the corner in the playroom. Being close to a horse, or galloping a horse, never frightened me after the accident, despite what had happened to Mum. Horses made me feel stronger, and they made me feel defiant too. They were a way of facing down the accident and all the sadness and horror it had brought with it. If anything, the accident made me want to ride more, not less. Giving up riding would have been a betrayal of the past and everything Mum had given us. It wasn't something I would contemplate. As a way of feeling close to her while her absence felt so strong, I wanted more horses in my life, not fewer, but I needed to ride harder, faster, and with more danger than I ever had done before.

Mum's rehabilitation wasn't working at all, but sometimes after I'd come in from riding I'd sit beside her on the sofa in the playroom, watching the news as Piper lay beside us, resting his soft head in Mum's lap. And if I didn't look at the swelling and scarring on her head or at her half-closed eye, and just stared at her strong hands,

I could almost imagine for a moment that she was still Mum. When the fire crackled and Piper sighed in his sleep, the television blurting white noise out into the room, it was as if none of this had happened.

Then a carer would come in from cooking Mum's supper in the kitchen, clucking, *Charlotte, time for your tea, my love, and we better change that pad before you have an accident,* breaking the spell.

There's a back route across the Ridgeway and over the Downs to Didcot, which I sometimes take from Baulking when I'm on my way to catch the train to Paddington for work. It's not a short cut, since it adds ten minutes to my drive to the station, but it's the route I like best if I'm not in a hurry and want to fill my head with horses before I'm swallowed up by the pavements of London.

Serious commuters, intent on catching the 06.28 a.m. fast train into town, might not see the sign outside Lambourne that says, 'Welcome to the Valley of the Racehorse', and if they're already lost in thoughts about their first meeting, will probably miss the white post and rails that flash alongside the road, shielding an all-weather gallop from the cars. In the winter, when the national hunt racing season is at its peak, I can leave the house just after dawn to reach the gallops as the cold morning light is thickening, to drive parallel to a string of horses thundering across the earth.

Racing is the living, thundering heart and spirit of the Ridgeway near Lambourne. In the summer, glossy-coated thoroughbreds with big bellies graze in the fields around the village, but through the winter these animals are speed machines. Leggy, hysterical, sensational thoroughbreds represent a completely different sort of romance for me to the clutch of scraggy black-and-white ponies hunched up against a thick hedge in the valley below, although they too hold a special place in my heart.

The energy of a thoroughbred mid-winter, when it's at the peak of fitness, is the souped-up thunder of high-octane adrenalin and brilliant, shiny, racing colours. This stretch of land on the Downs and running along the Ridgeway is driven by the thrum of that gallop.

The clatter of a string of horses through the village that I pass on the way to London still makes me feel shimmery with excitement and relief, the same sort of excitement I felt when I was first legged up onto a proper racehorse.

I was eighteen, and Minety as home was dissolving around us. Mum was in rehab almost all the time, and we were all deserting, because without Mum the house couldn't exist. A new feeling wrapped itself around me wherever I went, even when I was at Minety, of homesickness and a deep longing for a place that I couldn't find and wasn't even sure existed.

I didn't want to be at Minety any more, so I went to work for a racehorse trainer above Swindon. His yard was beside Barbury Castle, the Iron Age hill fort where Mum and Rick had used to drop Nell and me with our ponies to ride the Ridgeway. My accommodation was a concrete room beside his big American barn stables, where fifty horses nodded out of boxes. I joined half a dozen stable lads and two lasses, who lived in a communal building beside the stables, mucked out every morning and evening, and galloped the horses on the Downs every day.

I'd never ridden thoroughbreds before, and was wary of the tiny leather saddles, no bigger than a paperback book, and the light metal stirrups that were so different to the comfy riding saddles with high backs and padded knee rolls Mum had used.

The horses were completely different too. Leggy and rangy, they were shiny beauties who pranced and snorted when a pigeon flapped in the maybushes outside the yard, and who would whip around with the speed and ferocity of a fairground ride, which meant staying on was difficult if I didn't concentrate at all times and keep one finger slipped inside the neck strap around the horse's neck. I knew how to bridge my reins at a gallop so that if a horse pulled, it pulled against itself, rather than my arms, but riding with stirrups so short my heels were pulled up against my thighs was completely new. The trainer taught me how to sit down for the first two strides as the horse danced at the bottom of the gallops, then to stand up in the saddle as soon as the animal had 'jumped off', the term used to describe the moment a thoroughbred starts moving at speed up the gallops. The trainer would sit at the top of the gallops in his Subaru, binoculars trained on each animal as he evaluated its movement and speed given the firmness of the ground and the weight of each jockey on its back. I loved the feeling of galloping upsides with one of the boys from the yard, crouched over our saddles as the horses pounded across the Downs and the earth whizzed past, and I loved the seriousness of riding horses for work, not just playing with ponies. I rode three or four horses a day, developing muscles I hadn't known existed in my calves and thighs, while carting muck out of so many stables morning and evening made my arms grow strong with muscle.

There was a cooker, sink and shower in my room, which I made cosy with eiderdowns and cushions I'd taken from the playroom at Minety. Sometimes I ate pizza or toasted cheese sandwiches with the lads in their rooms across the yard, or cooked spaghetti or bacon and eggs for myself on the cooker, eating it alone sitting on the edge of my bed, listening to the sound of the wind outside, whipping across from Barbury Castle.

The boys I worked with were tough and funny. They only talked about sex or horses, nothing else, and I loved the feeling of moving to a new place with them. I didn't need to explain what had happened to my mum or to make the accident any part of my life. Jockeys fall off horses and have terrible accidents all the time.

I liked the stable lads who did all the hard work, but professional jockeys also came to the yard, purring up in silver sports cars to ride three or four horses very quickly, bringing an intense sort of concentration to the day, before spinning off to make a mid-afternoon race in Leominster. Once, after evening stables, a jockey returned to the yard having won a big race. Everyone was gone for the day, the lads cashing in at the bookies or celebrating in the pub down the road. I was about to go back to Minety for the evening to see Mum.

The jockey's hair was still plastered to his head. As with so many of his trade, he wasn't tall, his eyes almost parallel with mine, unblinking as he spoke to me. He smelt so good, of sweat and leather, and we talked about the horses, walking through to the stables to pass along the line, stroking the horses' velvet brown noses as we passed. At the end of the stables was a solid metal gate that looked out to a starry spread of sky flung above the Ridgeway, and suddenly he was pressing me against that gate, his mouth mashing against mine as he held me around my waist and then made me a part of him. There were specs of mud on his jodhpurs and a scratch of fresh blood across his cheek but nothing about him or what he did to me scared me. It was what I wanted.

On Saturday nights, after the lights were switched off in the American barn and the horses stood feeding in the warmth of their stables, I'd go back to Minety for a night, or drive out to a party with one of the boys who lived nearby. Sometimes that was back to the Ridgeway, since up on the Downs was where lots of the raves were happening. There was consolation in making my head swim and the present swirl into a peaky shape when I took ecstasy or MDMA. Once I went with a friend to a rave in Manchester, swallowing acid to sweat beside a giant speaker before he drove me back to my room on the Ridgeway. When I rode out with the lads the next day my world was still fuzzy and imprecise, although the power of the horse beneath me yanked me back into the moment.

All week, every week, I galloped and slept, galloped and slept, and that felt good, not thinking about anything much apart from keeping my fingers knotted tightly into the manes of the horses I was learning to understand. There was something intensely reassuring about moving at a gallop in one direction, only ever forwards, and never having to look back.

Four months after moving to the Ridgeway, I was faced with a decision I didn't want to make. Rick wanted me to apply to Oxford University, which meant leaving the racehorses and my concrete room at Barbury Castle to wrestle my essay-writing back into shape.

I didn't want to leave. Riding racehorses was like a shot of

adrenalin straight into my heart every day: just as exciting as the
drugs that gave me an alternative present, but with none of the
plummeting lows. And I didn't want to give up the pure, muscular
delight of a serious horse beneath me and time whistling past so
fast that for a moment I could escape it and gallop right into the
purest sense of the present, where the truths about Mum's condition
couldn't catch up. When I thought about Mum's horse, Joe, standing
in the field at Minety, or the little grey driving pony Annie hunched
up against a thick black hedge in the paddock, I felt cauterised with
sadness, but a thoroughbred was less specific, since Mum had never
owned one, giving me a portal into another world where things
like home and family were gone. But if I was going to be serious
about applying for university, I couldn't do it at the same time as
riding full-time.

I had to make a choice.

Late one morning in December 1993, after I'd ridden three
horses and the lads had driven down to the bookies, I went to the
house beyond the yard to talk to the trainer.

'You have a decision to make, Clover. You can stay here, and I'll
give you a job for as long as you like. I could give it my best shot
at turning you into a very good jockey,' he said. 'Or you can do what
your father would like, and go all out for that place at Oxford, which
is a different path that would probably take you far away from racing.'
He tipped his chin, looking down at his feet, and then raised his eyes
again, frowning slightly but not unkindly. 'I've no doubt you'd have
a glorious time, but giving yourself to a life in racing . . . It's not
something I'm sure I would actually encourage anyone to do.' He
gave a dry laugh, then smiled at me. 'Tea? You want one?'

His kitchen was cluttered with piles of dirty cups and plates, a
copy of the *Racing Post* folded over and propped up against a toaster
flecked with breadcrumbs. From one corner, on the TV, came the
low grumble of racing commentary from Lincoln as coloured silk
shirts streamed across the screen; beside the box a fat spaniel noisily
licked his balls on a collapsing sofa covered in faded William Morris
fabric.

'Race riding is punishing on the human body,' the trainer went on as he clinked mugs and the kettle wheezed. 'And even worse on a woman's. Even if you have some success and win a few races, you won't want to do it for ever, or even for very long. You'll probably end up running the office for a trainer who will fall in love with you. And then you'll marry him. And then, in a few years, you'll find yourself making cucumber sandwiches for Sheik Mohammed.'

He laughed again, flicking the *Racing Post* open and picking up a pair of glasses from the arm of the sofa. 'It's that, or university and the road it will take you down. That's not a decision I need to help you with.' He shrugged his shoulders. 'Now, I don't want to miss the 2.30 at Plumpton. I'll see you for evening stables later.'

I went back to Minety. Mrs Withers and Mrs Robbins gave me tutorials for the interview and I reread Keats's Odes and spent a month studying dystopian literature and what happens when worlds stop and are then recreated. Oxford was damp and gloomy, and my hands shook as I sat outside the tutor's room as I waited for the interview, but when I started talking to him, the fear had gone.

Afterwards, Nell took me to stay in the house she rented in south Oxford. She had Piper with her, and had shaved her long blonde hair off. On the High Street, scores of tourists swarming to find Christ Church parted as she approached, Piper loping at her heels. On Cornmarket Street she stopped to talk to a tall, dark-haired boy with a missing front tooth busking outside Miss Selfridge. A handful of coins lay inside the open guitar case as he belted out chords from an Irish ballad, his face cracking into a grin when he caught sight of Nell. He slung his guitar down, pulling a packet of rolling tobacco from his back pocket, making plans to meet Nell for a drink later that evening. When she introduced us, he smiled sideways at me and asked me about the interview and what I thought of Oxford, fixing me with a look so intent that later I had to shrug off the feeling he'd really cared. Talking to him, I felt awkward, dressed in a neat blue jacket for my interview, the younger sister up from school. He spoke with a strong Irish accent, and was so tall that when he kissed me on the cheek, he had to lean right down. He was dazzling.

'That's Dan, from Dublin,' Nell breathed to me as we walked back to her house, explaining that she'd met him when he was playing in a pub on the Cowley Road. He wasn't a student, but played in a band with several of her friends at another college. 'He's always turning up at the house in the middle of the night with a bottle of whisky. He's amazing. Everyone's in love with him. Come on, let's go and get something to eat. I'm starving.'

A few weeks later, a letter arrived at Minety to offer me a place at St Peter's College to study English, but not for another two years. Later, I learned my school had told the college about what had happened to Mum. The tutors felt I needed this time off before starting at university.

Nell must have told Dan, because he rang me at Minety, and told me he thought I was fucking brilliant to have got in, and that when I came to university he'd take me out to celebrate.

Three days later, Rick came back to Minety. Nell was in Oxford and Mum was away in rehab. Rick and I made a cottage pie and sat with it, plates on our knees, in front of the fire in his study. We watched *Kelly's Heroes* and Rick drank a bottle of red wine. The rest of the house was empty, most of the lights in other rooms turned off, but Rick's study felt cosy and it was snug, just us together.

After the film we watched a late-night chat show, and then Rick said he wanted to tell me something.

Minety was going to be sold.

Mum was moving into full-time nursing care.

I had thought this would probably happen, but knowing it for certain made my heart plunge and I burst into tears.

Some of Mum's friends were going to take the horses. 'But you can always go and ride any of them, whenever you want ... Change will be good for you, Bugsy,' said Rick, using my childhood nickname to make me feel less sad. 'We don't know what will come next but we have to move forward, all of us. We cannot make Minety into a hospital.' Outside the glassy blackness of the night reflected through a gap in the curtains behind the sofa, but I wanted to stay safe there with Rick for ever.

Everyone said I was so lucky. 'Two years off!' cackled Aisling, a friend of Nell's in Oxford. 'Lucky cow!'

Emma wanted me to enrol at a language school in France and then Italy so that I could become fluent in two languages, but I couldn't imagine going back to school anywhere. And while Dan didn't call me again, I couldn't forget him. He sometimes came to Minety with Nell and sang Irish music around a bonfire as everyone drank whisky. I'd never met someone as wild as Dan and his Irish accent made me think that if all the men in Ireland were like that, then that was where I wanted to go. I didn't want to think about Minety ever again, or our horses or the garden or my bedroom or the big kitchen with Mum's wooden table in the middle of it. I didn't want to think about any of those things so I just walked away, although remembering that astonishes me now.

I left Minety as it was put on the market, moving to Dublin to rent a room in a friend's house near the Liffey. Mark Palmer introduced me to a friend of a friend who helped me get a job as a waitress. The past and home were finished. I rode forward, never looking back.

CHAPTER 4

Beside our house in Baulking is a black wooden barn with a cobbled stone floor and thick oak beams. At night the blackness of the painted wood makes it look like a cut-out against the dark sky. The barn and the post-and-rail fence that runs around the tiny paddock makes me think of ranches and if I'm feeling lonely I imagine we're living on the plain in our homestead, and then it all makes better sense. In winter the wind howls relentlessly from the west and we light a fire in the sitting room every night, making yellow heat dance in the grate, so that at least one room is warm. The cottage is 200 years old, so insulation is non-existent, but with the fire lit it's cosy, and Dolly lies on her stomach in the sitting room doing her homework, while Dash and Evangeline burble around her like gnomes. It's exactly the home I wanted it to be for them, but during the daytime the house is permanently freezing. There are days of dense, grey skies and even the Ridgeway, right up there on the Downs and perfectly drained by the chalk, is greasy with mud. When I take Dash and Evangeline up there for a walk, they slip over within moments of leaving the car, lifting their muddy hands for me to admire. By March I give in, leaving the heating and television on for long stretches of the day.

I need something to lift my spirits above the relentlessness of the winter, so spend most evenings on a website called Dragon Driving. It's a sale site for driving ponies, along with gypsy paraphernalia like wagons, leather harness and flat carts. If you like driving ponies, it's more addictive than Facebook and it's where I find Trigger. He measures 12 hands high, but has the spirit of a racehorse. Dolly and I go to look at him in a yard near London. He has a thick, long mane down to his knees, and if you dipped him in pink dye he'd look like My Little Pony.

Driving a pony isn't like riding. When I ride, my legs, rather than my hands, provide the basic contact with the horse. My hands matter too, of course, but the pressure of my seat matters more. I don't have the luxury of this when I drive, and at first my contact with Trigger, sitting behind him in the cart he's pulling, feels too distant. Having good hands means you have soft, yielding hands that do not jag or pull a pony in the mouth. This is almost more important with driving than it is with riding, because the bit is the only point of physical contact between the pony and the human driving it. That's also the reason why driving ponies are taught to respond to a human voice more than riding ponies need to be. Driving Trigger around the three-mile circuit between Uffington and Baulking, I don't feel lonely, because I'm talking to him all the time, telling him he's a good boy, trotting on like that, and no, you don't need to look at that plastic bag in the ditch, just trot on.

Trigger is the kind of pony who likes work. He stamps and shakes his head when I pull the driving bridle, with its leather blinkers covering his eyes, over his head. The blinkers stop him from being scared by the cart behind him. It's a cheap harness, made of nylon webbing rather than leather, but it works for Trigger, who starts stepping on the spot, impatient to leave the yard, as soon as he's ready.

'Easy, boy, stand still now,' I tell him, making my voice strong and confident as he tries to lunge forward in the cart as I jump in the side. It's late winter when I first drive him up to the White Horse, and the puddles beside the road are glassy, the black winter grass on the verge still covered with frost.

On the straight road to Uffington I give him some more rein and he leans into the driving harness with his neck curving like a comma. A tractor passes, then a stream of three cars, then the bright-red pick-up of the gypsy who lives on the corner down the road. He keeps driving ponies in his back garden, and painted flat carts out the front. I cannot help but admire the way he lives. He is unapologetic about the pony he tethers on the thin strip of verge in the village outside his house, or the leggy greyhounds barking in his drive. On the back of his pick-up is a sign in gold swirly writing saying 'We Lead, You Follow' and there's a defiance about his life I find compelling.

He nods at me as he passes in his pick-up, the briefest acknowledgement that Trigger is quality, the kind of pony gypsies call flashy. I trot him through Uffington to the bottom of White Horse Hill, where the road starts to get steeper for the climb up onto the Ridgeway. Trigger's long white coat turns wriggly with sweat.

That last stretch up is steep, with the glacial valley of the Manger falling below and the White Horse lying dead flat on the hill above. I drive Trigger on so he's almost trotting to keep the momentum of the cart moving along behind us, but halfway up pull him over into a gateway so we can both catch our breath. The sun is scratching through the white morning as we round the last steep bend before the hill flattens. Trigger is strong and brave and doesn't stop, even when his metal shoes slip on the concrete. The rumble of the wooden wheels of the cart and the clop of Trigger's hooves on the road is almost the only sound, apart from snatches of a muffled conversation from some walkers further away across the sheep field running parallel to the road.

'Good boy, Trigger, good lad getting up the hill,' I say, sounding almost as proud of him for making it up the hill as I do when Jimmy comes home with good marks. Sweating, Trigger gives a huge shake and pushes his sweaty head against me before I step

back up into the cart and we walk along the road beside White
Horse Hill, which joins up with the Ridgeway. Trigger is no longer
pulling at his bit but has dropped his head, stepping quietly forward
into the harness. The outline of his thick tail and backside and then
the longer line of his back is traced by the length of the reins
running from his bridle. When I am riding a horse, I feel like I
must master that animal, but driving is different. It's more like being
a part of a team, together, and as we leave the road and pull onto
the rutted track of the Ridgeway, I feel Trigger understands me.

★

The pavements in Dublin were always wet, even when it wasn't
raining. Soft days, they called them, when a fine mist of water
covered everything. These soft days made my wavy hair turn into
wiry frizz, and as I walked to work across St Stephen's Green, I'd
pull the side of my coat up to cover my hair. Frizz wouldn't look
good in the restaurant. There, everything was sharp and shiny, and
I was expected to keep not only the black lacquer tables as polished
as glass but my appearance immaculate as well.

'Think of it as stepping onto a stage every evening. You have to
play a part,' said Caro, front of house, who'd been coaching me in
how to fuck up less often when on the floor. That's what they all
called it. 'Get out there on the floor and work some tips' was
something the waiting staff said to each other to keep ourselves
going in the middle of an eleven-hour shift.

As staff in Dublin's newest, shiniest restaurant, we were supposed
to be fast, friendly, occasionally funny and always efficient. Order
book tucked into tight black trousers, we wore thin white T-shirts
and tiny white aprons tied at the waist, and the best waitresses got
extra tips for carrying a tray of champagne glasses on the fingertips
of one upturned hand.

How hard can it really be? I asked myself, as I fumbled with my
order book, desperately trying to remember if that quiet Irish man
had asked for his steak rare or medium rare, and had his unsmiling

wife wanted a peppercorn or Béarnaise sauce? Was it skinny fries or mash he had ordered? And had she said spring greens or salad?

How hard can this be?

In my experience, very hard indeed.

Always be nice to waitresses. Say thank you, and look them in the eye, and try not to complain when they forget the extra mayo, because it's an impossible job. Sometimes it was simply because my writing was so illegible that I couldn't make out the order I'd scrawled in pencil across my pad, but sometimes I just forgot. I made the other waitresses scowl when I took their plates from the hot counter by mistake, and made the chefs scream when I left my orders sitting there too long.

The restaurant was Italian, owned by the band U2, who occasionally sauntered in to sit at the special private table in an alcove at the back, away from the public. The nights the band was in were full of an even harder glitter than already existed around those sharp, moneyed edges. There was a ledge around the table where the waiting staff were supposed to walk to refill the upheld champagne flutes of the rock stars' supermodel girlfriends.

I was terrible at the job, but it didn't really matter because Dublin was swallowing some of the sadness inside me, and the trials of life on the floor were just background noise and a way to pay my rent. I'd taken the ferry over as a foot-passenger, carrying nothing more than a black nylon sports bag stuffed with clothes and a brown woollen knitted cap, which proved useless in the rain. Nell was at university and everyone's lives had moved away from Minety, which was up for sale. Leaving had made me feel less strangled by what had happened because it made my life move forward, rather than just feel shaken around, out of control. I could invent whole chapters or leave out bits I didn't like.

I was staying in the spare room of a friend of a friend, but I was rarely there. Dublin is very small, and from the two or three names I'd scribbled in my diary as I left, I met a string of brand-new friends. Mostly they were students who were studying at Trinity College, or boys in bands who I met in the pubs around the Liffey.

Life in those three months in Dublin was a series of rooms I moved between: the pubs and sticky bars where men slipped ecstasy into my outstretched hand; the student bedrooms where I'd wake beside a naked body I didn't know; the cafés on Grafton Street where I'd sit with these new people, spinning time and the past into nothing. When they asked me why I'd come to live in Dublin, I'd simply say, 'Just for a change,' and nothing more than that.

If I didn't talk about Mum, I could almost convince myself I wasn't thinking of her; it was a trick I played on myself that worked some of the time, when I was drunk, or excited, or preoccupied by being someone new. It worked for prolonged moments, until I'd find myself walking around unfamiliar streets in the dark, looking for something I couldn't describe in a city that was completely unknown to me, with a broken longing for something I could never have echoing inside me.

Because even though I can pretend that going to Ireland had been my plan, Mum had been part of it. She might have been living in a nursing home, with no idea of who she, or I, was any more, but she was still the one who made me do it.

Mum loved Ireland, ever since we'd gone there for a riding trip when I was fifteen. We'd stayed with friends of hers near Galway, who loaned us their horses to ride together. She loved the dense green richness of the west coast landscape, and in the evening let me go to a pub with the teenage son of our friends' neighbour, who was playing music there. I'd sat at the bar beside a peat fire and watched him play fiddle, racing through jigs and reels as movement and sound in the room blurred into one shape.

It was the same music Nell's friend Dan had been playing when she'd introduced me to him in Oxford. Sometimes I heard snatches of it from the other side of pub doors in Dublin or from upper-floor windows. It was music that sounded like dancing, or breathing, but in Dublin it felt like it was always beyond reach somewhere else I couldn't get to. It was the mid-nineties and Dublin was a Celtic Tiger roaring into life as it strutted around, admiring its new beauty. Rock music and starry actors were the city's currency, and

for a while I was sleeping with a musician. He took taxis everywhere and played the saxophone and didn't notice that what I was
doing was imitating the way I thought a girl who was happy would
have behaved.

Once, on an afternoon off from waitressing, I took a bus to the
north side of Dublin to a junk market, wandering among trestle
tables piled with tangles of old woollen coats and ripped mackin-
toshes. There were boxes of books with their pages stuck together
and bits of broken china, dolls without eyes and a teddy with an
arm missing. Boys in tracksuit bottoms with pinched faces sold
packets of rolling tobacco from boxes stacked behind the tables, as
the tower blocks gloomed above and young women with babies
sucking bottles in buggies rifled through the broken toys.

It may have looked ugly and dirty, but after the sharp polished
tables at the restaurant with their neatly folded squares of white
linen, I felt relief concertina inside me to have found somewhere
as crumpled-looking as I really felt. Rain on frizzy hair didn't matter
here, and after wandering among the stalls I sat in a café, smoking
a chain of Marlboro Lights as moisture ran down both sides of the
windows. I didn't have a newspaper or book to read, and the luxury
of being able to hide behind the pretend urgency of a mobile phone
was a decade and a half in the future. So I just watched the rain
as I made a pattern with a handful of Irish twenty pences on the
Formica-topped table. They were pretty coins with the outline of
an Irish draught horse stamped onto them.

When Mum and I had been in Ireland she'd made a pendant
from one of these coins for me, by stamping a hole in it and
threading a piece of pink ribbon through. Now it was lost, all
vanished with Minety, like it had never existed.

I looked at the horse on the coin, then looked away, trying not
to remember anything or to let the past make me do something
so energetic as feel because once that pain started it could take a
long time to move on.

It was almost dark when I left the café and most of the boys
had packed away their broken wares in cardboard boxes, kicking

the legs of their trestle tables so that they folded down to be stacked into the back of flatbed vans. I had no business being there; the market was over. I was leaving the square to get the bus back to Grafton Street when I saw the horse.

It was black and white, like a gypsy pony, ridden by a boy with the hood on his sweatshirt pulled up; JUST DO IT was printed across the front. He had no saddle, instead his legs hung long and lean from the horse's back, tapering to trainers with frayed laces. The horse wasn't wearing a bridle, either, and the boy steered it gently between the tables on a halter with a plaited lead rope for reins. The horse must have been ridden through there many times, as it didn't flinch, even when the headlights of a bus flashed past in the gathering darkness. Men darted around the horse oblivious, shouting to one another as they loaded the last of the stalls away, slapping the backs of the vans as they reversed into loading bays, calling to one another for a hand, a lift, a light. The horse moved between them like a vision. And above the shouts of male voices, I could hear the clop of its hooves across the cobbles.

More than anything, I wanted to touch the horse and breathe in the warm smell of its mane, to feel the reassurance of its strength. The horse was a place I wanted to go to and very quickly, after that, I knew that I couldn't stay in Dublin any longer. I would go to Galway, I decided; to the same area of the coast where I'd been with Mum.

Now, when I look back, it seems so obvious. Wherever I went, I was always looking for her.

I could hear that music again as I walked towards the pub at the end of the quay. It had stopped raining, and the salt smell of the sea was sharp like a cold blade. I'd left Dublin five hours before, packing the few clothes and belongings I had into my bag before catching a train to Galway. I wanted to see the fields around the city and imagined I would stay in a youth hostel. I thought I might be there for a week. After that, I wasn't sure what I'd do but I'd work it out later.

I'd asked a man near the station where the best pub for Irish music was, and he pointed down the hill, to the quay. It was called the Roisin Dubh and was twinkling with yellow heat, fat pints lined up on the bar as I peered in one window before pushing the door open. There was a group of musicians playing by the fire: a frenetic fiddle player working beside a guitarist and a girl on a whistle. The other dozen or so people in the pub all faced the musicians, but the barman turned to look at me as I came in, rubbing raindrops from my hair and dropping my bag beside the bar.

'You're wet from the outside, then?' he said, as though he'd been waiting. He wasn't much taller than me, with wiry black hair and a thick accent and bitten nails. He pushed a packet of rolling tobacco across the bar towards me, nodding at it as he said, 'Here you go and what can I be getting you?'

It was fuggy with heat inside the pub, and the sound of the music and the chatter and clink of glasses suddenly seemed like the most delightful noise I'd ever heard. Everyone in the pub listened as the fiddler ran up and down his scales, but when the musicians stopped some of the punters came back to the bar for more drinks. The barman introduced me to them: a handful of people in their twenties wearing camouflage trousers and big leather boots. One of the men had a shaved head and a gold earring in each ear. He smiled at me like we'd met before, introducing himself as Seany, and he and his girlfriend, Clara, who had bleached-blonde dreadlocks, sat down beside me at the bar and asked the barman for a roll-up. Seany was from Limerick but Clara had grown up in Kent, and had met Seany when he'd been to England to do fruit picking the previous spring. It was easy talking to them, much easier than it had been with the sharp-looking waitresses in Dublin, and they told me they were staying on a New Age travellers' camp outside Galway. And when I asked them if there was a youth hostel in Galway they knew of, Seany shook his head.

'No need to couch down in a hostel,' said Clara. 'Someone on the site'll have a bed. And if not, there's a sofa in our van, as long as you don't mind sharing with the terrier. He won't bite.'

It was 2.30 a.m. before we left the pub, Seany weaving through deserted streets as Clara turned up The Clash on the radio, shouting he was driving too fast, then inciting him to drive faster. We left the city, driving away from the lights into the dense blackness with the coast on one side and fields and thick hedges on the other, until Seany suddenly turned a sharp right into a gateway.

'Lucky you've got proper boots on,' he said, looking down at my long leather boots worn over jeans as we scrambled out of the car and into a muddy field, where I could hear the soft sound of the slap of water on rocks nearby. Seany caught sight of me looking at the water. 'Beautiful, ain't it? Mussels for tea tomorrow too. They grow all out there on the rocks and we can rip them off when the tide's down.'

In the moonlight I saw a field with vans and trucks parked across it and the smoking embers of campfires where dogs, roused from their sleep, stood up to bark at us as we walked past.

'Don't mind them, they're all friends,' said Seany as we stopped at a wooden horsebox where he swung up into the cab, then reached down to give Clara, then me, a lift in. The horsebox had been converted into a room, with a bed above the cab and a kitchen with a double gas ring and sink under one window. Dream catchers hung at the windows, and a tie-dyed rug was slung across a sofa at the end of the room beside a wood-burning stove that was still warm.

'Make yourself at home,' said Seany, as he yawned and rubbed the back of his neck. 'Clara'll show you how to make a cup of tea. I like mine white, two sugars, but not too early.' Then he winked at us both, slapping Clara on her bum so she jumped forward before he scrambled up onto the bed above the cab, letting his boots drop onto the floor below with a thump.

I stayed on the travellers' site with Seany and Clara for two months, living on savings I had from the racing job in England and the waitressing in Dublin. Their van looked out to the ocean and at low tide we'd walk out over the greasy rocks and brown seaweed to the mussel beds, pulling up handfuls of the blue shells to cook in a saucepan over the fire.

The travellers' site had been permanent for about a year and a half, after a handful of people had parked up their vans and sound systems for a rave, and never left. Every week or so, new vans or converted trucks rumbled into the camp, mostly English or Irish people in their twenties or thirties looking for a place to park for a few days or scouting for another party. They all wore a sort of uniform – the men had blunt shaved hair and camo trousers while the girls wore tie-dyed skirts with thick leggings over lace-up leather boots – and everyone smoked roll-ups. Some of them had babies or young children with them, and almost all the girls had long dreadlocks they'd pull back in the imitation of a ponytail. It was very muddy, and the hard techno energy of the camp wasn't the music I'd been looking for that first night I'd arrived in Galway, but I was happy to spend large parts of every day doing little more than keeping the camp-fire going. There was wood to collect from the copse of trees on one side of the camp, and ceaseless cups of tea to be made.

'She asked me what I did all day, so I told her: sit around the fire and keep the kettle boiling,' said Seany, cackling, palms stretched out to the flames, as he recounted an interview he'd had at the job centre one afternoon.

One of the girls on the camp had two horses that she kept tethered along the verge. Sometimes she let me ride them bareback down to the sea, and I loved leaving the mud of the camp and riding down into the water to the crash and splash of the horse's hooves across the rocks and into the sea.

I was eighteen years old. Mum's accident was two years in the past. What was going to happen to me tomorrow, let alone next week or month, barely seemed to register. Instead the days washed through me because they were all I could hold, and the muscle memory of the previous two years washed away, right out there to the horizon, with the tide.

★

By the late spring of 1994 Seany and Clara were restless and planning to leave the site. I wasn't ready to go back to England, and no part of me wanted to be in Dublin again, either. But I did have a sort of plan.

The previous summer, just before A levels, I'd met a horse-drawn traveller called Brad. He'd been helping Mark Palmer with his horses, and in return Mark let him keep his own driving ponies in one of his fields and park his wagon in his yard. Brad had left school at fifteen and had been a horse-drawn traveller for ten years when I met him. He wasn't a gypsy, but had started out as a New Age traveller, moving in a convoy across southern England in the late eighties. But it was horses he really loved, and so he taught himself to ride on some of the ponies of other horse-drawn travellers he met on the road, then started buying and breeding his own heavy cobs. He knew Ireland, and had travelled on the road there a few years previously, but when I met him at Mark Palmer's in Gloucestershire, he was planning to go back to Ireland.

'Just for the summer. Like a little holiday, I suppose,' he'd said. 'And I've a mind to go to the west coast, to do some horse trading. For a change from England, for a while. There's a horse fair I want to go to, near Cork, called Cahirmee. You can do some good dealing there.'

'With gypsies, you mean?' I'd asked, wide-eyed and country. Mark's kitchen was squashed with people huddled around the big table and talking over their glasses in front of the Aga. His wife Catherine held court at the end of the table talking about astronomy and astrology and the phases of the moon, her laughter rising above the hum of voices around her. Brad leant forward to pour us both another glass of wine. A shock of dark hair fell across his broad, strong face and when he grinned it made me feel good.

''Course I mean gypsies. What other sort of horse fairs did you think I'd mean? You should come. Next summer. I'll meet you there, in Tipperary, if you like.'

Brad had written to me when I was in Galway so I knew where to find him, catching a bus to Tipperary and then on to a village called Golden. A herd of brown-and-white cows stared at me over a stone wall in the village as the bus spewed me out, and just for a moment I doubted myself because while I trusted Brad, I barely knew him.

It wasn't hard to find him. Even in Ireland, where horse life is thicker than in England, people don't forget a burgundy-and-yellow flat cart with two piebald ponies tethered beside it. A man on a tractor pointed down the road outside the village, and I could see Brad's campfire and the horses tied up beside it in the distance, before I saw him. His dogs, two wire-haired lurchers called Minny and Blaze, ran up to me, barking as they lolloped along the road, then curled their bodies around my legs as I leant down to pat them. Midges danced in the unusually hot evening air; Brad had taken his top off, a sledgehammer slung over one shoulder. He'd been hammering in a tethering stake to move the horses to a fresh stretch of grass on the verge. The horse stood facing him, so that man and animal mirrored each other, silhouetted against the high evening light. Brad finished hammering in the stake, wrapping the horse's chain around it, and the horse nodded its head, snorting into Brad's outstretched hand. Then Brad looked towards me and smiled, although he didn't look surprised.

'So, you're coming to Cahirmee then?'

Because he was only planning on spending a summer in Ireland, Brad had left the horse-drawn wagon he usually lived in back in England, but was travelling with a flat cart and a bender he'd build in every camp from willow branches bent into the shape of a tent then covered with a piece of tarpaulin. He'd made a summer on the road in Ireland sound like a vacation, or holiday camp, but on the third day I was with him, when Eddie, the big black-and-white stallion I'd seen him with that first evening, stood up on his hind legs and reared in the shafts, I felt something pass into me that was wild and strange and new.

Nell and I had done some driving with Annie after Mum sent her to Mark Palmer's, so I knew how to tack a driving pony up and hook it into the shafts of a cart, but I was more accustomed to the tight, speedy rhythm of a racehorse than a gypsy cob. Brad had a three-year-old filly called Moon he'd bought the day he'd arrived in Ireland 'just because I liked her eyes, she looked like the right sort'. Moon didn't cause any trouble, and spent most of the time tied onto the back of the cart, stopping whenever we stopped, and trotting forward as soon as Brad clicked his tongue. Brad's driving animal was Eddie, a boss of a horse, a stallion standing at little over 14 hands high, but who wanted to tower. He'd spook and snort at plastic bags caught in a hedge or stop stock still in the road when he spotted a cat sitting on a fence post. He had the thick, fluffy white hair around his hooves that gypsies call 'feather', which gave him a flashy glamour.

He and Brad fought all the time. He'd shake his head and lift his ears out of reach when Brad tried to slip the driving bridle over his head, turning round to bump Brad in the stomach with his Roman nose, so that Brad would punch his neck and shout at him that he was an ignorant fuck and throw the bridle down at his feet, turning his back on the horse, who'd drop his head and snort in defeat. Then he and Brad would make up, Eddie breathing into Brad's outstretched hand as Brad turned to stroke his velvet muzzle, whispering words into Eddie's big ears for him alone.

Eddie never liked standing still and would career forward as soon as he was in the shafts, sometimes sending the kettle or a box of saucepans clattering into the road. Harnesses, cooking implements and bedding were piled onto the cart under a sheet of green tarpaulin and I threw my bag up there too. Brad knew how to shoe his own horses, where to find the best verges for grazing, how to thump a steel tethering pin so deep into the ground with a sledgehammer that even Eddie at his wildest couldn't pull it out, how to fix his own harness and make rabbit stew. When it was sunny and the horses were grazing and there was no more road ahead of us, he'd take a battered saxophone he carried everywhere and walk to a far corner of the field to practise. He liked singing some of the Irish folk songs I'd heard as we walked down the road.

The road had given Brad the freedom of living just to keep on moving, but what he loved best was the sweet wet smell of the dew in the early morning before anyone else had walked on it. He liked drinking and drugs a lot too, since – as much as the road is romantic – there were long periods when we'd been camped up in the rain for two days when it was extremely boring.

'Because what else are we expected to do on a verge but tether the horses and drink a bottle of vodka?' he'd say on a wet Tuesday afternoon when we'd walked twelve miles and even the dogs looked sullen. Then he'd spin the lid off a cheap bottle of vodka, crushing the metal and slinging it into the fire because there was no going back until it was all gone.

When you live on the road there's nothing to do but keep moving and that makes you exist right in the very moment. Sometimes, walking behind the cart as Brad walked ahead with the reins hooked over his shoulder, I'd imagine I could cup the moment like a tiny pool of cold clear water in my hand. The passing time slowed right down so that it felt like the pace of Eddie and Moon clomping steadily down the road. Every day we'd make a new camp on a new grass verge and sleep for the night. If it was wet, we slept under the cart, but when it didn't rain we lay on the back of the cart under tarpaulin with nothing but space and the velvet blue sky around us. Then the harness would be piled under the cart and Minny and Blaze would lie loose beside it. 'You need the dogs there, close by, in case there are visitors in the night,' Brad said, breaking up damp sticks for kindling to make a fire. There were a lot of visitors all the time, at least during the day: the gypsies in their pick-ups and 4x4s who stopped at the camp all the time, rolling out of their trucks to see if there was any dealing to do.

'How much for the dog? The pony? The cart? How much for the cast-iron kettle? The tarp? The harness?' they'd ask, greasy shirts straining across button-bursting bellies as they pointed to our life with the end of a wooden stick. Brad would reel off prices so high you could cut them in half and there would still be too many noughts, because it was all an elaborate game. They wouldn't buy anything but they might be back in the night to steal it. And sometimes they'd all laugh and say, 'How much for the girl?' and I never quite knew if they were serious or not.

Brad knew a lot of the gypsies on the road and I think they had a begrudging respect for him because of the way he was with the horses and the look of his turn-out, with his shiny leather driving harness and the horses themselves, who looked strong and proud. They didn't ignore the fact he knew all the best pull-ins to tether his horses or the way some publicans let us tie the horses in their back gardens while we stopped for pints of lemonade and vodka shots. Once, near Limerick, we passed a gypsy site near a dual carriageway where horses stood tied and boys on two-wheel racing trolleys called sulkies hammered through the traffic. They seemed fearless, driving leggy ponies past lorries and buses with their heads up to the sky, oblivious to the honked horns and shouted abuse, even when a horse careered sideways, making the car behind slam on the brakes. Brad knew a lot of the boys on that site, and as we passed he stopped to talk to them about a mare he'd sold them a few years before. I was tired, whining at Brad that it must be time to stop, and couldn't we just stop for the night.

'Not very fucking likely we're going to stop with this lot,' Brad said quickly to me under his breath, although he was always friendly to the gypsies. Limerick was rough, he later told me, rougher than anywhere in Ireland, so we trotted on past, even though it was almost dark and cars splashed past us with their headlights on, spattering my leggings with muddy water.

Being cold and uncomfortable, or wearing damp clothes or not eating hot food or taking baths very regularly at all was just part of being on the road. When we washed, it was after boiling a series of kettles and pans over the campfire, then stripping down to wash with a flannel. I stopped washing my hair altogether, because outdoors, without a mirror, my wavy blonde hair stopped irritating me but wriggled into blonde clumps I'd rake my fingers through to prevent forming dreadlocks. Sometimes I'd run my fingers over the calluses that had formed on my palms when the ground was hard and I'd had to hammer in a tethering stake to tie the horses out. I lived in a leather jacket worn over a mid-thigh dress covered in sprigs of flowers, worn with knee-length, flat brown boots with thick leather soles that never wore out, even though we'd walked miles. Once, walking through a village, a man emerged from his garage holding an oily rag, his eyes tracking me as I walked beside Moon behind the cart. When Brad had passed out of earshot, he called out to me, tipping his chin, 'Traveller's whore,' then disappeared back inside the garage to polish his car. I laughed, putting my hand out to Moon's flank, because that man knew nothing of the halls of freedom echoing inside me.

For most of the time, we travelled alone, stopping when we found a verge wide enough to tether two horses for a night, or even two or three nights if we were feeling worn out by the constant motion forward and wanted to spend a couple of days in camp. After days of movement there was relief in simply sitting by the campfire to discuss the best way to cook a curry in a tin bucket over a fire, walking the dogs at dusk to hunt for rabbits, or finding a river to strip off and swim in on a warm afternoon. Living outside felt like inhabiting a new skin. Brad taught me how to fix the harness when Eddie reared up, snapping the belly strap, and how to collect the best-sized kindling for lighting a campfire, and how to tie Moon onto the shafts beside Eddie if we came to a steep hill. We were just friends to start with, but when it rained at night I pulled myself closer to him in the bender and soon that sense of safety he'd first given me when I met him at Mark Palmer's became a stronger sense of needing and wanting him and the place he'd created for me within his camp.

Brad showed me how to cook over a campfire, frying eggs for breakfast that we'd eat scooped onto slices of toast grilled over the flames so that they tasted of smoke and early morning. Once we travelled with a friend of his, a woman called Anya who had thick brown hair down to her waist. She'd known Brad when he'd last been living in Ireland. There was a ragged glamour to the way she'd sit on the back of the cart, waiting for the morning kettle to boil, carefully writing a spidery line of black eyeliner onto each lid. She had a gold tooth and usually wore a purple velour hooded top with tight black jeans and buckled-up boots. I wanted to have her confidence as she tacked up her skewbald pony, or her dexterity in the way she always managed to avoid getting blood on her clothes as she skinned a rabbit, cutting it into joints that she'd fry in a pan over the fire, eating it with boiled potatoes and sliced-up cucumber. Unlike a lot of the harder New Age travellers, who seemed to have a point to prove, she was friendly too.

'He's practically like a son to me, and a friend of Brad's is a friend of mine,' she'd say, and I wondered how many times she might have said it before to other girls. She was living on the New Age camp near Cork when we first pulled in, playing the role of mediator when fights broke out between the younger couples around the campfires or in their wagons.

I'd have preferred to stay in the temporary camps we made for ourselves on the wide verges, but Brad knew a lot of New Age travellers and wanted to catch up with friends. Their camps were usually in deserted areas, far from towns or villages, because no one wants a travellers' site, New Age or not, in their back garden. The sites needed to be remote too, because of the sound systems most of the New Agers carried in their trucks, and their propensity for loud, repetitive beats. We stayed on a peat bog for a few days in Tipperary, surrounded by forest so thick no sound could permeate it.

Within the shelter of the forest, over a dozen painted horse-drawn carts and wagons were dotted over a couple of acres. Leggy lurchers roamed the site, where gangs of children with shaved hair ran from one campfire to another. Between the lines of washing and wood smoke, it was sometimes idyllic. Brad knew almost everyone from the years he'd lived in Ireland before, and everyone had a nickname: Trivet John, who made the three-legged, triangular trivets used to balance a kettle or pan over a fire; German Chris, with his dark, difficult eyes; and John the Bus, who drove a truck painted with psychedelic images of the zodiac.

Some of these New Age travellers were horse-drawn, living in wagons pulled by heavy cobs tethered across the site, but sometimes vehicle travellers, in converted trucks or Bedford vans, pulled in too. That was when the fights broke out, after a drug dealer had arrived for the night and crack pipes had sent the travellers in vehicles demented. Looking after an animal as big and demanding as a horse means that horse-drawn travellers have to keep their game together. All of us, without exception, took amphetamines like speed and ecstasy, which were relatively cheap and were just a way of staying up later and dancing for longer. Very few of the horse-drawn crowd habitually used crack or heroin and none of them had proper drug addictions, since regularly lunching out for days on end chasing the endless chemical high or narcotic low of a really strong, dirty drug like that isn't possible if you want to keep your horses healthy and capable of the hard work you expect them to do on the road. Horses need moving on their tethers, buckets of fresh water, and the love and care that the hardest drugs like crack and heroin obliterate. That was the reason why the New Agers in vehicles tended to stick to their own crowd, and the horse-drawn crew were, generally, easier to live with.

But when the drug dealer's vehicles arrived, the harmony of the campfire would be broken. I could snort amphetamines until my throat stung and take ecstasy until my head rattled like a pill bottle, but was scared of the persistent filth and lingering guilt of crack. After it had been around, the campfire, normally the heart of daily life, would be destroyed, with smashed glasses in the mud, cans of Special Brew burnt out in the ashes, the chairs and stools of the previous evening lying on their backs in puddles. But saddest of all was the sight of the horses on the far side of the field, nodding on the end of their tethers, still optimistic that soon the day would actually begin.

Brad said he didn't want any of that any more, anyway. We pulled out from the field the day after a particularly bad fight had broken out. It had happened on dole day.

'Watch it, money always brings fights to the camp,' Brad had told me that morning, reaching to the hot handle of the kettle over the fire with a rag, while ignoring the muffled shouts from the truck beside us, where two couples were fighting.

Though plenty of New Age travellers did it, Brad didn't believe in signing on. 'I can make what I need selling nags anyway, why would I tie myself to that false promise?' he told me. It was one of the reasons why the gypsies liked him, because he always had a harness, the odd dog, chickens or tools he'd trade with them. Because he shod his own horses, he never had to pay a blacksmith, so apart from the vodka his life on the road wasn't expensive.

The rest of the camp, who lived on the dole, viewed signing-on day as a sort of celebration, a break in the two-week cycle that saw them mostly skint and always on the blag. It was probably the reason why dole day was usually such a disaster, since very few of them would return with any cash. Instead they'd roll into town on their horse and carts, then spend the day at the pub after the formalities of the dole office were over. It was a sight: the line of painted carts and patient black-and-white ponies standing tied up in the pub car park, as New Age travellers stumbled in and out, juggling black pints of Guinness, orange cider and clear shots like water. There was always a fight, either in the pub or later, back at the site, over hurt feelings, borrowed money, flirtation.

The day we left, there were broken noses and blood spattered across angry faces, glowing bright metallic red against the greening brown of the peat bog. We hitched up Eddie and rode out that same afternoon.

Once a week or sometimes less I called home, gathering a handful of ten-pence pieces to slot into a phone box. Minety was in the process of being sold and the last time I ever called the house, my sisters told me I was speaking to them as they stood in empty rooms stacked with packing boxes. Outside the phone box, I could see Brad adjusting Eddie's harness as Moon stood patiently, tied on the back of the cart. My sister's voice sounded disconcertingly close by, as if she was standing in the phone box with me. I asked how Mum was, and could hear her trying to sound bright as she said Mum was moving to a new nursing home near Milton Keynes, but that, no, she hadn't really changed or improved. I tried to concentrate on the outline of Eddie's black-and-white jigsaw colours as I heard her voice echoing around the space where our life had been, and I made quick excuses about having to get on because the horses were getting impatient.

Brad and I walked on in silence for the rest of the afternoon after that. I tried not to think about Minety at all but instead concentrated on the verge beside us and the stone wall running parallel to the road. We had slowed the horses to a walk as we'd been trotting all morning, and the pace was gentle enough for me to count the rocks piled up on top of one another, and to examine it in detail. It was strong enough to hold a field of cattle in, but beautiful too, and fragile enough that between the rocks there were holes where the light got in.

'Clover, did you hear me? You've been in Ireland for, what, nearly seven months? You should go back,' Brad said eventually, turning his face towards me so I could hear his voice over the sound of Eddie's hooves. 'You'll regret not seeing your family home one more time. Not seeing it ever again. That's something to lose.'

I made excuses about not being able to afford the travel home, and when Brad offered to pay for my ticket I just ignored him, dropping back to put the space of the cart and horse between us. To me, Minety was already gone and home did not exist.

I was a coward too. I let my brother and sisters do it because I didn't want to see the house with empty walls and rooms, with their furniture and belongings vanished. I hated the thought of the bright patches of wall left where Mum's paintings had been, and the shelves in her kitchen emptied of her pans and plates. If I thought of Mum's horses being led out from their stables to a new home my heart clenched into a fist that beat me from the inside. It was easier to imagine it wasn't happening, because late at night, lying under the tarpaulin with the white pinpricks of stars above me and the quiet sound of Eddie moving on his tether just across the grass, I could imagine that my younger self, as a child, was still there at Minety.

It's the same now, in fact. If I close my eyes and sit quietly with memory and time seeping into one another, I can sense myself back there – with Mum. In that way I can imagine nothing has gone, and I can keep us both safe in a box in the past.

In Ireland, the space around the campfire became home instead. There was a comfort in the bent black arm of the cast-iron kettle and the metallic chinking sound of Brad hammering a tethering spike into the earth. And when it rained, and we slept beneath the cart, the drum of water overhead drowned out the thump of my heart every time my mind veered close to the dangerous edge where the thought of Mum existed.

There were always the horses too. Close to Limerick, Brad had bought a black five-year-old gelding called Buckle from a dealer on a travellers' site.

'I felt sorry for him more than anything,' Brad remarked, reaching out to stroke Buckle's soft nose as we refilled the horses' buckets of water from a trough in a field beside the verge. Eddie and Moon had eaten the grass short around their tethers like the most method-ical mowers, but Buckle had left patches of long grass. He didn't settle on his tether as Eddie did, often stopping mid-mouthful to raise his head and scream into the distance for the horses he'd left behind in Limerick.

'Do you think he remembers where he's from? Wants to go back?' I asked Brad.

'Not likely he'd want to go back there, is it, lad?' said Brad, addressing Buckle directly. Dusk was bleeding across the sky in patches of streaked orange, and after a day of rain it was at last warm and still. I shifted in my sodden boots as I felt wetness from the grass seeping through the leather. Minny danced back through the long grass to Brad, wagging a greeting with her whole body, and Brad knelt down in the grass beside her.

'It's a good evening for riding. Cloudless and it'll be a big moon tonight,' he said, more to himself than me.

We didn't have any saddles, but threw bridles onto the ponies, then trotted towards some woodland, where the thickening darkness was mottled with the shadows of the branches as Minny and Blaze bounded along, ahead of the thump of the horses' hooves. The moon was white and almost ghastly above us, but its light was clear too, sending the long shadows of the horses darting between the trees. I couldn't see the ground in the dark but kept my finger knotted through Buckle's thick mane, following Brad and Eddie's single outline as they cantered away from us. There was no time to be scared as Buckle stretched into a gallop as the woodland rushed past. I could hear my own breathing, like it was somewhere distant from the rest of my body, as I dodged the branches of the trees that suddenly swooped down to meet me in the darkness, kicking Buckle forward with my heels and gripping onto his damp sides with my legs.

But then, without me noticing, a branch swooped lower than those before it and the breath was knocked from me as I slipped off Buckle's back. I felt something on my face as I fell, but the ground was soft enough to cushion my fall. I kept my hand clasped through Buckle's slippery rein, desperate not to lose him in the darkness. Eddie and Brad were far ahead, but in the moonlight Buckle turned back around to face me, as if checking I was safe. He snorted, then dropped his head and sighed deeply, so I could make out two plumes of his breath in the night.

I was angry with myself for falling off, but the adrenalin kicked me forward so I had no time to feel pain or regret. Around me the woodland was thick and black, and I shivered, gathering my breath as somewhere distant a fox howled. I led Buckle over to a fallen tree, using it as a step to scramble onto his back, before gathering up the reins to prove to myself I wasn't afraid. I kicked him on into a canter again and he moved faster than before. I felt myself vanish into the outline of my pony, so that there was nothing more than the damp, fresh summer night around me and the sound of pounding hooves beneath me as I flew through the night.

I was nineteen that summer. I hadn't told Brad about my birthday, since being someone without a past or a future was like cool spring

air blowing through my life. But it was hot that day, and the unfamiliar warmth made us throw rugs down in the grass, lying on
our backs beneath a cloudless sky. Brad had bought batteries for
his radio in a village shop and we did nothing but lie on the grass,
winding from one station to another to find the music we wanted.

'It's a perfect day, isn't it,' Brad said, a statement not a question,
rolling over onto his front as a bee hummed in the grass beside us.
Nothing could spoil it, and the radio crackled, jumping to a song
by The Kinks we both knew.

For a moment the swelling sound of the music and the heat of
the sun and the sounds in the grass beside my head made me feel
like I was wide open to everything that was happening about me,
as close to the best version of myself that I'd ever been, but when
the words started I felt something tumbling over. The man's voice
was clear and pure and addressing someone he loved. He sang about
the loss of endless, sacred days together that seemed as if they'd
never end. He promised not to forget a single day, and suddenly
Mum's figure was walking across a far corner of my vision. I felt
the familiar, silent pressure descending as it snatched that beautiful,
sunny afternoon lying in the grass and screwed it into angry nothing.

Brad's smile had gone as the past I'd been resisting since going
to Ireland was all around me. The song went on, terrible and irresistible as the man sang of his sense of blessing that the beloved
had bestowed on him, and that not a day together would be forgotten.

Brad reached across to touch my face but I turned away, tears
blinding me, as a dreadful sickness drenched through my body,
which had felt so heavy and sweetly easy moments before.

'Don't cry, Clover. It's a good song, not a sad one . . .' started Brad.

'No, it's not, it's not . . .' I choked, but as I tried to put together
the words to explain to him what my tears were for, he interrupted.

'I love you, Clover, you know that now? I love your wildness,
coming out here all on your own. I love that in you and I . . .' he
said, putting his hand across my cheek to hold my face, but I
shrugged him off, furious.

'Don't say that, please don't say that. Please don't tell me that,' I cried, pushing him away and standing up, brushing dried grass off my arms and my skirt. Brad sat up, baffled, as he switched the radio off. I walked over to Eddie and buried my head in the warm fur lying underneath his mane. He stood very still and waited as my tears drenched his thick hair, dropping his neck down so that I could lean my whole body into his.

Brad was boiling a kettle over the fire when I walked back to the camp. After that I told him everything about Mum, elaborating on the bits I'd briefly told him when I first met him, about how she was alive but also lost and how mad and sad that made me feel, because I had no idea where she was or whether I'd find her again.

I told him that quite a lot of the time my heart felt like I was standing on the edge of a precipice, and he seemed to know what I was talking about. He said that sometimes I'd woken in the night with a violent start, and had sat up screaming and pulling at the bedclothes, then gone straight back to sleep without waking up.

'I knew there was something about you that was breaking inside,' he said calmly, pulling the hissing kettle from the flames and pouring its contents into a smoky-blue enamel teapot. 'That's why I never asked. Sometimes it's better not to have to explain.' He patted Minny's head and handed me a cup of tea. 'It'll be a nice evening. Shall we take the horses out?'

By the middle of summer we were close to Buttevant, the market town where Cahirmee horse fair is held every year on 12 July. Brad had sold horses here before so, for him, the white caravans parked on the verges, where children played with plastic toys beside tethered horses, weren't exceptional, but I felt increasingly excited as we got closer to the town. We still never camped with the gypsies, but in the days leading up to the fair would be visited in camp many times as they and Brad kept up their dealer patter. Brad didn't want to sell the kettle or the dog or even me, but he was impatient to make some money on Eddie, Moon and Buckle so he could go back to England and his field of horses in Gloucestershire.

'One summer in Ireland and I remember exactly why I left last time,' said Brad, as we sheltered from the rain in an empty barn beside the road. Brad passed me the cigarette we'd been sharing. 'And the raves are better in England anyway. They don't really know how to do it here.'

But leaving depended on selling the horses, since transporting them back to England was too expensive. Buckle and Moon would never make big money, but Brad was looking to make some proper cash on Eddie, whom he'd bought for £1,000.

'I need to sell him for at least £4,000,' he told me, looking uncharacteristically serious. 'Not easy at all.'

As we pulled out of our camp on the last day before the fair, a red pick-up slowed down beside us, the window lowering like it might reveal a mafia don. Instead, a gypsy with sandy corkscrew curls and a doughy complexion nodded at Brad, who pulled Eddie to stand, with Buckle tied neatly on the back of the cart. They talked quietly for ten minutes, Brad leaning against the side of the pick-up as I held Eddie. Numbers were thrown around and then Brad reached inside the van and slapped the gypsy's hand. Silently, a girl with dark hair to her waist, wearing skintight denim and over-the-knee black suede boots, got out of the van. She gave Brad a special smile as he unhitched Buckle from the back of the wagon, handing the lead rope to the girl, who walked past me, down the road in the direction of the fair.

'But I never even said goodbye to him!' I shouted at Brad, as he grabbed Eddie's reins from me, walking on ahead. 'You sold him and I didn't say goodbye to him.'

Brad shrugged.

'He's a horse, Clover. No point in getting sentimental over a horse. There's plenty more to break your heart over in life. I thought you would know that.'

I was still smarting the next day when Brad vanished in a rage to the pub. He'd sold Moon to an Englishwoman looking for a family pony early that morning, making an extra £200 on the £500 he'd paid for her. But Eddie had been harder to sell, and by early afternoon Brad was sick of the gypsies and their endless backchat. 'Five thousand pounds? You must be joking, aren't you? For that yoke?' He was annoyed with me too, still sulking about Buckle, and he told me he deeply regretted ever having come back to Ireland.

'And anyway, why don't you fucking well try and sell this horse?' he eventually shouted at me thrusting Eddie's reins into my hands.

The horse fair was concentrated in one field on the edge of the town, but the gypsies spilled onto the streets, leading ponies on strings, or queuing for fish and chips or piling into pubs to nurse pints of Guinness. Horses covered the field, from hairy Shetlands driven by gypsy children no more than seven or eight years old, to fat men holding a string of half a dozen ponies, to teenage boys who rode bareback, just like the boy I'd seen in Dublin. All the men were overweight: the older ones' girths straining under mismatched suits; the younger adopting a uniform of tracksuit bottoms and woollen jumpers worn with trainers. Middle-aged women with hardened faces pushed grandchildren in buggies through the field, but the younger girls were different. They dressed up, some of them in skintight lacy ruffle dresses and thigh-high boots, revealing startling flashes of goose-pimpled thighs. They dazzled, leaving me feeling I was looking in on a world where they were getting it all right.

Most of the girls had gone by the time I walked Eddie slowly around the edge of the field. The grass had turned to a slick of mud, chip wrappers whipping along the hedgerow surrounding the field, where the horses had thinned right out. I knew I couldn't talk to the gypsies, or at least that they wouldn't talk to me, and I was about to lead Eddie back to our camp when I saw a man with wiry white hair wearing a green tweed jacket approaching. He smiled with both his hands out like he was a prophet, and suddenly I recognised him. He was called Walter; he was a horse dealer who lived down the coast. I'd met him four years before, when I'd been in Ireland with Mum. He was in his sixties but had a young son and daughter with a girl who was a friend of Mark Palmer. They dealt horses from a yard near Galway, and the dilapidated romance of their life had imprinted itself onto my fifteen-year-old self's mind. Walter clearly hadn't forgotten Mum, either.

'It's Clover, isn't it? Clover? Am I right? With the remarkable mother?' he asked in the soft, loping Irish accent I'd heard in the villages. 'And where is your mother, I ask you? Is she here?' he asked, looking around us. I knew I would disappoint him, but I didn't want to explain what had happened, either. I didn't want the accident to be suddenly present in the field, here with us, nor to face the unanswerable questions that would follow about whether Mum was getting better.

'She's not here, not this time, but I'm here to sell this horse. Are you buying?' I asked, pushing the accident away and keeping our conversation moving forward. Walter bought and sold horses at the same speed most people buy pints of milk – and he wasn't completely honest. The family we'd stayed with in Galway had told us Walter was known to sell a horse one day, only to steal it back days later, then re-sell it again to a new customer, or even the same person again.

Now he walked around Eddie, inspecting his hocks, running gnarled hands down his legs and clucking as he ran his fingers behind his ears. Eddie, thoroughly bored by a day of being prodded and poked, didn't flinch.

'A stallion, cut late, I see? Good presence, nice-looking animal. Nice-looking horse,' said Walter, then he paused, putting one hand on my shoulder. 'Now, come here, Clover, listen to me. You want to sell this animal and I have an idea.'

He had a friend, he said, a girl with more money than she knew what to do with, looking for something she could use to pull a wagon. What was the price I was wanting for this stallion?

'Six and a half thousand,' I said quickly. Walter nodded and went on without flinching at this ridiculous price.

'Now, you and I know that's more than this yoke is worth. Could ever fetch. But the girl I have wants an animal like this and she will pay. I say six for the horse and nothing more. Give one thousand of that to me, and you'll have your profit.'

The numbers dizzied me. Four thousand pounds was more than Brad had ever thought he could make on Eddie, so another thousand was a fortune. I shifted, running my hand across Eddie's broad shoulder as if hesitating, just to keep Walter guessing. Eddie nuzzled in my pocket, but you couldn't be sentimental, that was what Brad had said. He's just a horse.

Honest or not, Walter was good for his word. When Brad stomped out of the pub, I didn't have a horse to hand back to him, but £5,000 in £20 notes. Brad thought I'd been stung to start with, but then he took the cash, running his thumb through the thick wad of notes as a smile slowly spread across his face.

'You're a fucking horse dealer now, Clover,' he said, laughing so hard he bent over double. 'Who'd have fucking thought it?'

Later that evening, he swapped the cart for a Renault 5, in which we packed the harness and saucepans and the dogs, before heading to the ferry back to England.

We spent the rest of that summer on the Ridgeway. After the endless rain and gypsies, and the mud and the fights and Brad's regrets he'd ever gone back to Ireland, travelling horse-drawn in England through a hot summer felt like one long party. After nights sleeping under a flat cart in Ireland, Brad's elegant barrel-top wagon was as glamorous as the Ritz. When it rained we could light a fire in the stove in the corner and play cards and drink hot whisky. There were cupboards for my clothes and a place to leave my boots inside so they were always dry. We saw lots of friends too, since the novelty of life in a horse-drawn wagon meant there were always visitors, and this time none of them were gypsies. Brad was proud of his big mare, Kim, and her daughter, Midnight, but quickly bought another pony called Romey and a two-wheeler for her to pull, so as well as a wagon to sleep in, I had my own cart to drive too.

We travelled south, heading off the road and moving along the high track of the Ridgeway as often as possible. The string of white chalk cutting across the Downs is made for horses, their hooves melding into the same ground where horses have travelled for thousands of years. There were places where the deep dried ruts made it impossible for a wagon to pass, but for long stretches we could leave the concrete and passing cars, moving up onto the hills where skylarks burst from the skies and the grass was springy, where sheep with their lambs had cropped it short.

The Ridgeway is steep but Brad taught me the best way to get a horse and cart up a high hill is to attack it with speed and strength, rather than gently ease your way up. He'd make Romey almost canter up the steepest part of the hill so that the momentum of the cart wheels would help push her up until she was leaning right into the collar, her hooves slipping on the steep concrete. Only then did the square iron block Brad insisted I carry up the hill behind the wagon make sense.

'You have to run fast enough to stay so close to the wagon you can touch the back of it but you must *never* hold on to it,' he said. When the hill got really steep, and Romey would be forced to stop, he'd scream at me to block the back wheel so that she wouldn't be pulled backwards by the weight of the wagon.

'It's a tonne, this wagon, remember, Clover. A fucking tonne,' he'd said when I whined at him that the block was too heavy and the hill too steep for me to run all the way up. 'You fail to block the wagon and Romey'll be pulled backwards by a tonne of wood and canvas. In which case it can't be too heavy, got that?'

That summer, England was throbbing with parties as ravers revelled in another summer of love. The peace convoy of the 1980s that Brad had been part of – the cavalcade of trucks and vans that a tangle of New Age travellers moved around in – had long been broken up, but during a few summers in the mid-nineties there was a bedraggled contingent criss-crossing the roads and tracks of the south of England to converge, like magic, on the same spot for one night, to set up sound systems and dance. At that time in my life I could see no downsides to taking ecstasy, and it was the painkiller I needed after I came back to the camp having seen Mum.

She'd been moved to a rehabilitation centre in Milton Keynes. She still could not talk or communicate, but she could walk and her arms were strong, so that when I took her for a walk around the garden she would grasp my arm so hard that it hurt, although she never hugged me, or stroked my face, or did any of the affectionate things she'd once done to show her love when she'd really been my mother. Instead her movements were tense and sudden, and she often looked hunted. Although she was incapable of communicating, she'd sometimes make noises at me as if she was trying to say something. Then I'd sit with her, trying to tease words out of her by suggestion, handing her a pen to write things down or even draw what she was feeling, but she could not convey any meaning at all. I'd follow a trail of guesses in my head, trying to piece together an explanation about how Mum might be feeling or what she was thinking, but it never went anywhere.

She had her own room with a cupboard filled with some of her old clothes from Minety, but also tracksuit bottoms and soft cotton tops in pastel colours. I sat in her room with her and talked to her about Ireland and meeting Walter. Her head was still very swollen and her right eye partially closed, and she stared at me beadily as I spoke. I had a few photographs of Eddie and Buckle but when I handed them to her she turned them over and left them face down on the table between us, muttering inaudible sounds to herself as she stood up and walked to the door, rattling the handle.

It was locked. She was now living in a secure unit after she'd been found walking down a main road in Milton Keynes. At first her wandering hadn't worried the home too much. She'd stayed in the garden or sometimes walked to a church one field away, a remnant of a village life that had otherwise been swallowed up by a mass of roundabouts. Sometimes she'd even gone to services there, and occasionally I'd found the order of service for someone's marriage or funeral in her room. Later, I walked to the church myself and met the parish priest and his wife.

'Charlotte, your mother seems to enjoy our services. She's welcome here,' he'd said, smiling kindly. 'It must be a very hard thing on you all, what has happened. We hope she can find some peace in the church at least.'

Mum's overriding desire to go to church made us all feel optimistic for her future. I often went to stay with Emma and we talked about Mum a lot. Didn't this prove that she could get better? If she liked church, maybe she'd find her way back to everything else she'd lost.

In church, her lost words came back to her too, because although Mum couldn't speak at all, or communicate yes or no with any meaning, she was able to recite the words to the Lord's Prayer and even tried to sing some of the more familiar hymns. Clearly, we told each other, it was a sign that she could learn to talk again, in time, that she would get better.

Being in church certainly did stir up something inside her, because a few months later she started to try to escape the nursing home – which was when she was found walking down a dual carriageway in Milton Keynes. And after that, when I went to visit one day, she had a black eye. The home said she'd fallen while out walking. Following these incidents, she was locked into the secure unit.

Concentrate on the positive, I always told myself as I drove to see her, knowing that every visit was only painful and horrifying. I would sit with her to talk to her about what had been happening, making my voice sound light and positive as I tried to break through to her strange, internal world. Walking with her in the garden was good, and she'd seem to want to walk on and on, round the large garden with an artificial pond and conifers running down one side, even when I knew she must be exhausted, or her pads needed changing.

On one visit the staff showed me drawings she had been doing in art therapy classes. Her handwriting was unchanged, and she drew with strong, confident lines.

'She drew this, just last week,' said the art therapist, who had thick blonde hair the colour of honey and wore a necklace of chunky amber beads. She handed me a picture of a horse's head with a bold, curved neck.

Underneath it, in the only sentence Mum ever communicated in all of the years after the accident that made any sense, my mother had written: 'I wrecked myself.'

The camp, the horses, the wagon and the wild feeling of England all around me was like a blanket of anaesthesia I wrapped myself in. I rode across the Downs barefoot and bareback on Romey and felt the embrace of the world, huge and free and undemanding. Brad and I travelled to raves with the horses, tethering them in a field beside the party, sometimes riding them in the night, bareback, to feel the thrill of darkness and drugs and horses all mixing up into one raw moment. Once, we were chased by police helicopters that shone spotlights over the Downs as we rode across the hills hunting a sound system we'd heard from our camp. Nothing was out of bounds: I stripped naked and galloped Romey across the Downs with nothing but the coldness of the night and my horse's back against me.

But that party did come to an end, because they all have to. One year slid into another but eventually, in October 1995, I had to take up my place at university. Brad dropped me in Oxford in the wagon, and it was nice when Rick came to have a drink with us in a pub in the middle of the city, with the horses tied outside. Afterwards I tried not to cry when Brad left, clopping down the high street as he waved goodbye. Seeing the horses vanishing was awful, but I was excited too. Rick took me to a department store and bought me a blue and white duvet cover and a toaster. He helped me find my room in the halls of residence and when he hugged me goodbye, he told me he was proud of me.

Brad went back to the road, and sometimes I talked to him as he travelled through Wiltshire, close to Wayland's Smithy. I see him still, at Stow Horse Fair, or round the kitchen table at Mark Palmer's, and his presence is always reassuring because it reminds me of how he taught me to be braver and all the good that can come from snatches of life we share together.

When I walk up on the Downs now, I can feel a memory of the days with the horses, living up there on the Ridgeway. But a memory is all it is. Big stones have been moved in front of the gateways to the tracks that criss-cross the huge fields now. They're too big to move, at least without heavy machinery, and they're there to stop the parties. All this open, empty space has always attracted people up here, thousands of years before ravers brought their sound systems onto the Ridgeway and split open the sky with their repetitive beats, but it's getting harder. I know the arguments against it. The ravers hardly do themselves any favours. They leave litter, water bottles and those little metal gas canisters for laughing gas. The landowners don't like it, and why should they? The ravers make a mess, those people with their music and their drugs and their dogs on strings and heavy boots amongst the crops. Why can't these people have their parties in the city, where they belong?

But the landowners ignore the black plastic silage wrappers clinging to stretches of barbed wire fence beside the White Horse, the pesticides drenching this ancient land, and the pasture outside the village they've just sold for 100 new houses.

CHAPTER 5

April, and the white hard days of winter have sliced back into the earth, which looks creamy with the cow parsley and elderflower blossoms that froth over the verges. On White Horse Hill, skylarks punctuate the clouds, sending a thrill of chorus down to the ground. If the chalk horse seemed to gallop through the winter, now, in the basking spring warmth, it stretches, shakes its head and leans down to graze.

This is a relief. The months of winter after we'd moved to Baulking were like hard bones, but in April the earth sighs and rolls over. The darkness lifts, the landscape sings and April is our prize.

*

Three years of university had come and gone. I'd read books, taken notes in lectures, enjoyed brief flings and laughed at parties, generally giving quite a convincing impression of being a girl whose life was moving in the right direction, even if the first few months had been like acting. Moving from a gypsy wagon into halls of residence in the middle of a city was like the jolt of stepping into ice-cold water. For the first few weeks, I had photographs of Romey and Brad on the Ridgeway pinned up on the wall of my student room.

'Who's *that*?' a girl called Eliza had asked, peering at a picture of Brad and me on the horses, bareback at dusk. It was out of focus so Eliza had to peer right up at it, pausing between mouthfuls of a cream-cheese-and-ham bagel she'd made in the shared kitchen at the end of the corridor.

'Just some friends, ages ago, you know . . .' I'd replied. 'Ages and ages ago. Look, do you know when that essay on Yeats is due in?'

My life on the road with the horses and Brad felt like a piece of a puzzle covered in dust that I'd found under a bed. I didn't know how it fitted into the rest of the story.

By half term I'd taken the photographs down and hung in their place a purple feather boa and plastic silver crown I'd bought for a fancy dress party. I stopped wearing the brown leather boots I'd walked down the road in and bought some tight black dresses and a red fur jacket. I wanted to be a different person.

Actually, I tangled through it, sometimes coming face to face with the person I'd been in Ireland, but at other times convincing myself she never existed. If I walked forward, I thought I could move past the trauma that rippled as constantly as waves on an ocean through my life. Even when I couldn't see them, they were always there, beneath the surface.

Without Minety to go home to, I spent the holidays moving between Rick's new home in London and Emma's home in Norfolk, where she and Matthew were living with her two young daughters. The excitement I'd felt about seeing Emma as a young child had never gone away. Sometimes I took friends from university with me, driving up late to arrive in the middle of the night, or catching a train alone so that Emma would pick me up from the station. I'd known Matthew since I was twelve and he often felt almost like a brother. When we all became worried about how suitable the rehabilitation centre was for Mum in Milton Keynes, Emma found a Sue Ryder nursing home near her own house on the coast in

Norfolk that we moved Mum to. After that, visits to Emma's also became about seeing Mum. Emma and I would drive off to see her on a Saturday morning, sitting with her and talking together as Mum watched us, because it was so hard keeping up a monologue to Mum that she never answered.

Afterwards, back at the house, we'd talk obsessively about Mum's progress, or lack of it, until one of Emma's daughters would run in to drag her outside to see some new chicks, or to swim in the pool with them, and then time would be forced forward as Matthew would make lunch, which we'd eat in the garden, or we'd go to swim at the beach at Cley that Mum had once loved.

Sometimes, though, I'd walk through their house feeling stunned. Mum's pictures on the walls and her china in the cupboards and her eiderdowns on the beds seemed to watch me. I felt like a refugee, surrounded by things that had been home but that had got lost. Sometimes it was beautiful to see Mum's sugar pot on the kitchen table, or to hold a dress that she had loved, but it also made me terrified with disbelief: what had happened to the past? She wasn't dead, so where was she? I would sit in the half-light of the sitting room with her books in the shelves and an antique French carpet she'd loved on the floor, tears pouring down my face as I tried to feel her soul.

I made some new friends at university. Some of them had been students with Nell, who'd only left the year before I arrived; although there were times that being Nell's younger sister again grated, it had advantages. Several times a term, I met up with Dan, and those were the nights I looked forward to most. Like Nell, most of his friends had graduated and moved to London, but since he wasn't actually a student, he'd stayed in Oxford, rarely leaving the Irish pubs on the Cowley Road where he was ringleader at the lock-ins happening most nights. They were the sort of pubs that don't really exist any more. One of them, the Bullingdon Arms, even had sawdust on the floor of the dark back bar where people played pool and it was hard to see from one side of the room to the other through the cigarette smoke.

Dan would usually come and find me in college, and after quickly dismissing the student bar as too well-lit, we'd take a bus to the Elm Tree, where bricklayers and scaffolders drank beside old academics, and almost everyone had a strong Irish accent. Dan did too. He talked like the boys I'd heard at that market on the north side of Dublin, and on the Cowley Road he was a sort of hero. He sometimes worked behind the bar, or, at least, was often seen pouring drinks there, and he played music most nights. He sounded like Shane MacGowan on a good night as he belted out tunes like 'Leaving of Liverpool', 'Dirty Old Town' and 'The Fields of Athenry'. Everyone loved it when Dan sang, and at the front of the stage there would always be more than a handful of girls whom Dan was playing as deftly as his guitar.

The music that really makes me think of Dan is the stuff he played late at night, when the pub was almost empty and the landlord had pulled down the blinds, locking the doors. Dan had the kind of voice that can make a grown man weep. He understood those haunting Irish songs – the rebel songs and folk songs about battles and famine and misery – in a way that made you believe he was actually feeling that hurt. I loved the pain in his voice, and craved the dazzle of his attention, basking in it for an evening and always hoping this would be the night he'd hold me under a street-light and kiss me, before he'd vanish, without telling anyone, and I'd spend some more months wishing he'd come back.

Rick usually came to see me once a term, to take me for supper at a restaurant that had been a flower shop he and Mum had used to go to when they'd lived in Oxford before we moved to Minety. Sometimes, he'd talk about her and how he had loved the person she had been, but then tenses would switch and we'd talk about what might happen and who she might become. In my second year, he arrived unexpectedly one evening to tell me something about Mum.

Since the accident, Mum had been on a strong daily dose of

anti-convulsants and painkillers to treat the epilepsy, infections and other health problems she'd developed after the fall. They were serious drugs, administered by a nurse, but this time she'd managed to get into the medical cupboard at the nursing home, and taken a big overdose. Now she was in a coma again.

'She may have thought they were sweets, Smarties or something,' Rick said, looking down at his hands. I felt like the room had shifted slightly; unsure of my balance, I gripped the edge of the table we were sitting at, just to steady myself because it seemed impossible we were back in the land of comas. 'She may just have got confused.'

His reasoning wasn't impossible, since her accident had left her with an insatiable thirst and hunger, so that if a tray of tea and biscuits was put in front of her, she'd eat and drink absolutely everything on the tray. Rick was trying to make me feel less sad but we both knew that it wasn't true that the overdose had been an accident. Because while Mum wasn't capable of talking or doing anything for herself at all, it seemed clear she had been trying to kill herself.

She was in a coma for three days; nothing compared to the three months she'd spent unconscious in Bristol, but when she woke up it became clear she was more damaged. She certainly couldn't walk to church now and she moved far more slowly, until eventually she gave up walking altogether, unless she was heaved out of her seat by her nurses, or Emma and Nell and me when we went to visit. Before the overdose she could make hissing and mumbling noises, which meant nothing but which were still a sort of connection, but after her second coma the sounds she made became more muffled.

Whenever we were all together as a family, we didn't stop talking about when Mum would get better. We had to have that optimism, because thinking about Mum was like carrying a boulder of acute heart pain that could never be put down. It was sadness and trauma and yearning and pain tied together with guilt. Guilt that she was living in a nursing home because she needed round-the-clock expert care, guilt that she might be scared, and guilt that she was missing out on so much life. Guilt too that I might be happy, might be laughing or walking outside when she was sitting alone, and guilt because I had not been able to face visiting her for over three months.

I think I was very strange in those days because the pain was so intense and always so present, and I know I was very angry too. One evening a friend's mother visited Oxford to take a group of us out for supper. It was cheerful, and she ordered several bottles of wine for us and didn't mind when we smoked at the table. But afterwards, when she'd dropped us back in college, my friend rolled her eyes and made a tutting sound when I asked about her mother.

'God, she's so bossy. She always wants to be part of my life,' she sighed as we lay on her bed. 'Sometimes I wish she'd just back off a bit.'

'No but . . . You should feel . . . I would do anything . . . You have no idea . . .' I started, then dug my nails onto my palm to crush the anger I felt as the thought of Mum coming to visit me to take me out for supper suddenly rushed up to me on the bed and then rushed far away, forever out of reach. I pushed myself up from the bed and pulled on my coat. 'Say thanks to your mum for me, will you? It was really great of her.'

It was hardest at the start and end of term, when the narrow road outside my college would be blocked with Volvo Estates, boots open, as mothers loaded in books and bedding to drive their children home. It was a sight that made me giddy with a violent jealousy because I wanted those mothers so badly for myself. Instead, to take away that anger, I used the close comfort of men, or boys really, as a way of not thinking about all the things I'd lost in the fire. There were no horses in my life at that time, but there were other diversions that excited me.

When the flash of finals was over, I felt flung out and lost, divorced from myself. I wandered around the city, stunned, watching my friends tumble off to parties or spread out on college lawns at champagne picnics, or stand outside pubs juggling pints, always laughing, open-mouthed. Life seemed like it was happening to other people, and I had no idea how to become one of them. At a college ball I sat in a student bedroom with four friends, taking coke beneath peeling posters, regretting everything that had happened to me at university. Slipping across the muddy college lawn, most of all I regretted having spent £100 on a pair of red Calvin Klein high-heeled sandals that were now covered with mud.

I left university in 1998. It was the dot-com era, and there was a certain sense of hysteria that my friends who were joining start-ups were soon going to be rich, despite the fact that the internet still wasn't the blanket over everyone's life that it is today. Very few of my friends had mobile phones or email addresses, and 'www' wasn't yet a familiar prefix. Everyone was moving to London. I had a degree in English but absolutely no sense of where that would take me.

'Publishing, maybe?' suggested my father, who I'd been staying with in London. He'd cooked prawns and pasta and we were drinking white wine with the Thames below us. After Minety was sold, Rick moved to a houseboat in London. All that outside life at Minety, with the horses and the big garden and the chickens, had been Mum's world, and Rick, who grew up in London and is most at home in Soho or Chelsea, embraced it because he loved Mum.

Buying a houseboat was inspired, because it was as beautiful as Minety, yet wasn't trying to replicate it. In the previous few months, the boat had changed. Pink lustreware china had appeared on the shelves where Rick kept books about the Second World War, and there was a pair of black satin stilettoes at the bottom of the stairs. There had been a moment when it looked as if the accident would freeze all our lives in a single moment in time, but now Rick's life was moving forward. Mum could no longer be a wife to Rick, just as she could no longer be a mother to any of us, and when he met Alexandra, dazzlingly glamorous in satin and fur, Nell and I were only happy for him.

Alexandra moved onto the boat, hanging colourful paintings and arranging rows of delicate gold china along the shelves. She liked the boat to be really hot, cooking asparagus risotto barefoot in the kitchen. She was funny and brilliant company, and we shared long gossipy evenings over bottles of wine. Rick and her lives were completely focused on London, and though I felt sad when I realised the photograph Rick had of Mum wasn't on his desk any more, I knew that the past cannot define the present. A few years later, Rick got divorced from Mum and he and Alexandra married at Chelsea Town Hall. Her son Daniel and Nell and I were the only guests, and afterwards we had lunch at the Chelsea Arts Club. It was a new feeling of family.

That evening, though, Alexandra was out at a work event, so Rick and I were alone. Rick poured us both another glass and took a gulp.

'You might be good in publishing. You know how to say no,' Rick suggested, but I looked away so that he couldn't see my face. There were plenty of things I wasn't good at saying no to, and I shifted in my chair.

'I don't want to just go and live in London and be in an office and do that for ever. I need to do something physical, using my body, not my head. Just for a bit. And I need to go somewhere different. You know, that feeling of wanting to be away?' I said, as Rick smiled at me.

'Of course, Bugsy,' he said, using my childhood nickname. 'Well, maybe that's what you should do. If you really feel you need to. Shall we open another bottle?'

That night, Rick and I listened to Willie Nelson and Emmylou Harris and all the old songs on his CD player. We watched the Robert Altman movie *Nashville*, and when Rick fell asleep in his chair, I changed the film to *Sweet Dreams*, about the life of Patsy Kline. I'd watched it many times before, but the moment Patsy dances to country music beside a parked pick-up with her husband Charlie as their lives are falling apart made me cry until my whole body was shaking. I felt drunk as country music washed over me, leaving me with its yearning and its loss that felt so familiar it was almost like seeing home from a distance. I wanted to go there.

Again, I left. I had money saved up from holiday work at a publishing company, and Rick bought me a ticket to New York. This was pre-9/11, when arriving in America with a one-way ticket and nothing more than a handful of addresses of friends of friends of friends scattered across the States was easy.

It was like waking up in a brand-new film, with the old life all behind me. In New York a truck driver pulled up beside me and yelled, 'Girl, you too pretty to be walking around on your own.' I stayed with a friend of a friend of my brother's on the Upper East Side. It was August, wet hot, and he took me to an Irish pub. The man said, 'I want to take you to bed and make you scream,' which really made me want to walk away from him, but he had coke too, so I stayed with him for a week as the steaming city breathed around me.

A week later, I took a Greyhound to Colorado, to a dude ranch in the mountains that a friend of a friend had told me about. It was a play ranch for millionaires, and I found myself changing the Egyptian cotton sheets of rich men who slept beneath real fur Calvin Klein rugs. The owner said I could look after the horses in return for lodgings, but the air stank of money and it made me feel claustrophobic. Instead I criss-crossed Colorado and Montana, staying in motels while reaching for something solid like fool's gold that seemed always beyond reach. I thought I might go home, until I found a T-shirt in a junk shop with TEXAS IS THE REASON in tiny gold letters across the front, and then I caught the next bus to Dallas.

When we were children, country music ran through our lives. From my bedroom I'd hear scratched records Rick played of Merle Haggard and Gram Parsons. Before I understood what any of their songs were about, I'd sing along to stories of outlaws and cowboys, and of girls on bar stools and rodeo queens. Even as a child, before any of the jagged confusion of what happened to Mum changed the way I thought about everything, country music communicated a yearning that still speaks to me and only gets stronger the more I listen to it.

So finding myself on a Greyhound to Dallas didn't come from nowhere. For the first eight hours I sat next to a girl called Kacey-Louise, who told me about working as a prostitute in motels for her step-grandfather when she was twelve. When the bus stopped in a gas station at midnight we shared cigarettes in the heat, crickets chirping over the growl of trucks edging in and out as we drank Kool-Aid.

'Why are you going down to Dallas anyway?' she asked, grinding the cigarette butt into the floor, and I wasn't sure how to explain about the cowboys I'd been thinking about when I was twelve, but it didn't matter; when I looked up at her to answer, she'd already trailed off to blag a cigarette from another passenger.

Before I'd left England a friend had given me the number of a friend called Mary living in Dallas, and I'd called her to ask if I could stay for a few days. I was sitting on the pavement, trying to avoid cockroaches in the heat, when she pulled up at Dallas bus station in a black sports car with a dented bonnet and just shouted, 'Get in!'

'How did you know it was me?' I asked, as Mary put her foot down through the traffic then snorted at my question.

'I'm English, like you, Clover,' she said in a precise, clipped voice that made me feel like she was pecking me. 'How could I not have known you were you?'

Mary looked the same age as me with short black hair that fell across one eye and bright-red lips. She looked a lot like Winona Ryder, and had a ragged energy that made me feel we could do literally anything together. She was living with a religious organisation while researching televangelism, which meant getting up at dawn for daily prayer meetings and helping out in their communal kitchen. She had a boyfriend who also worked for the cult, and she let me sleep on a mattress in her shared house in the Dallas suburbs.

I stayed with her for a month, reluctantly dragging myself to the prayer meetings. Mary didn't like me calling it a cult but I knew she was wild and so the zeal with which she approached religious life surprised me. I went along, but had my own weakness anyway.

Several evenings a week, I'd take a taxi to a nightclub on the edge of the city to dance with strangers. The clubs were called The Red Fox and Country 2000, full of couples waltzing to top-ten country hits. I'd wear a denim mini-skirt and blue cowboy boots with skulls on the side that I'd bought in a vintage shop, and I'd only have to lean against the bar for a few moments before a stranger in a Stetson would ask me to dance. Don't mistake the two-step with line dancing. I'd never line dance, but two-step is romantic and sexy, where couples twirl around one another, bodies pressed against each other.

The men were called Carl or Billy or Clarke and it really didn't matter to me that while they looked like cowboys in their boots and big hats, they were actually construction workers. For a few weeks, it was high fantasy, and I could imagine I was Patsy Kline, dancing to country in a parking lot.

But I was desperate to find a real ranch. Living in cowboy country, where the rhythm of the music that had always called to me pounded from every street corner, a nugget of a dream had taken root inside me. I wanted to live that wild life I'd heard sung about so often; to ride horses with cowboys in the red dust of Texas, on a ranch, and abandon myself to the physical need of both myself and my animal.

A few weeks after I arrived in Dallas, a friend of Mary's told us about a man living outside the city who was looking for some help with a few horses and some acres where he kept cows. He was in his fifties and his son, a huge and morose man with a pistol beneath his heaving belly, was the local sheriff. The owner let me ride and the novelty of a big Western saddle and a barn full of horses was diverting. I was so desperate to find the cowboys for this new ambition of mine that it seemed like a start, so I tried to ignore the pictures of models in black or red lace underwear hanging on the man's sitting-room wall. I concentrated on his horses for a week and was grateful when my new boss showed me how to swing a lasso – or rope, as it's really called – and took me out in his pick-up, driving among mesquite bushes through dusty, rutted pastures to check his cattle. I ignored everything else but the horses – until one evening the man crept into my room, pressing his doughy body against mine, his erection poking me through the pink velour bedspread, murmuring that surely the good Lord had sent me so that things could develop between us. By midnight Mary had driven out from Dallas and picked me up.

Mary had a friend of a friend who had worked on a ranch called the Pitchfork, and although she'd never met him, she knew his name.

'For all they know, he could be my best friend,' she said as we sat on the porch, smoking and working out our next move. She called the ranch, telling the lady who answered that her close friend had told her we were invited out there.

'Ya'all, we really don't encourage girls to come out and ride with the cowboys,' the woman replied, loudly chewing gum. But Mary is difficult to say no to, persuading the woman to pass the phone to her husband, the ranch foreman, who agreed that we could come. (Mary always has this effect on people. Years later, when I'd take a new boyfriend to meet her, it would always be her they would talk about. Even last year, at Dash's christening, when Mary stood by the font as his godmother, my friend Toby later asked me, 'That girl with the black hair, is she married? Who *is* she?' She has a darting, mercurial glamour that makes you want to hold on to her.)

We drove to west Texas, past Lubbock and out onto the flat open prairie where windmills pumping water spun in the wind and oil jacks nodded their heads. Hours and hours passed on the road where we'd see nothing but horizon, until a gas station would shimmer into view like a distant mirage and we'd stop for packets of Twinkies and vats of Dr Pepper. Shortly before we reached our destination we ate fried steak and green beans with pints of iced tea at a diner, before we drove seven miles along a dirt road and arrived at the ranch.

An unsmiling woman in tight jeans showed us the wooden ranch guesthouse. Later that evening, the foreman introduced himself briefly, but other than that there was no sign of either cowboys or horses. The foreman told us to come down to the pen at dawn.

'Over yonder,' he said, motioning to some barns in the distance.

There were lots of cowboys there in the morning, more even than my fantasies held, although none of them spoke, apart from the foreman, who handed us the reins of two quarter horses tacked up with big Western saddles. The dark morning air was ringing with the jingle of spurs and bits and the thud of horses' hooves on the dry ground as we rode away from the barns. The foreman told us nothing except that we would be moving a herd of cattle from one section of the ranch to another, and should follow the directions of the cowboy in front of us.

It was like a dream unfolding in front of me. The men wore big hats, their jeans stacked low over cowboy boots, and when they looked sideways I caught a profile of their faces with their thick moustaches. The horses danced around the cattle as the cowboys neck-reined their animals, pushing them up against the herd to form a seamless band holding the cows in. The cattle moved slowly, not at the breakneck gallop that I'd expected from watching Westerns.

We spent all morning in the saddle, shadowing the cowboys, and trotting behind them as they pushed the cattle forward. The green smell of mesquite bushes crushed by the cattle filled the air, and when I ran my hand across my face, red dust coated my palm. The cowboys and their horses were beautiful, their leather bridles and Western saddles inscribed with patterns or dates punched into the leather, their chaps fringed from the top of the thigh to the point where it met their long stirrups. They were polite to Mary and me, calling us 'ma'am' when we asked a question, but mostly they worked in silence, except to make noises at the cattle when they threatened to break from the herd. By early afternoon the move was finished, and we jogged back to the ranch, the foreman trotting beside me.

'Begging your pardon, ma'am, but girls don't do this job, at least not in west Texas,' he said as his chestnut pony pranced beside me. 'But there's plenty of dude ranches that might take a stable hand on.'

A dude ranch is a play ranch, either set up as a holiday destination or owned by a rich and usually absent owner, like the one in Colorado, and it wasn't what I wanted. I wanted to stay on the ranch – but the foreman made it quite clear our day trip was over, albeit politely. We were putting our bags into Mary's car when one of the cowboys approached us, asking if I'd accompany him to a rodeo that weekend.

'Down in Lubbock, if you'd like that, ma'am,' he said, tipping his hat at me. He was called Jake, and later I found out from his friend Lyle that he was called Jake the Snake ''cos he's kinda slippery, if you get what I'm saying, ma'am'.

The following weekend, I caught a bus from Dallas to Lubbock to a rodeo where men rode bucking horses and rounded up cattle in a dusty arena, and the finale was a bull-riding competition. After the rodeo finished we sat in the back of Jake's pick-up and drank cans of beer under a blood-red sky. When the beer ran out he found a bottle of bourbon among the back copies of *Playboy* behind the seat in his cab. It was a hot Texan evening in early September, and later that evening a band played nearby on the back of a truck. I already knew how to two-step after all those nights dancing in Dallas, and Jake and I twirled around the concrete floor under a canvas awning strung with fairy lights that twinkled brighter than the stars. Afterwards, we drove out to the flatlands, away from the town, and an electric storm split the sky open.

Jake was unusual. Unlike the ranch foreman, he didn't think what I was trying to do was ridiculous, or completely impossible, either, and after that I went to stay with him at the bunkhouse when the foreman was away. We cooked steaks outside on a fire, and at night the narrow bunkbeds squeaked as he held his body against mine, pressing me into the sheets, but even in the darkness I could see the big tattoo Jake had of a horse's head on his chest.

'Darn it, Clover, you sure are determined,' he said one evening, when we'd driven to a distant pasture to check the mares and foals and I was outlining my plan, for the tenth or eleventh time, of trying to find a ranch – any ranch – that might give me a chance. Jake wrote down every single ranch he knew, and for three weeks I sat in Dallas, posting dimes into slots to telephone every one of them. All the foremen I spoke to made it clear their world was not open to me, was too tough, too hard, too masculine for a girl, especially an English girl.

In Dallas, I sweltered on the pavements. I no longer pretended to share Mary's enthusiasm for life in the cult and now that I'd met Jake, dancing with the bricklayers at The Red Fox wasn't romantic. When I called Jake in the bunkhouse at the Pitchfork I could hear him grinning through his thick accent.

'If things get too bad, I guess you could try that lesbian ranch I heard talk of in east Texas,' he said. 'Or the Slash Y. Down near Alpine, by the Mexican border. Big Bend country. It's kinda wild down there, Clover. It'd suit you.'

The Slash Y was owned by a man called Bill, or Big Bill, as he was known. He lived in Dallas, but flew to the ranch in his jet once a week; he called me for an interview in Fort Worth, the old cattle trading town beside Dallas. While receptionists with great hair teetered in and out of his office to offer him iced tea, he questioned me about what I was doing, and seemed amused, more than anything, by my ambitions. I thought about Mum, as it was a bit like meeting J. R. Ewing.

'So you're trying to live your dream,' he said, when I outlined my plan. 'I admire it. Easy enough to dream it, but takes a certain sort of determination to go after it. And wanting to make it on a ranch in west Texas, well, lady, you have *cojones*, I'll say that for you. And if you want in on my operation, you're in.'

★

I stayed at the Slash Y for three months, living in an Airstream
trailer beneath the Big Bend mountains, right beside a log cabin
where a cowboy called Chuck lived with his girlfriend Dusty, who
worked in Alpine as a primary school teacher. Bill's huge ranch
house was a mile away, but he rarely turned up, occasionally appearing
to jog around the ranch with his pneumatic blonde personal trainer.

'You bet she's personal,' Dusty would snigger as we sat on their
porch eating grilled chicken in the evenings. My job involved
looking after a dozen horses and my favourite task was being sent
to herd them back to the barns on horseback, a procedure called
jingling. I sometimes rode out to check the cattle with Chuck or
one of the local cowboys who worked for Bill. I'd thought Texas
would be flat but there were mountains around the ranch which
cut jagged zips through the orange sun when it dipped over the
horizon, although the foreground was always fuzzy with mesquite
bushes. Beyond Alpine was Marfa, no more than a few houses
clustered together, but famous for the white lights that appeared
from nowhere, blinking, every evening.

Even if the work wasn't as exciting as I'd hoped, Alpine itself
was wild. It was the Western town of all my fantasies, with real-life
cowboys fresh from the surrounding local ranches striding down
the town boardwalks most evenings. The Mexican border was close
by, so it felt lawless, with a railroad track running through the middle
and two bars: the Crystal Bar, with swing doors and a dance floor
playing pure country, and The Moody Blues, a bikers' bar full of
men in bandanas with thick arms covered in tattoos. At the Crystal
Bar I met a big-boned girl with her red curly hair pulled into a
high ponytail working behind the bar.

'Cara,' she said, plonking a Bud Light on the bar in front of me.
'I'm one loud-mouthed broad and I'll be your best friend if you
buy me a beer.' She'd been at college in Alpine and knew everyone,
from the cowboys to the truck drivers, the girls who worked in
the beauty salon to the man who ran the steak house. We'd drive
with a handful of her friends into the desert, with black peaks of
mountains glooming above us, to shoot road signs and coyotes and

light a bonfire to drink beside until dawn. They were all obsessed with gambling, so we drove to the casinos at the border towns, and there were rodeos everywhere. Cara only ever laughed, even when the cowboys brawled and we had to stop and buy ice and frozen steaks to slap onto their black eyes. We drank and danced and gambled, and I lost my best red knickers at a rodeo in El Paso. I could rarely call home as it was so expensive. I only thought about Mum when I was alone in my trailer at night and coyotes were howling somewhere very distant outside.

Horses were my consolation if I was lonely. In between the parties there were just enough of them at Bill's ranch to keep me occupied; and then I met Shay and later I wondered, if things had worked out differently, I might have stayed in Alpine for ever.

Shay smelt of tobacco and the green brush on the ranch land and cherry chapstick, because it was so hot and windy out there, it killed your lips. I knew he smelt of all these things before he ever kissed me, as soon as he walked into the Crystal Bar, where I sat drinking Bud Light with Cara. Shay wore a battered palm-leaf cowboy hat with a band of sweat around the rim over his short cropped brown hair and he brought all of the openness of the ranch where he'd been working in with him.

He knew Cara from way back, she later told me, so he sat with us and when she stood up to start her shift behind the bar, he just moved his stool closer to mine. We talked without stopping and he made me laugh, telling me about a colt he'd been breaking that morning who had bucked him off five times in a row. He was open in a way that reminded me of my friends back home and we didn't stop talking all evening.

After midnight, when the bar had shut, we sat on the tailgate of his pick-up outside, drinking cold bottles of beer that he'd bought from Cara, with his radio turned up loud playing Patsy Kline numbers. He took my hand and pulled me out onto the tarmac, holding me close against his body as we danced under the moonlight, until he said, 'Spend the night with me,' and of course I did.

Shay lived outside town and after that I spent nights with him at his wooden house with a veranda running all the way around it, where he lived alone with two dogs who slept on the porch. It was a rented house and he broke broncs for a living, so had built a round pen for breaking and some wooden corrals where a dozen horses nodded in the shade of a big wooden barn. He could weld hollow pipe into fencing and fix his truck himself when it broke down.

I would fall asleep pressed into his hot skin, but would wake alone, the window beyond the bed flung open to where I could see his figure in one of the pens on the back of a horse as he galloped it around and around to break it in. It was as if he knew when I was watching him, as he'd always look up, flashing that smile that was knowing and vulnerable at the same time.

I stayed at his house more often than I stayed at the trailer on the ranch. He'd light a fire in the pit outside his house, cooking steaks we'd eat in the dark and the heat as the nights shifted onwards, country music playing on the radio in the kitchen window. One night, just to escape Alpine, we drove together into the mountains in his pick-up, until he parked up in the thick blackness with nothing around but the yellow dots of stars dizzying above us. We didn't sleep at all then, but we talked and drank until he pulled me towards him so that I knelt across his lap and he pulled my skirt up, pushing me against the steering wheel. I felt like I was dissolving around myself, beyond the cab but into landscape and on beyond that into the bleeding dawn sky.

Later, as the pale morning sun split the darkness and daylight arrived, he folded up his faded yellow Carhartt coat to make a pillow as I lay across his lap and he put his hand in my hair. There was nothing to say because we were just existing for a perfect moment with our breathing and the morning arriving, before it was time to drive back to the ranch.

'Horses to jingle,' he said, running his hands through my hair. 'Come on. Wake up, wild one.'

As we drove back, the truck cast broken shadows onto the mesquite bushes beside the tracks, and Shay glanced across at me so I could almost touch his presence, even though he didn't say anything. When we got back to the horse barns, there was a wild turkey feather lying beside the gate and I thought: This is freedom like I've never known it.

Lots of the country-and-western songs are about cowboys riding off into the distance with your heart in their pocket. I thought that was just for the songs but it's what Shay did to me and it changed the way I thought about Alpine. There were many nights together at his house, or out with Cara at a rodeo by the Mexican border and then alone on the plain in the brush with the lights of Marfa blinking mysteriously in the distance. And then one afternoon he came to my trailer but his truck looked different, because in the back there was his bedroll and some bags packed up and all his saddles and some coils of rope. He had his trailer on the truck and four horses in the back.

'You going somewhere, Shay?' I asked, standing in the door of my trailer. He didn't answer for a moment, but tipped his hat down to the ground as he moved his boot across the dust making a deep mark.

'Reckon so,' he said at last, smiling a bit at the same time so that for a moment I didn't know if he really meant it. He'd been offered work breaking broncs near Santa Rosa, New Mexico, and it was good money. Enough to get him set up with his own yard next year.

'Here, near Alpine?' I asked, trying to figure out what he was really telling me, and he shrugged.

'Maybe. An' maybe out near Santa Rosa. I can't say anything for sure now,' he replied, then turned away. 'I'm real sorry, darlin'. Believe me, I'm real sorry. You've been one helluva girl, a great girl, these last few weeks, but these kinds of jobs don't come up so often for people like me. But I'm real sorry. You got to know that much.'

He looked back at me without moving his eyes from mine, then walked over, taking my face in his hands, kissing me really hard so that our teeth touched and for a few moments all of him was close to me and that felt so good.

Then he turned and swung into the cab, his truck and trailer vanishing down the long drive in the dust that his wheels kicked up.

Alpine was too lonely after that. Sometimes I went to the casinos in the desert with Cara but everywhere I looked I saw him, only he wasn't there. Winter was coming too and the wind screaming around my trailer was spooky. From the bunkhouse at the Pitchfork, Jake helped me again, telling me about the T Bar ranch, up in Panhandle, near Amarillo.

'Owned by a lady, and a real good lady I hear. Proper operation the T Bar is, though,' said Jake down the phone. 'Randy, the manager there, you should call him. He might give you a chance.'

If I'd arrived in Dallas wanting to dance with anyone who wore a Stetson, four months in west Texas had refined my sense of what cowboy culture was. The big operations like the Pitchfork, where Jake worked, were the historical ranches woven through the history of west Texas and through the history of America. Then there were the newer operations, like Bill's. Living in Alpine had helped me to understand the difference between them, but as we left the main road as we drove to the T Bar, turning onto a track snaking cross-country into the far distance, I realised I was crossing into a landscape that was bigger, redder and wilder than anything I'd ridden through before.

'Hey, y'all, you ready for this?' said Maria, the ranch cook, who'd picked me up from Amarillo bus station in her huge pick-up, water bottles and bags of Wal-Mart shopping slung in the back. She was a glamorous mass of black hair and silver and turquoise jewellery, and her hands on the steering wheel were soft and small, each nail filed into a painted point. The pick-up jolted and bounced over the ruts so hard that I had to press my hands into the seat to stop myself being thrown around the cab, as Maria explained that she was the ranch cook, and was married to a cowboy from the ranch called Sandy Paul, and that together they had three children, Colt, Bronc and RJ.

In the wing mirror I could see the dusty hills giving way to scrubby pastures dotted with brush and bright cacti, straight out of a cartoon. Maria kept her foot down, thundering over a cattle grid and through pastures fenced with barbed wire as two small yellow coyotes darted out of the bushes.

'Damn coyotes,' she hooted. 'They'd eat a calf right out of its momma as it's being born. The boys shoot them often enough but they're pests. They need to be ridden out of here.'

'Do you ride, Maria?' I asked.

'Lordy, no,' she said, laughing and turning to look at me in the cab. 'I mean I did, when I was small. My daddy ran a few sections of land so helping out was part of being a kid for me. But not any more. It's a man's world here, and you know what they say?'

'Not really,' I replied.

'The pioneers said it. "Texas is hell on women and horses." Some truth in that, I guess.' She stared back at the track, and then reached over, patting me on the thigh. 'Quit your worrying, though. Now, headquarters, that's where we all live, is another five miles along this route. This is the horse pasture we're driving through now. It's five thousand acres, or thereabouts. To the left of us – see that real wild-looking country? – that's the canyon.'

The track left the horse pasture and ran along the edge of a steep escarpment that fell away to a bowl of red rock met by bright-blue sky, the land like a scene from a Wild West film. 'See those buildings, way over in the distance?' said Maria, pointing to some tiny dots nestled between the edge of the canyon and the plains. 'That's headquarters, near the edge of the river, see? Come on, the kids will be excited to meet you.'

It was a Sunday, and the ranch cowboys and their families were sitting on the porch that ran along one side of the cookhouse. Above the door was a bull's skull, green gingham curtains hung at the windows, and propped against the glass was a painted sign with a picture of a cowboy hat reading: 'Y'all welcome here.' Maria introduced me to the foreman, Randy, a man with crooked teeth and a broad smile, and his wife Sarah, who had blonde hair like candy floss, as well as their daughters, Amy and Christine, and then another cowboy, Red, who had a wide handlebar moustache, and his wife Jackie and their sons Donnie and Shy. All of the men wore cowboy hats and jeans, boots and spurs; their sons dressed identically.

After the introductions had been made, Red's twelve-year-old son Donnie, looking very small in a wide-brimmed hat, showed me to the cabin where I would be living, proudly pointing out a picture at the entrance of a man in a black suit. That was Charles Goodnight, Donnie told me, who became one of America's first cattle barons from the ranch.

'Pretty neat, huh?' he said, smiling shyly at me as he opened the door to the cabin. It had a small sitting room with a big stone fireplace dominating one wall, and a bedroom upstairs with a patchwork quilt on the bed. The cabin was attached to the back of the main house, and Donnie showed me the door through the porch that led to a hall with Indian rugs flung across the wooden floors, a panelled sitting room lined with books and a dining room with a long table flanked by antelopes' heads staring listlessly into the silence.

'This is Eleanor's home,' said Donnie, running his hand enviously over the smooth table surface. 'Real pretty, ain't it? If I owned this place, I'd be here all the time. Eleanor's a real neat lady – one of the very best, my dad says – but she's not here all the time. She has a house in town and another ranch up in Montana.'

Donnie had grown up at the T Bar. He had a restless, animated energy, excitedly telling me the names of some of his favourite places on the ranch: the hill covered in dark-green sage brush called Mitchell's Peak in the canyon; and Coogill Falls, where an angry chuck-wagon cook was said to have driven a team of mules off the hill when the cow boss complained his beans were overcooked. He told me about the flat land around Battle Creek and Griffin Hills, and how, when they weren't killing rattlesnakes or shooting coyotes, he and his brother Shy liked to take a teepee and camp in the canyon in the spring.

'The spring, it's prettiest here, when the wildflowers are so high,' he said, holding out his hand to waist height. 'I reckon you'll like it here.'

We walked back to the cabin and I told him that I bet I would. I was about to go inside to unpack when I realised that he was lingering by the door.

'Ma'am, do you mind me asking, but do you have roads in England? And have you met the Queen? And what do you all do for ranches there?'

'This is God's country,' said Randy, the foreman, the first time we rode out from headquarters. The pastures were massive, and we'd ride through rough country with creeks that appeared from nowhere and dropped 100 feet to cedar breaks hiding cattle as wild as the buffalo who had once owned this landscape. Randy showed me where to find arrowheads left by the Native Americans in the bottom of the riverbed, which ran through the deepest part of the canyon. It was called the Salt Fork of the Red River, and after a long day's work we'd ride the horses through the water to cool them off. Riding beside Red or Randy or Sandy Paul, with no sound but the chink of their spurs as the horses' hooves splashed through the clear water, I felt happiest, and furthest from the past.

After I'd been working a month or so, and knew my way from Coogill Falls to Griffin Hills, Randy told me the thing he'd worried most about when he'd considered taking me on was the thought I might get lost on a drive. A cowboy had done the same thing on a cattle drive a couple of years before, when the heat of the sun and momentary panic in that huge landscape had disorientated the lost cowboy, who rode blindly for three days until he was found on a neighbouring ranch, dehydrated and exhausted, hallucinating on his experience.

'He went completely loco,' Randy told me, shaking his head slowly as we leant against the pick-up at the end of a day's work.

'And now he's a goddamn builder,' said Sandy Paul, who'd caught the end of a story he knew well, snorting with derision as he spat out a mouthful of tobacco juice.

'You do know how to locate your compass points, right?' Randy interrupted, and I nodded.

'Of course I do,' I lied.

I'd told Randy I knew how to ride a horse and wanted to work hard, but there was a lot more to learn about being a cowgirl than just looking good in a Stetson. And anyway, none of the cowboys wore Stetsons; they preferred black felt Resistol hats and Wranglers above Levi's too. One of the girls took me to Amarillo, where we visited a Western store called Cactus Jack's, with rows and rows of boots covering the walls and racks full of Carhartt jackets. Working boots were not the fearsomely pointed winkle-pickers J.R. and Bill had worn, but knee-length boots that fitted tight around the calf with rounded toes and stacked heels. The men tucked their jeans into their boots to help protect their legs from the spiky mesquite bushes we rode through, and also from rattle-snakes, as they were everywhere. They wore denim shirts, or plain white shirts with poppers, and looking 'punchy' was important. Red showed me how to crease my hat over a steaming kettle, curving the sides right up so that they were almost vertical to the sides of my head. I was given a pair of leather half chaps for working, to protect my legs from the thorny mesquite bushes that covered the plains. The chaps were also protection against the coiled length of rope Randy showed me how to tie onto the front of my saddle. It was for roping cattle, and often Randy would spend hours with me outside the bunkhouse, patiently teaching me how to swing the thick, stiff rope that makes up these lassos. I practised on the roping dummy, made from a plastic cow's head stuck onto a bale of hay, standing to loop and throw, loop and throw, again and again, usually missing the head, until one of the children would pass, pick up a rope and hook the head within seconds.

'Don't get frustrated, sister,' Randy said, shaking his head when I threw my rope to the ground crossly. 'These boys have been carrying a rope since they could crawl. It's second nature to them.'

Randy was patient with me. Each morning the cowboys would gather in the cookhouse to discuss the day. On big work days, when there was branding to do, Maria would make plates of pancakes and biscuits, bacon and fried eggs for us all to eat at long tables lined with oilcloth in the cookhouse, where yellowing photographs of men roping cattle and busting broncs stared down from the walls above. In the summer, we'd meet as early as half past three in the morning, to avoid the heat, but the cookhouse wasn't a place for socialising, and I'd eat in silence, listening to Randy as he told Sandy Paul about the broken windmill that needed fixing. Later, after a long day, Randy would drive me around the ranch, showing me paths through the canyon, and teaching me how to tell the differ-ence between male and female calves, how to approach a pasture full of bulls, and where I'd find the spots on the ranch that the horses liked grazing the most. He taught me how to sit deep in the saddle and neck-rein my pony around a bull; they were huge, as big as trucks, and even Sandy Paul looked nervous when he was sent out to rope the couple that had broken through fencing into the canyon. Sandy Paul didn't smile as much as Red, but when it snowed, he carried one of the calves from his sections of land and nursed it in front of the fire in their sitting room, speaking to it like it was his own child.

Sometimes, after work, I forgot to make the switch back to being a girl. The families would often socialise together, gathering to grill steaks outside, even when there was snow on the ground, or to play music in one of the barns, or to drive to Amarillo on a Friday night for beers and Mexican food at one of the drive-ins. One evening, after a long work day, we were at Red's house and I was outside talking about a horse with Red and Randy. Red sent me back into the kitchen for more beers for the three of us, but his wife Jackie stopped cutting up onions and wiped her hands on her apron as I came in, and reached for only two beers from the fridge.

'You know, usually we just let the guys get on and drink alone,' she said pointedly. 'Let me get Colt to take these out and you can have an iced tea in the kitchen here.'

The cowboys called the far extremes of the ranch 'the concrete', because that was the road that led to the nearest small town, Clarendon. It was a drive I did once a week with Maria, or in the school holidays with a fourteen-year-old called Brandon, who came to work on the ranch when he wasn't at school. Randy said he'd never met a teenager like Brandon, as all he wanted to do was be out on the land on a horse. Brandon and I spent a lot of time together, especially when Randy was away for a day as Sandy Paul would send us out to do the jobs he hated, like checking frozen tanks in the furthest pastures or maintaining the fencing in the fiercest heat of summer. We were enlisted to rip out miles of the old, rusting, barbed wire fences some of the first pioneers had erected when the range was parcelled up. We'd park the pick-up and turn Country FM on really loud to distract ourselves from the stinging as the wire ripped through our heavy leather gloves, making our palms bleed. Sometimes we'd stop to sit in the pick-up cab with the air conditioning turned right up and drink cans of Coke, stunned by heat. Then Brandon would tell me about his stepfather, who had beaten him until Brandon had suddenly grown taller than him, and how all he wanted to do was be a cowboy.

If we were lucky, we'd borrow a pick-up to drive to Clarendon for beer and cigarettes. The beer store was actually ten miles beyond the town, across the county line, for Clarendon was officially 'dry', and was subsequently full of alcoholics. None of the cowboys liked lending us their trucks, so sometimes Brandon would cobble together an excuse that Sandy Paul couldn't say no to.

'Tumbleweed here's got to go and get herself some female para-phernalia down the drugstore,' Brandon would tell Sandy Paul, and he'd reluctantly let us go. We'd drive into town to go to the Mexican café near the bus station, which reminded me of the play cafés Nell and I used to set up at Minety. The peeling walls were bare, apart from a ripped poster with a picture of a cliff diver in Acapulco and some hanging baskets filled with dusty plastic flowers. Small square tables covered with fraying purple oilcloth were set across the room, and overhead fans sliced through the stagnant air. I half expected to see a child dressed as a waitress come and take our order of cheese-and-chilli enchiladas as Brandon talked without drawing breath about cowboy life, because he knew I'd always drink it in.

Afterwards we'd drive home with the music turned right up, Brandon steering with one hand, the other crooked over the open window as we worked our way through my packet of Camel Lights. The music was so loud we didn't need to speak, and I pushed right back in my seat so that some of my hair flew out of the window and beyond my own reflection in the big wing mirror I could see the image of the canyon spinning away behind us in the red dust kicked up by the pick-up's wheels. Staring at my reflection with the landscape changing behind me, I was pressed right up close against myself, but my real life felt a million miles away and far out of reach.

I'd lied to Randy when I told him I knew my compass points, and I lied to him again when I said I'd ridden unbroken horses in England. Of course, I had ridden a lot of horses, and I'd certainly ridden a lot of young, flighty thoroughbreds when I'd been working in the racing yard, but I'd never actually broken in a horse before. I had to lie, though, because otherwise Randy would have gone on putting me on the children's horses, like the big chestnut Squirrel, who would stand rock solid as an armchair even when a rattlesnake reared up between his legs. I knew too that Randy had my best interests at heart and wanted me to stay safe, but I was looking for the opposite. In Ireland I'd always have chosen to ride Eddie over Buckle, because Eddie might have been more wilful and difficult, but he wasn't predict-able like Buckle. He excited me and made me feel alive. And danger increasingly felt like a necessary part of my relationship with the horses.

I didn't care if I was hurt. I *wanted* to be hurt, if it meant I could get closer to what being a cowboy really meant, beyond the hat and the pick-up. Later, Randy would laugh and say I seemed like

I was craving it when I'd arrived at the ranch, but he was reluctant to take that risk at first.

'Oh no, Clover, let me tell you now that is one wreck I'm not going to be responsible for,' Randy said, shaking his head after I'd suggested he might let me try starting one of his unbroken horses. But I worked on him, spending hours in the metal round pen below the main yard, where I'd started halter-breaking some of his one-year-old colts.

'All the handling they can get at this age is money in the bank,' Randy told me when he allowed me to run some of them into the round pen to let them get used to human contact. At first they'd run from me, but the sand was deep in the pen, and after they tired they'd slowly turn to face me, sides panting, big brown eyes blinking. It was a slow process: by the summer they'd be turned back out in the canyon again, and the process repeated a year later when they were two-year-olds.

Breaking them – or starting, as the cowboys called it – was faster and sometimes more violent. Red could start an unbroken colt and have a saddle on it within one day, and Sandy Paul might tie a horse's leg up with a rope, leaving it standing for an afternoon to force it to relinquish control.

I didn't really mind how we did it, as long as Randy would let me try to ride a bronc. Finally, after months of halter-breaking, he conceded to let me try a small bay colt called Amigo.

'He looks gentle enough,' Randy said, sitting on the edge of the round pen with his feet hooked through the bars, instructing me as I ran Amigo around in the sand. 'A good horse to start on. He shouldn't give you too much hell.'

It was early evening, and Jackie had joined Red beside the round pen to watch. Powder, a cowboy from a neighbouring ranch, had stopped by to pick up some hay and now he watched too, arms looped over the outside of the round pen. By the barn, I could hear the children returning from school, the sound of the swing door of the cookhouse banging and Maria calling to her kids Bronc, Colt and RJ to come in for something to eat before they did their homework.

When Amigo eventually dropped his head and walked towards me in the sand, Randy said it was time to try him under a saddle. He quivered when I pulled the girth up, spinning away from the pressure around his belly as Randy held tight on his bridle, murmuring, 'Easy, boy, easy now,' as Amigo's eyes bulged round and wild.

'Keep your focus now, Clover,' said Randy as I stood beside Amigo, one arm on his saddle. 'Focus is what riding a bronc is all about. Don't stop concentrating for one moment or he'll bury you. Put your hand through that strap on the front of your saddle to help you stay on, the sugar strap, and keep your head. I'll leg you up, crouch down as you get in the saddle, he'll be plumb terrified of the sight of you above him, see.'

I felt a cool trickle of sweat running between my shoulder blades as I jammed my hat down on my head, pulling my gloves tight on my hands. Randy suddenly caught my arm and said, 'And Clover, you don't have to do this, now. I won't be offended.'

I looked down in the sand and took a deep breath.

'I know that, but I'm not doing this for you. I'm doing this for me.'

Then Randy lightly threw me into the saddle, slipping the rope from the bridle so that Amigo was free in the round pen, and suddenly everything around me was silent.

When Nell and I were children we used to make our ponies buck as we rode through the fields around Minety. We'd press on our ponies' soft skin behind their saddles, or run our fingers under their tight girths, so that they'd flick their back legs forward, because it was exciting. Amigo didn't move like this, but instead jumped across the ring in one huge movement, sending me flying up in the saddle just as I had slipped my hand through the sugar strap. He snorted and kicked, all four feet off the ground, throwing himself against the high metal railings of the pen, before pitching his head down between his legs and lurching across the sand.

Afterwards, Powder told me Red had been whistling and whooping, and Randy had started to clap his hands slowly over his head, but I didn't hear that, or the muffled thump of Amigo's hooves in the sand, as all I could hear was the sound of blood pumping through my head. All I saw was a flash of his brown mane and a glint of his wild white eye as Amigo flung his head backwards like he was trying to see me, before the sand was suddenly rushing up to meet my outstretched hands, and Amigo was bucking towards the far side of the pen with an empty saddle on his back. I struggled to my feet, legs wobbling, as Randy jumped down from the railings, crouching down in the sand beside me.

'Man, that sucker can pitch,' he grinned, but looking anxious. 'He cheated you there. You alright?'

Adrenalin coursed through me as I nodded quickly at Randy, gasping, my hands prickling with a sting like the feeling of falling off my bike on the gravel at Minety when I was a child.

'Again,' I said quickly, breathless, before Randy could argue with me. 'I want to get on again. I need to get on again, to show him he hasn't beaten me.'

Red had jumped down into the pen, grabbing Amigo's bridle, so before there was time to pause or hesitate, Randy legged me back into the saddle, and this time I was ready, with my hand tucked tighter through the sugar strap as Amigo snorted and bucked around the ring, throwing his weight against the walls. Second time around I felt like I was riding, rather than just participating, and I remembered what Randy had told me in the past: that a good bronc rider is not a passenger, but a pilot, in control of the ride and his destiny. Gradually, Amigo started moving around the pen in a half trot, half gallop, skittering across the pen like he was trying to run away from the shape of me on his back, until he dropped his head, snorting, then beaten. My mouth felt like sandpaper and my hands were shaking as the rest of the world came back into focus; I caught sight of Red throwing his hat into the air and Jackie standing with one hand to her brow, saying, 'Well, I'll be darned.'

Afterwards, I limped across the pen towards them and my legs felt collapsed, as if the ground was spinning. A dull metallic sound was thumping in my brain and my hands were shaking so hard that I dropped the cigarette Red gave me. Powder shook his head as he watched us unbuckling Amigo's girth.

'You got some kind of personal vendetta against horses then, Clover?' he said, and Red laughed.

'She's been craving this since she arrived, I just knew it,' said Randy, letting Amigo loose into the main horse pen, and I didn't contradict him. I didn't think about getting hurt, and if I did, I didn't care about it. Much more important than keeping safe was the thought that I was taking myself to the furthest extreme of this trip. As soon as I'd arrived at the ranch – even in Texas itself – I knew my life there had to be as real as possible. I wanted to feel and inhabit every part of myself while in Texas. The idea of an easy holiday, a year out, just made me feel annoyed. If I was hurt, at least it would have meant I was pushing myself as far as I could go so that I could never have said, 'I'm too scared.'

But Powder was wrong if he thought I had a personal vendetta, as what I really felt with the horse was a special sort of closeness, to myself and to the heart of the matter, which only horses could ever give me. And maybe the more dangerous the places the horses took me to, the closer I felt to Mum, since what I really craved was to find her.

As we turned Amigo back out into the horse field, and I slung the bridle over my shoulder, a sense of completeness flooded through me. It wasn't just the adrenalin of riding a bucking horse making me feel sky-high, but the feeling of having grasped the moment as tightly as I could, and not let go.

The sun had dipped right down below the horizon but it was still warm, one of those heavy Texan evenings when nothing moves and the air clings to your skin. I wiped beads of sweat off my upper lip with my forearm, leaving a mark of dust across my shirt sleeve. As I made to go back to my cabin, Randy paused. 'You'll be sore later, with the bruising, after you're down from all that excitement. Get yourself a long bath before you go to sleep.'

I nodded, swallowing, holding my hands out to see how much

they were shaking. 'And thanks, Randy,' I said. 'For giving me this chance.'

'Now I should be the one thanking you, for saving me from breaking my old bones on that wild sucker.' He stared out to the horse pasture, where Amigo had joined the herd and was grazing, the only sign of what had happened a darker mark of sweat where his saddle had been. 'And you sure have earned your spurs now,' he added as he swung into his truck.

That night, I lay in the bath, one hand on my heart to feel the adrenalin still coursing through my body. Every part of me ached but I had never felt so alive. Sitting on the edge of the bath, a towel wrapped around me, I examined the vivid bruises running inside my thighs. My skin was turning purple and blue as the bruises spread beneath my skin. It was the same colour Mum's eyes had been that first night when we'd seen her in a coma.

My bruises, though, were beautiful, and, in the night, when I woke up, I turned the light on, pulling the covers back to run my fingers over the marks.

A week later, Red rattled the door handle of the cabin, shouting that Randy wanted to talk to me over at his house.

'Reckon you're in some kind of trouble now, crazy girl,' he said, vanishing in the direction of Randy's house.

Everyone was gathered in the small sitting room. They turned to look at me as the door slammed behind me, making the dog snoozing on the verandah jump. Randy was leaning up against the mantelpiece, but when I came in he did something he'd never done before, and took his hat off. Straight away he started talking, saying he sure was grateful for the hard work I was putting in at the ranch, and how surprised he was – they all had been – when I'd first arrived, and even more surprised when I hadn't whined once, even after I'd been sent out fencing.

'But your bronc riding has to be the biggest surprise of all,' he said, handing me a brown paper bag. 'Here, these are for you.'

Inside was a pair of intricate metal spurs with the ranch brand TI and CLOVER marked out in silver around the metal band.

They had heart-shaped buttons attached to ornate leather straps, and I felt my face flush as Randy hugged me again, and Red nodded and said I sure enough was a bronc rider now. Only Sandy Paul, on the far side of the room, hung back, waiting until each of the children had played with the spurs and the girls had traced the shapes of the hearts around them with their long painted nails. Then he leaned forward and shook my hand.

'Congratulations, dude,' he said, reluctantly. 'Seems like you really deserve them.' Then he pushed open the door, spat out a mouthful of tobacco into the yard and left the room.

I keep the spurs on a shelf in my bedroom. Sometimes, when it feels lonely and I want to reach backwards, I take them down and flick the rowels so that they make that heavy metallic sound of spurs on flagstone floors, which always sends me spinning backwards to the way that Texas felt all around me.

In west Texas, I lost myself. I could sidestep the bits I wanted to forget, and then the sky and the plains swallowed me, along with the pain that sometimes, in England, had felt like it was encasing me. I loved the quiet, still comfort of being around the horses every day and the hours and hours I spent every week in a saddle. I loved the way the cowboys talked to their favourite animals – Packman and Brown Jug, Bar Stool and Happy – and the way those horses allowed me to belong to them too.

I was fitter than I've ever been, and in the bath would press on the calluses running across my palms as my hands wrinkled in the water and condensation dripped down the walls. My body felt strong, like it was looking after me, like I could do anything.

I didn't call home often. Occasionally, I spoke to Emma or Rick, who told me about Mum's progress in Norfolk. There was no progress. She wasn't getting better and, since the overdose, she moved around less, no longer walking to church. She was completely incontinent all the time. I used Eleanor's phone for these infrequent calls, sitting in the big house with the buffalo staring down at me as Rick's voice, very distant, told me about it all. But I felt like an ocean and a lifetime separated us, so I'd stare beyond the windows, into the mesquite bushes leading to the canyon, letting the words flood away from me like I was standing in deep water but the water was all draining away.

When Brandon wasn't there, I was often lonely, sitting on the porch in the evenings, gazing mindlessly at the yellowing stars pricking the velvet dark sky, nothing but miles beneath them, as coyotes howled, also alone, in the distance. Homesickness was there, but I didn't know where home was any more, or what it was. Without Mum to tether it to a place, I had no home to go to.

Sometimes, at dusk, I'd walk out into the landscape, down the long red drive from headquarters and over the cattle grid, out into the wildness to let it all dissolve away, or at least dilute into the heat and dust and the huge, huge sky. Until Texas, I had felt that the acute sadness of what had happened to Mum and to Minety and to the family we had once been would only ever define me. Texas gave me the advantage over the accident, so that for the first time I could pull away and be someone different. I couldn't imagine my life before Texas. It was as if nothing else mattered except for the massive plains and the red canyon and my sense of being alone, spinning around, at the still centre of them.

In the spring of 1999 I went back to England for a month because Nell was getting married. After the scale of west Texas, England looked like a fairy's garden, nimbly furnished with tiny, domesticated flowers. Daffodils and tulips flourished beneath stone walls that separated neat gardens from orchards of apple trees.

Nell was married in the church next to Emma and Matthew's house in Norfolk, and the party was in their garden, with 100 guests sitting down at long tables in a white canvas tent. There were plates of lobster, then speeches and dancing. Dan and his Irish band played the music, and Nell's first dance was to 'Dirty Old Town', before everyone flung off their high heels and danced on the grass.

Later, Dan snatched the cowboy hat I'd been wearing, taking my hand to pull me barefoot out into the field behind the house, to kiss me. I left the wedding with him, prolonging the holiday a bit longer, and we drove to Ireland, stopping at pubs on the west coast where Dan would play in sessions and I'd feel completely giddy in love with him, even before I'd drunk anything. I cried when I left England, but I knew I wanted to go back to Texas, because the summer brought with it the rodeo season; and anyway, Dan promised he'd write.

'A chance to play at bull riding,' Randy joked as we drove to the rodeo.

It was so hot that night of the rodeo in Clarendon. I sat in the bleachers with Brandon's older brother, Levi, eating corn chips and drinking Coors Light. Levi's wide-brimmed hat covered his eyes, but he'd never take it off. I knew he wore it all the time, even in the bath, because some nights in the spring he'd taken me out to see his broncs by his cabin beyond Clarendon. Then I'd shared his bed; we'd since stopped sleeping together, but were still friends.

'And now the event you've all been waiting for, folks, because we know y'all are just dying to see which of these brave young cowboys will bring home $500 in their Wranglers tonight. So let's give a big Texan welcome to all the competitors . . .'

On the far side of the arena, rows of cowboys were hanging over the rails of the holding pens by the main chute, swigging from cans of beer as girls buzzed around them in the heat. These girls wore the tightest jeans, like they'd been melted down and poured into them, and fitted shirts with big belts studded with diamanté.

Beside me, Levi was distracted, trying to catch the eye of a redhead in the seats below us, but she ignored him. He yawned, and the inside of his mouth looked very red.

'Got any smokes there, Clover?' he said lazily, stretching back in the seats with his arms spread out along their backs.

'Sure,' I said, passing him a crumpled packet of Marlboro Lights. 'Something else, this rodeo, isn't it?' I enthused.

Levi looked at me and scoffed.

'I've been around rodeo all my life, it's not exactly as if this is a new game for me,' he said, and yawned again. I felt put in my place, and an urge to take myself away. 'I'm going to get a beer from the pick-up, you want one?' I offered, and he shook his head. I dusted my hands off and left Levi to the redhead.

I wandered away from the noise of the arena to the parking lot. It was full of pick-ups with their tailgates down, groups of men drinking beer as they listened to the snatches of country songs and rock music that drifted from inside the cabs. Sometimes it was Willie Nelson, sometimes AC/DC. My arms prickled with sunburn and I felt tired.

At the end of the row of pick-ups, I could see Brandon, surrounded by a handful of other teenagers. I didn't want to go back to the bleachers, but I didn't belong with Brandon, either. Instead I swung into the cab of the ranch pick-up, flipping on the radio as I sat and watched the arena from a distance, as the cowboys thundered around and the crowd went wild.

I stayed in the truck on my own until the last prize-giving buckle was presented and the arena emptied as people started moving to the barn beside the arena, where there would be a dance that evening. I sat in the cab, feeling sleepy and not part of things, until Red and Jackie saw me, and pulled me out of the cab to introduce me to everyone. It should have been the kind of evening I loved, but I felt agitated, suddenly impatient with the feeling growing inside me of looking in from the outside.

From the edge of the dance floor, I watched Red and Jackie dancing, feeling a stab of envy for the close way they held one another. Later I danced with Red's sons and with Little Paul, the tallest man I'd ever met, and Randy's brother Smithy and Levi too, but something had changed. I was too far away on the outside. This wasn't my life. I felt like I was watching a film I had no part in and I knew my story in Texas was finishing.

The next evening, I walked out from the ranch, the air singing with the hot, hypnotic sound of cicadas. On the verges either side of the track, before the rusty barbed wire fences, blankets of waist-high yellow flowers nodded their heavy heads at passing shadows, their velvety petals drooping in the heat. The silence was broken by a faint rumble, far away in the distance, of a pick-up moving slowly along a distant ranch track. I stopped, leaning up against the gate near the horse pasture. In the dust below the gate was a dead lizard: its back was caked with dirt, but its belly was bright green, almost the colour of an emerald.

Back at the barns, behind me, I could hear the sound of Red and Jackie playing football with their children. I could have gone and joined them, but I knew their life would never be mine. I looked down at my feet instead, making an arc in the red dust with the end of my boot. I loved Texas, but I didn't belong there, however much I told myself I was making it mine.

For a moment, I thought of the wet, low-lying field behind the house at Minety with its thick blackthorn hedge, and the corner near the pond where the nettles grew higher than the barbed wire fence. That was the landscape I really knew, which was really in my blood and my bones and my heart. Standing on the red dust track, I somehow felt like I was being watched, and more than anything I wanted to go home.

I left a month later, in late summer 1999, as the rodeo season was drawing to a close. Levi and Brandon took me to a rodeo on my last night, stopping on the way back so that I could get TEXAS tattooed on my left bicep. Those last few weeks on the ranch were like living in multicolour. Before I'd even left, I was already missing Mitchell's Peak and Coogill Falls, the feeling of spending the whole day in the saddle, and the jokes I shared with Red and Randy. Even Sandy Paul, perhaps sensing the end was in sight, softened a bit. Once, untacking our horses after driving a hundred head of cattle out of the canyon, he nodded at me as he passed me on his way to the tack room, saying, 'You done good today, sister.'

Saying goodbye to any of them was hard, but hardest of all was leaving Donnie and Brandon, because for a while they'd almost felt like my brothers and suddenly that was all ending. And when I told Brandon that taking my spurs off made me want to cry, he just said, 'Well, hell, put them back on again and get back out here, Tumbleweed.'

My return to England felt like a holiday, at least to start with. I had been in America for over a year and a half, and I was twenty-three years old. It was autumn 1999 when I came home, and now there were no calves to brand or fences to fix. Postponing real life, I went to work for Mark Palmer when I got back. I moved into a flat above his stables, and helped him ride his horses. Best of all, Dan was there.

Now I was back in England, I became his girlfriend and he came to live with me in the stable flat, the two of us sharing the place with the rats who lived in the sofa. I covered the walls with some of Mum's old pictures and Dan played music in the local pub, where I waitressed in the evenings to earn some extra cash. I bought a big, unbroken grey mare called Ghost and broke her in from Mark's yard, wearing the black chaps with silver hearts on the belt that I'd worn in Texas. It was almost hypnotically easy work, and meant I could postpone the moment I had to work out what I'd really do.

That winter it was the Millennium, and the entire country went on a huge bender. Three days later, I was still being sick and on 3 January 2000, I sat on the edge of the bath in Mark Palmer's house, holding a plastic stick with two straight blue lines running across it, which told me I was expecting a baby.

CHAPTER 6

The bright yellow of the oilseed rape fields I pass as I drive Trigger from Baulking to Uffington is the same colour Mum painted all her kitchens. That rich yolk yellow looked even brighter behind the willow-pattern plates she'd prop up on her dresser and as Trigger's shoes rattle, insistently metal against the concrete, I can half close my eyes and touch the past. There's no breeze and England is warming for summer as the sticky-sweet smell of rape seeds surrounds me, as if their pollen is clinging to me. I slow Trigger to a walk, the breeching on the cart that runs around his hind quarters pulling tight as he drops his head and snorts, pausing for a moment to rub his long mane on his outstretched leg. Beyond Uffington the outline of White Horse Hill stretches ahead, outcrops of trees puncturing the sky.

I flip the reins to make Trigger trot on again and soon we're at the base of the hill. It's steep and now I have to ask a lot of Trigger to get up there, slapping the reins harder on his back to keep him moving. At the top I rein Trigger into a layby, leaning up against his side as we both struggle for breath. The valley of the White

Horse is flung below us and the horizon stretches west, from the grey mass of Swindon far to the east, where in the very distance I can see the darker outline of the Chiltern hills. A red kite wheels above me as flat-bottomed clouds scoot across the blue sky. Trigger is pleased to stop after the steep incline, so I close my eyes and now I'm standing here, fifteen years before, with another horse, and another cart, on the day before my son Jimmy was born.

★

Jimmy brought absolute happiness into my life but I didn't know that when I first saw the two blue lines on the white stick. Then, all I felt was extremely scared. Sitting on the edge of the claw-footed bath in Mark's bathroom, my hands shook as the two blue lines throbbed at me. I ripped open the second pack, sitting on the loo to pee onto another stick. There's really no way of cheating a positive pregnancy test, though, and as I walked back across the yard to the flat above the stables, a question lodged itself in my brain.

What on earth do I do now?

I was twenty-four, living in a stable flat with a mattress on the floor, paid £150 a week by Mark to ride his horses each morning. The job was something to do and the flat somewhere to live while I worked out the next bit of my life, which I'd imagined would involve moving to London, 'proper work', a rented flat, ambition. I loved the riding, and although life was chaotic and formless, I hadn't really minded about that until the moment with the two blue lines. Evenings spent around the wooden table in the Palmers' kitchen, with the dogs stretched out on the stone floor beside us as rapidly emptying bottles covered the table and Dan sang his songs, felt like a home of sorts. And then there was Dan, of course. Always Dan. Because I'd first met him when I was seventeen, we'd been friends for almost seven years by that point, which seemed like a significantly long time. We'd been properly together for almost four months and I was reassured on those jolly evenings that leaving Texas had been the right thing to do.

Before the two blue lines, mornings were often a hangover, not just at the weekend; but the thumping, sweating paranoia of coming down wasn't the easy trip through a lost day that it had once been when I was taking drugs in my late teens. Now, panic would creep in, galloping through my veins as I woke, early, after broken amphetamine sleep, but usually Dan would roll over and make a joke, and somehow everything would seem OK again.

That was the time I started dreaming of homes too: fast, tense knots of dreams where I was forever losing and finding houses which were unfamiliar, but also where I wanted to be. Sometimes the houses I dreamed about were Minety, or versions of Minety where it had changed, with unfamiliar wings of rooms added where my bedroom had once been. Sometimes I woke with my face wet with tears, or started awake, as if falling, and often in dreams I'd find myself clinging to the edge of a high building as the ground swirled below. Then I'd wake feeling rumpled and lost, with that terrible sense you get when you know you've lost something really important.

It was the lost mother I wanted more than anything when the test said I was pregnant.

'I always wanted to have kids!' was what Dan said when I showed him the plastic stick, throwing his head back and bursting into laughter. 'It's great! We're going to have a baby!' He laughed again, picking me up and whirling me around in his arms. 'All I ever wanted was to be a dad. And now I am. Brilliant.'

I loved him even more then, for his enthusiasm and heart, but I needed a mother to tell me what to do. The vast size of the decision in front of me seemed too large to answer on my own.

A baby?

It hadn't been an accident. There had been no slip-up, no forgotten pill or split condom, nothing as well organised as that. There had been no contraception, and I'd had sex with enough people and not got pregnant until then to know exactly how it worked.

I was sick and terrified by what had happened. But it was not as if I hadn't wanted it too; always. It would be neat, when tying up the frayed edges of my life, to say I'd got pregnant to replace what had been lost. Maybe some of that is true – grow a new version of the thing that's gone – but I'd also wanted to have babies even while I was still almost a baby myself. I was the eleven-year-old child at lunch parties at Minety running the crèche and looking after the visiting children. I'd talked to Mum about it sometimes when I was a young teenager and she'd always liked the thought. 'When you have a baby, we are going to have so much fun together, buying nappies and muslins. You'll just love having a baby' was what she would say.

I think Mum might have loved us all best when we were babies, at eight or nine months when we were big enough to sit on her lap eating a banana but not yet big enough to slip away from her and toddle off. 'Having a baby is like a love affair,' she told me. 'It's the obsession you feel when you fall in love and you just want to be in the same room as that person all the time and look at their face. That's what having a baby feels like.'

She wasn't a woman to complain about broken sleep, exhaustion, boredom, loneliness. While some women describe childbirth as a terrible, scary secret never to be disclosed to the expectant mother until after the event, Mum taught us to love it. When my brother-in-law Matthew called her to tell her Emma had gone into labour with her first child, Mum had said, 'Oh, lucky her, I am so, *so* envious.'

So as soon as those two blue lines appeared, I was angry with her. So furious I could have killed her because I wanted her so much.

'Please tell me what to do, tell me what to do,' I said aloud as I drove through the villages near Mark's house, trying to work out my route through what lay ahead. I couldn't really have a baby, could I? Before this had happened, I'd wanted something very different. I wanted to go on riding, but I also knew that working with horses is no way to make a living, unless you want to sacrifice your life to it completely. And I wanted to be able to go to them, but leave them too.

Retching up bile over the loo in the stable flat each morning, I desperately wanted someone to tell me how to be a mother. The smell and sight of a cup of coffee or a fried egg made me spin with sickness, but I devoured slices of white bread and butter, soft and neutral and demanding nothing from me when my body was asking me questions I'd never heard before. The questions woke me at 5 a.m. as Dan slept, so that I'd leave the flat at dawn to tack up Ghost and trot along the lanes slicing across the cold winter world near Mark's house. Dan was really pleased at our news and had started celebrating all the time, but in the stables below the flat my hands would shake as I pulled a bridle onto a thoroughbred, pushing the leather throat lash into keepers, throwing the saddle over the horse's back.

I didn't tell my family but I told Mark, tears coursing down my cheeks as I rubbed a currycomb over his favourite dappled grey gelding.

'Just keep on riding,' he said, leaning up against the stable door. 'Keep on riding and you'll work it out. Horses are the best influence in your life when it feels out of control because they force you to keep yourself together. They force you not to fall apart. Horses have saved my life and they can save yours too.'

I didn't know just how pregnant I was. The previous weeks had been such a blur, even before I'd found out. It was Christmas 1999, and everyone was in alcoholic collapse with the talk of millennium bugs and an excited fear the world might be about to end. I had no memory of when my last period had been so the GP sent me for a dating scan at the hospital in Oxford. Before the scan, I was ushered in to meet a family counsellor, an Irish lady with short brown hair wearing a heavy knitted jacket, with a clipboard and a questionnaire on her lap. She looked solid and sensible. She might know the answer to my question.

'So your husband, does he . . .' she started.

'My boyfriend,' I interrupted. 'He's my boyfriend, not my husband.'

'And how long have you been together?' she said as she readjusted her glasses, glancing down at her papers and picking up her pen to prove she was now really concentrating.

'Almost three months,' I replied, looking down at my hands. 'I haven't told anyone; my family, I mean. They'd be shocked, definitely. They might not like it.'

'And your boyfriend. Does he know? That you're pregnant?' she asked, head tipped onto one side.

'Yes. He knows. He's happy about it.'

'And you? How do you feel about becoming a parent?'

I paused. For a moment I wasn't quite sure who she was talking about as 'becoming a parent' sounded much more grown-up than I felt at that moment. I stared out to the car park, watching smudge-coloured cars lining up to find a space.

'Me? I'm happy too . . . I mean, I'm sort of pretty scared, actually. We've been together such a short time and we don't really have any money or proper jobs . . .' Then I told her, in a monologue that lasted several minutes, about the things I was worried about. The lack of money or life plans. The fact my mum was absent when I was wanting her most because of an accident she'd had. My worry because my boyfriend drank quite a bit; in fact, most days. 'And I don't know what to do. I don't know if it's just a thing now, or if he will drink less if we had a child. Became parents. If my mum was here I could talk to her. But she can't talk about anything because of this accident she had. And I don't know what to do. I just don't know what I should do.'

She watched me, sometimes scribbling notes, sometimes asking more questions about my lifestyle, always glancing up to me then looking quickly back to her paper. Afterwards, she flicked through her notes then put her Biro down on the table between us, running her palm backwards and forwards over it so that it clicked across the table.

'Because of what you've told me, about the alcohol consumption, and your concerns about it, and the lack of support or structure, in my opinion your wisest route would be an abortion.'

I went for the scan straight afterwards, as even while booking me in for an abortion, the hospital still needed to know how pregnant I was. A nurse squirted clear gel on my bare tummy and as she spun the television screen towards me, a watery scene emerged. Grey shapes of liquid spooled around, sometimes moving into slow motion as she froze the screen, dragging a cursor across the shapes to measure them. *It's just a bunch of cells*, I told myself.

'You won't be able to make out much. The shape is imprecise at the moment,' she said, staring intently at her screen, pressing down a little harder on my stomach with the head of the ultrasound. 'Now, where are you?' she said quietly, but shocking me too as I realised she was not addressing me. 'Six weeks. I make that six weeks. And there you are, found you!'

She sounded triumphant as a small white dot pulsated at me, insistent and absolutely present. 'That's the heartbeat.'

And in that instant I knew exactly what I was supposed to do.

I was almost five months pregnant when Dan and I moved from Mark's stable flat to the house in Oxford I'd lived in as a student. It was a tiny two-up, two-down Rick had bought for Mum, for when she got better, but which she'd never been to. Nell and I had both lived there as students. Now I painted the walls bright yellow with a thick band of pink around the top, like rhubarb and custard. I found a job with the university, answering phones and entering data in the admissions office. Dan wasn't always in Oxford but instead was working for Nell. She and her husband had started a circus, throwing together a show with a dancing horse and high-wire act. She roped in friends to do the lighting or build sets, salvaging costumes from the remnants of the dressing-up box we'd played with as children. For two months over that summer I was pregnant, Dan became her musical director, playing the same jigs and reels he'd played in the pubs of Oxford.

We planned a wedding in the Catholic church in St Giles that spring. We invited everyone we knew and all our family, with cousins and aunts and uncles arriving to celebrate with the Irish scaffolders and publicans Dan knew from the Cowley Road. At first, the idea had made him look slightly worried, until a couple of weeks before the wedding, when he slipped out, telling me there was something he urgently needed to do.

In Oxford, he was known as Irish Dan or Dublin Dan and although his hard north-side Dublin accent had softened a little bit, it was still very obvious. But that night he went out to tell his friends that his family, whom they would all meet at our wedding, might not sound quite as Irish as he did. Might not, in fact, sound Irish at all.

He kept the accent up all the time until then, even when he took me to Hereford to meet his family. If I'd fallen hard for Dan, I fell equally hard for his younger brothers and sisters and his parents too. He was the eldest of five, and his siblings tumbled out of their tall redbrick house, each more charming and accomplished than the last, trilling off A-star exam results while playing Grade 8 piano concertos to impress their elder brother. His mother was warm and smiled all the time as she cooked fish pie, laying the table to be ready when his father got home from his job as head of an art college. It was the warm, cosy, family-kitchen life I'd craved, and I fell into it with both arms wide open.

They surprised me too. Dan had always created the impression he'd come from a tough, working-class family, and told me that his missing front tooth was the result of a boxing injury when he was a child.

'Did he really say that?' his mother said, draining peas to go with the steaming fish pie. 'No, no, he fell off a tricycle when he was a little boy. Oh, Danny!'

Everyone laughed and after supper we all went to the pub to hear Dan playing, where Dan's father's eyes glistened when he sang 'The Leaving of Liverpool'.

I was entirely in love with Dan. I loved the way he sang and he spoke, the way he walked towards me and the way he stood at the bar waiting for a pint and a shot. I loved the fact he made me laugh about fifteen times a day and I loved his kindness towards complete strangers. I didn't care that he wasn't really from Dublin and had been a little creative about his background; I'd done the same in America at times. Once, in a bar in Tucson, I'd met a businessman on his way to California and told him I was married to a bull rider on the professional rodeo circuit. For an evening, I'd inhabited an entirely different life. I understood the need to invent and reinvent. And Dan hadn't really lied, either. His mother's side of his family were from Ireland before Liverpool, so he had some long-distant relatives in Connemara. It wasn't complete fiction. He still had a great accent and could sing with more soul and spirit than anyone I'd met in the whole year I'd lived in Ireland.

Sometimes I worried a bit about how much he hated getting up in the mornings and the fact he could easily sleep until one or two in the afternoon, and that he didn't seem overly worried about working. But that was OK, I told myself, as a life with Dan was always going to be unconventional. I didn't want normal. Life with him would be an exciting, romantic tangle, and most of all it would be a real family of my own. Anyway, he was a musician. Being unconventional is what they do for a living. And once the baby was born, he'd start taking life more seriously.

We married on a cold sunny day in that Catholic church in Oxford in mid-April. Dan played four gigs in two nights so we had enough money to buy some cases of wine and hire a hall, but my sisters and closest friends, and the new family I'd found in Dan's helped me with almost everything else. My naughtiest friend, Etain, who had always been a partner in crime, cooked roast chickens and home-made mayonnaise, and Sophia made my pink-and-red wedding dress, copied from something similar I'd seen on Loretta Lynn in a documentary about her made in the sixties. Jackie brought her camera and took photographs, and Dan's sisters made cupcakes, and his mother, lovely and beaming, arrived with a wedding cake she'd made, covered in whipped white icing and petals.

With their help, we put a wedding together for a few hundred pounds. It wasn't what I'd imagined my wedding might be like, when as a child I'd draped a strip of nylon netting over my face and stood silently in front of my bedroom mirror, the only sound my breath behind my netting veil. It wasn't like the wedding scenes I'd seen in films, either, with a big wedding brunch and mother-of-the-bride moments. Mum wasn't there. It was never going to be like that.

Instead, it was something else. Nell and Emma and my stepmother Alexandra tied pink ribbons in my hair because I didn't have a veil, and I bought a green-and-pink cut-glass necklace from a junk shop in Oxford. The Catholic church sparkled with golden jewelled icons, which beckoned me as I stood at the bottom of the aisle, where what I felt was imprecise and tangled. Afterwards Mark Palmer met us out of the church with his black-and-white pony and painted cart, piling the bridesmaids onto the back to trot through Oxford to the hall, where Dan and his band played the first song.

The next morning we caught 5 a.m. flights to Pisa and drove a hired car into Tuscany, where we'd rented a room in a villa for a week. I was exhausted, slumping onto the bed beside my suitcase, and as Dan opened a bottle of wine, throwing open French doors onto a little terrace, a thought arrived in my chest and sat there.

What have I done? This is forever. The rest of my life. What the fuck have I done?

A cold, hard, precise dread sat on me for about three minutes, until I fell asleep. When I woke up, fifteen hours later, the thought had gone.

Dan was a dream on honeymoon. One afternoon, when I was sleeping after a long walk around a hill town, he went out and bought me a pink scarf because I'd said I was cold. We sat out late on the terrace every night while Dan smoked, eating fish he'd grilled on a barbeque and imagining what lay ahead. He made me laugh all the time and he made me feel loved too.

We didn't have very much money at all so we were lucky, when we returned from honeymoon, to have the house in Oxford to live in. We bought a sofa from a charity shop and one afternoon Dan dragged some cabinets home from a skip which we used in the kitchen. I found some faded Indian rugs, eaten ragged by moths, which had been salvaged from Minety, and we painted not just the kitchen but the whole house bright colours. When I lit a fire in the grate in the sitting room, and Dan cooked and sang music, I felt it was the best place to be in all of Oxford.

I got used to my card being refused at the till or spat back out at me at the cashpoint. I knew how to shop in the late afternoon at the weekly market for cheap deals on fruit and vegetables, and once a week would drive to a budget supermarket on the ring road where dry food was sold loose without packaging. I bought washing-up liquid and soap powder from Kwik Save, which also sold cheap alcohol. When he knew I was going there, Dan would sit up in bed, rummaging through his jeans to find a crumpled ten-pound note to thrust at me.

'Get me cider. The cheap stuff. White Lightning, maybe.'

'White Lightning?' I giggled. 'Last time I drank that I was fourteen.'

'Yeah, that's fine. Anything like that,' he'd say and then he'd wink at me and I'd find myself, despite myself, smiling back. 'Love you, Clo.'

Up on the Ridgeway with Trigger, a decade and a half later, the air is clean and warm. Trigger rubs his head against my arm because sweating has made him itchy. It's what all driving horses like to do when they get hot, and it's the same thing another horse did to me when I walked up here with Dan, the day before our baby was born.

It was September then, a hot Sunday afternoon on the first weekend in the month, and the promise of a proper Indian summer was unfolding luxuriously across the countryside. I was thirty-nine-and-a-half weeks pregnant, my belly so huge and tight I couldn't see my feet, and I was restless, impatient to meet the child whose heart was beating inside me. Sleeping was uncomfortable and I paced the house, dragging chests of drawers and tables into new positions, flipping pale-blue paint onto the bathroom walls, washing and rehanging the thin cotton curtains in our bedroom.

That afternoon we wanted to get out of the city, so Dan made sandwiches from the cold lamb he'd roasted the night before, wrapping them carefully in greaseproof paper and packing them in a canvas bag with some digestive biscuits and apples and a bottle of cider he bought from the corner shop at the end of the road.

We drove out of Oxford to Candida's house in Uffington, tacking up her skewbald cob, Axle, to trot up to White Horse Hill, looking over the hedges from the high seat of her two-wheeled dog cart.

If I concentrate, I can touch that day. I can feel the soft cotton of the faded purple vest I was wearing, and the swish around my knees of the flower skirt I'd bought in Topshop. I can hear Candida's laugh as we pulled out of her drive in the cart – 'Just *look* at you three!' – and the rumble of the metal wheels on the road. We jogged up the hill in the cart, but both jumped out as the hill rose more sharply, and I can feel the memory of the heat of Axle walking beside me at that moment. There's my laugh too. I'm laughing at Dan, who's pretending to be a gypsy in his best, thickest Irish accent, as we crest the hill.

We bumped along the Ridgeway north of Wayland's Smithy, down a stretch of byway now closed off with a locked gate. The track vanished into the long, burned, late-summer grass so it felt like we were driving Axle across an open field or prairie. It felt like escape.

A little way down the track were some barns and a cottage with blue-painted window frames. I sometimes pass it now with the children if we're walking or riding on the Ridgeway, and just as it was that day with Dan, it's framed in my mind as a place we went with Candida for picnics when we were children.

In the dusk of that day, the day before Jimmy, swallows darted and wheeled around the eaves, but the sky was still as the shadows lengthened. Dan lay down in the grass, dizzy with the solidified heat of evening, and pulled the bottle of cider from his backpack.

'No further anyway, Clo, or the baby might be born up here,' he said as I tied Axle on a long rein close to the fence so he could graze beside us. We lay in the grass and ate the sandwiches, posing together for photographs while Axle watched us, sometimes nodding his head before returning to concentrate on the grass.

The next morning I woke up at dawn with the first light of morning seeping under the curtains, sitting straight up in bed in Oxford with a persistent thought of Mum around me. Then it started and Jimmy was born, five days early, that afternoon. The complete and absolute rightness of his existence flooded into my life like a pot of golden poster paint tipped all over a white floor.

When Jimmy was a month old I took him to see Mum in her nursing home in Norfolk. I'd go through a stage of seeing her at least every month and at other times I'd feel defeated by the hours and years I'd spent in homes, sitting beside her and telling her about my life passing as she stared at me in silence, and I wouldn't feel able to go.

On a visit to Mum, she'd tap her feet gently while I spoke, looking away at the tea trolley sliding past her view to reach for a plate of shortbread biscuits. She'd had to have all her teeth taken out because she refused to brush her teeth, or let anyone else do it. She'd got abscesses in her jaw, but since she could never manage false teeth, the only way to avoid a serious infection was to take all her teeth out. I didn't like the sight of the inside of her mouth when she smiled, or made a strange retching noise after she'd drunk a cup of tea. Her bare gums were pink and raw and scared me.

It wasn't just her teeth. There were always questions to deal with about her health. Should her epilepsy medication, which was giving her urinary tract infections, be reduced, or would that put her at greater risk from a fit? Was her eczema going to become infected due to her incontinence pads? When she had flu, how could bed sores be avoided?

Her nurses in the Sue Ryder home we had moved her to were angels. Literally, they were not normal girls or women, but gave everything to the elderly disabled patients they looked after. They loved it when I brought Jimmy in, taking it in turns to pass him around the sitting room so they could all hold him and coo at his tiny, perfect features.

Mum was less infatuated. When I'd gone to see her when I was pregnant, she'd looked almost shocked or angry for a moment, making strange hissing and sighing noises when she saw me, then grabbing my arm as if to turn me around and push me away from her. That was painful, but not as painful as the moment I arrived with my baby. When I showed her Jimmy, she looked at him in my arms, then back at me, studying my face as her eyes flicked back to the baby. She muttered inaudible sounds and turned her face away.

'This is Jimmy, my baby, Mum,' I said. 'Isn't he beautiful? Isn't he the most lovely baby?'

Mum looked at me and pointed to the far side of the room.

'Charlotte, he's your grandson,' one of the nurses purred beside her, stroking her arm and gently squeezing her hand. 'Hasn't he got your eyes, Charlotte? What a little smasher. I'll leave your tea here now, so you can enjoy it later,' she went on, leaving two cups of milky tea on the dark wooden sidetable, before bustling off to attend to the man dozing gently in the window. Mum turned her shoulders away from me, reaching towards the teacup, then slumped back in her seat.

'Mum, would you like to hold him?' I said quietly. 'I could help you support him. Please will you hold him?'

She looked at me again and made a groaning noise. Then she slipped her hands beneath her legs, very deliberately sitting on them. I swallowed, a stab in the back of my throat that felt all dry like I was about to cry.

'OK, we'll just sit here and then you can just look at Jimmy. You're right, that's probably easier,' I said, pretending to relax into the stool I was perched on beside her. 'It's so lovely having him, Mum. You were right about it all. Do you think he looks like me? Did I look like this when I was a baby?' I smiled at her, like we were a mother and daughter having a chat in the sitting room at home.

Beside me, Mum stared out through the French windows to the nursing-home garden, where the late-summer leaves were turning to brown. She sighed, tapping her foot gently, her hands tucked beneath her.

Jimmy was my life and all my good dreams made real. He was a focus for all my love and he was the missing part of a broken jigsaw I was putting back together. And Dan loved us both so much.

When Jimmy was a few weeks old, a neighbour gave me a brown Silver Cross pram she'd had in her garage since the early eighties. We rubbed the dust off it and Dan polished the brake and wheels until they gleamed. She wasn't the only one to help. I'd never lost the childhood friendship I'd had with Candida and Rupert and their five children in the years just after Mum's accident, but Candida walked very purposefully back into my life after I had Jimmy. Candida saw, very clearly, how my son's arrival had opened fresh wounds in the scars around Mum's absence. She visited me several times in the days immediately after he was born and I think she was consciously keeping a sense of Mum absolutely present for me, repeating the rituals of friendship with me that they had shared together as women when their children had been born. When I got back from hospital, she'd left a bunch of wild flowers on my doorstep in a blue enamel jug with a multicoloured crochet blanket and a note:

Darling,

I didn't want to disturb you and the bubba but I brought you these. Your mum was walking beside me through the garden as I picked them.

All my love, Cand

PS The blanket is something I made for the baby, ignore the dropped stitches.

Dan wrapped Jimmy in the blanket, cradling him gently into the new pram to push him down the road in the sunshine.

'I've never seen a father looking as proud as your husband did that morning,' the neighbour told me later. 'His pride. That's a sight I'll never forget.'

I loved my baby Jimmy, but the feeling of being tethered to the kitchen table also made me crave the animal smell and thunder of a horse. When Jimmy was about one and a half I started riding out for another racehorse trainer who had a yard close to the Ridgeway at Wantage. It was only about twenty-five minutes from Oxford and I'd leave early, at 6.30 in the morning, while Dan was still sleeping, with Jimmy strapped, blinking, surprised, into his baby seat. The wife of one of the stable lads looked after him while I rode two or three horses. It was a serious operation, with sixty sleek thoroughbreds like bullets to shoot up the gallops every morning and a string of lads working full time. I was only there a couple of mornings a week, so didn't share the same camaraderie I'd had with the stable lads I'd worked with at the yard near Barbury Castle when I was eighteen. I was there, anyway, purely for the horses.

The racehorses arrived back in my life like liberators when motherhood made me feel like a kitchen hostage. Zipped into my leather chaps, I drank in the moment of stillness in the stable while I pulled up the horse's girth, running my palms over his velvety sides as he cocked his ears at me, my own image reflected back, fish-eye, in the pool of his eyes.

The power of the horses scared me but I craved the time I could steal with them. Jumping off – that moment a racehorse starts to canter at full speed up the gallops – was what terrified me the most, but was what I wanted to feel again and again and again. The moment before jumping off is also the time when the horse is most likely to spook by bucking or whipping round, so a sort of tension solidified between the lads and me as we approached the start of the gallops. Once the horse moves into a canter, there's no going back, so the horse has to be pointed straight as an arrow at the gallop before him. Jumping off at the bottom of the gallops made me shed motherhood, and being married, and even being my mother's daughter, and gallop at a thunder directly out of the past and straight into my very own present.

Being married to Dan was a blast – most of the time – too.

There were endless late nights and early mornings when Dan came home at dawn from another gig. Then he'd get up at teatime, trailing Golden Virginia tobacco across the kitchen floor and telling me jokes as I spooned pasta into Jimmy's open mouth. If we could afford a babysitter, I'd put on tight jeans and cowboy boots and go to see him play a gig.

'Look at you. You're with the band,' a friend visiting from London said as we stood at the bar in a dark pub, the ice in my vodka rattling in the glass as I raised it to my mouth. Being with the band was exciting and made up for the grains of worry growing inside me. Because what I tried not to think about was the drinking that was going on every day inside our marriage. I didn't tell anyone because I thought that way they might not notice. I didn't talk to my sisters about it and blocked it out like background music. Everyone drank when they were young, and because we were only in our mid-twenties, all my friends were drinking hard back then. Everyone was getting wasted a lot of the time, and if anything I felt lucky. Dan had never ever suggested I do anything but have the baby. He'd only ever wanted to step up to the challenge of becoming parents when most of our friends were another decade away from it. And so his drinking, I convinced myself, wasn't really that different from anyone else's.

If he could haul himself out of bed after a gig, Dan worked on building sites, returning with hair matted with concrete dust, big leather boots crusted with mud. Later he started doing night shifts at a hostel for homeless people. He enjoyed helping people, and the night-time hours suited him. I'd stopped working for the university after Jimmy was born, and in the hours in which he slept, or during the evenings when Dan was out, I started writing. I bought a computer, a huge lump of white plastic that sat on an old table I'd had in my bedroom at Minety, and someone who knew Dan from the pub gave me some work researching the lives of great artists for a website; I had to write their potted biographies into bite-size pieces of copy.

'Maybe you should write about Texas,' my stepmother Alexandra said one Sunday afternoon when she and Rick were visiting and I'd shown her the notebooks I'd filled in America.

'It would make a good newspaper article,' she said. 'Write it up as a story, the sort of thing you might read in a magazine.'

It worked, and a magazine bought it for £500.

'Everyone on features loved the story,' the editor emailed me afterwards. 'Come and see us next time you're in town.'

'In town' meant being in London, and since I didn't have a nanny or any proper childcare I took Jimmy with me. I dressed him in his most appealing Fair Isle jersey and faded green corduroy trousers and took him through the polished revolving doors of a huge magazine company near Oxford Street. The editor took me to a Japanese restaurant for soft shell crab and noodles as Jimmy slept in his buggy. Afterwards she clattered back to her shiny office scented with huge white lilies.

'Send me some more ideas. I love your writing.'

If we fought, or when times were hard, I told myself that the toddler years were always supposed to be the hardest. It would get easier. But I was three months pregnant with my second child when I started going to Al-Anon. Jimmy was two and a half. That summer Jimmy, Dan and I had spent a holiday with Emma and Matthew and some friends of theirs in a rented house in France, and Dan had drunk especially hard, pairing up with the husband of one of Emma's friends to stay up all night, sinking bottle after bottle until it got light. Dan also sang beautifully almost every night after supper, so he was always forgiven for the huge pile of empties, but at the end of the holiday, the wife of the man Dan had been drinking with pulled me aside to talk quietly.

'Al-Anon is a benign place to find support when you are married to an alcoholic,' she told me, as we stood in the baking heat in the dusty drive of the French farmhouse. I really wasn't sure what she was talking about. Dan was such good fun to be with, and I imagined Al-Anon would be full of women with black eyes married to drunken thugs.

'"Al-Anon"? No point in that, seriously,' said Dan when I told him about it back in England. 'You think *I'm* an alcoholic? Go to Al-Anon and then you'll meet people with serious problems. People married to real alcoholics. Waste of time.'

As if to prove it to me, he promised he'd go to an AA meeting too.

I felt self-conscious, hiding behind a scarf and a coat with a tall collar, arriving in the community hall to sit on plastic chairs arranged in a circle. I thought Dan would probably be right, and that the people I would meet would really be suffering, not like me. So I sat and listened to their stories of living with addiction. Very ordinary people, just like myself, talking about the confusion and betrayal and utter disorientation of living with someone who loved drink more than they loved you. And I found out Dan was wrong. The stories I heard were just like mine, only mine was often much worse. I hugged my arms across my chest and sat in silence as the reality of the extent of the addiction I was dealing with solidified around me.

Back at home, later that evening, Dan was sitting in front of the fire, drinking a bottle of wine. He'd been to AA.

'Me? Have a problem? Seriously, Clover, I went to AA, and everyone there was so much worse than me that I left halfway through. I'm not an alcoholic. Forget about it. I just like a drink. Seriously, stop worrying about it.'

I'd never missed Mum as much as I did when my daughter Dolly was born. She arrived two weeks early, a perfect, tiny bud of a girl who blinked up at me with the darkest eyes, as if she already saw into my soul. It seemed impossible I'd be able to reproduce that brand of love I'd first experienced holding Jimmy in my arms, but Dolly brought it all back to me with the same intensity. The end of my pregnancy had been nerve-wracking, as I'd lost a lot of fluid in the final month, and was being monitored every couple of days at the hospital in Oxford. Earlier in my pregnancy too I'd got a huge electric shock from a wire deer fence walking on a hill with my friend Claudia at her home in Devon. Later, Jimmy said it might be the reason Dolly is so singular and unusual, and we gave her the name Electra as her middle name.

Dolly was born in the same hospital where Jimmy had been born, and where Nell and I were born too. Being there made me feel closer to Mum and completely in love with Dolly. I wanted to stay swaddled in the clean white light of the hospital for as long as possible after she was born. The sound of the ward around me at 1 a.m. reminded me of the comfort of drifting off to sleep upstairs as I heard the grown-ups talking downstairs when I was a child. I was part of it all but did not have to participate. I could be alone with my daughter as my body felt its way into a new role as a mother of both a son and daughter. Sitting up in the half-light of the hospital bed, with Dolly tucked into my shoulder; I felt exhilarated and delighted to have her, but also sadder than I've almost ever felt in my life, since Mum's loss was tangible. People talk about the loss of someone you love as the removal of something, but I felt that my mother's absence then was more like the presence of another fierce and very real emotion, which wrapped itself all around me until it was the only certainty I knew.

I took my new baby home and life went on. But sometimes, when Dan hadn't been working but still continued to sleep during the day and I was up with my children, I wanted to stab my husband's sleeping head. I wanted to hurt him. I wanted to do that most of all on the children's birthdays; first when Jimmy was one, and Dan didn't bother to get up as he said Jimmy would never know, anyway. But he did it again when Jimmy was two, and on his third birthday, just after Dolly was born, he stayed in bed once more.

After I'd helped Jimmy unwrap the presents I'd wrapped for him the previous night, I took both of the children to the super-market to buy ingredients to make a birthday tea. Unloading the car afterwards, one of the plastic bags split, weeping half a dozen oranges like big fat comic tears all over the road, and I sat down on the pavement with Dolly strapped into her seat screaming, and Jimmy in the house looking out at me from the sitting-room window, and I cried and I cried. It was three in the afternoon on our son's birthday, Dan was still in bed, and it wasn't supposed to be like this.

Because I loved Jimmy and Dolly with every part of me and I loved Dan too, I wasn't expecting what happened between us. It should not have come as a shock, since it wasn't something that started overnight but was always there. Once, towards the end, I found some credit-card statements stuffed down the side of the fridge and, even by Dan's standards, the quantities surprised me, although the list of benefactors didn't: Moody's Pool Bar, Twelve Bar, Coach and Horses, Whites, Half Moon, Elm Tree, Bullingdon Arms, High Low Jamaican. Each transaction was in three figures – £175, £122, £279, £333, £102, £289 – which meant that he'd been gambling as well as drinking. Until then, the gambling hadn't worried me as much as the drinking, since it seemed so much more benign. I'd imagined it to be the odd fiver here and there, Dan seduced by the whirr of the flashing machines. They didn't make me feel sick like the smell of old wine and stale beer did. Gambling didn't hurt me or enrage me like vodka. But those three-digit numbers showed it had its own dangerous decline that could eat away at our life together.

Alcoholism was my sickness as much as Dan's, though, since I believed I could make things better for him and help him find the person he could be without vodka distorting it all. Even when he called me a fucking bitch, I felt like I was fully engaged with him and we were connecting. Even the shouting and the smashing of glass on the kitchen floor meant he was really there. The writing was on the wall, but at that time I had forgotten how to read.

In the end, we broke without me realising. I should have been able to feel that end approaching quicker than I did, as then I might have protected the children from some of the chaos in our lives. But by the time Dolly was born, that chaos was like a physical presence that was yellow and spongy and got bigger and bigger when I wasn't looking.

I wanted to hold this yellow chaos in my hands, and stuff it back down the black hole that was boring away in the middle of the sitting room or the kitchen, or the children's bedroom. It didn't matter which room we were in: the black hole was always there. Even in the car. And while the chaos was growing like some horrible puffy amphibian in a misty green tank, the black hole was swallowing up all the parts of my life I liked best, making me panic with claustrophobia.

And even if I thought I could evade the hole, that my legs were just long enough to step over it, I should have known the children were about to fall into it if I didn't do something quickly.

I should have known, but I was blind.

I'm strong. I can take this, I told myself, after another fight about money left the six wooden chairs we'd been given as a wedding present in splinters on the sitting-room floor. I thought Mum's accident had made me very tough, so I resisted admitting to myself – let alone to family or friends – that I could not cope with my marriage.

I was also completely confused because life with Dan was a trip I wanted to be on. Even at its very worst, there were still many moments during every day when he would make me laugh more than anyone. And that was what made the route out of my marriage feel like a baffling maze. My fear about what was happening was like the Minotaur, waiting for me around every corner. I didn't know when it would roar out at me, but I knew it was there.

At that time, I did not talk to anyone about the cracks that were breaking the house apart. I was dishonest. I pretended that Dan got up and went to work every day. I pretended we were in, together, on a Friday night, when really he was at the pub spending the few hundred pounds he'd made that week, slotting school lunch money and the electric bill into a fruit machine.

At the school gates, I pretended the entire time. Once I was asked to go and hold a song sheet up at Jimmy's sharing assembly, so I had to pretend all was absolutely calm inside me, even though I was shaking with rage because Dan was at home in bed, refusing to go to either work or the assembly for Jimmy.

I was fine, until the children started singing and I saw Jimmy, cross-legged, in the front row, his mouth a wide red O as he sang the words to 'Lord of the Dance': 'I am the life that will never never die.' Holding the word sheet up at the front of the assembly hall, I tried to sing along to the words until I felt the sides of my mouth pulling downwards, like I had no control of them at all. My throat felt tight and tears fell down my cheeks. I couldn't wipe them away as I was holding the song sheet, so I just smiled shakily at the children staring up at me, as teardrops bounced down my jersey and onto the floor. Some of the children in the front row stopped singing, their mouths wide open as they stared at me, like I was a fascinatingly horrible exhibit in a museum. At that moment, I felt like a rat's skull in a sweaty child's hand, or a shrunken head in the Pitt Rivers Museum. I was grateful Jimmy could not see me, sitting on the far end of the row, for even when the song ended and I went to sit down on the small benches reserved for parents at the back of the hall, the tears kept coming.

Before I got married, before I ever even met Dan, I remember thinking about divorce, and wondering, *how do you actually do it?* There was the same exoticism to it that there was to marriage, but instead of being imbued with a sugary pink glow, the word was shimmering with something glassy and black, like a cracked pane of glass in a dark upstairs window. How does a person go about getting divorced? How bad does it have to get before you can reasonably say, 'Enough is enough'? What does that point feel like?

It was a Thursday and Dan had texted me to say he was stopping with the boys from the building site on the way back from work for a quick pint. By now I'd learned that no pint was ever quick and calling it that was a lie, so I wasn't surprised it was late when he got home, almost eleven, although I was still disappointed. His eyes had that intense sparkle of heavy drinking. He pulled his coat off, rubbing rain from his thick hair, smiling at me glassily.

'I bought you these,' he said, holding out a cellophane packet of purple chrysanthemums with a sticker saying 'reduced to 50p' on it. The children had been asleep for hours. They'd bounced on the beds with excitement after their bath, but by nine were ripped with tiredness.

I was upstairs in the bathroom, brushing my teeth, when Dan came home.

'Clover, darlin', I bought you these,' he said again. 'Alright?'

I hadn't bothered to come downstairs when he got back, so he had come up to the landing and was thrusting the flowers into my arms. But I was surly and knotted with anger and disappointment and so although I took the flowers, I turned away from him and went back into the bathroom, discarding them on the edge of the bath. I heard him following me. Despite my fury, I was glad he was still there.

'I made supper ages ago,' I said flatly, standing in front of the bathroom mirror, watching him in the reflection.

'You buy anything to drink?' he hiccupped, leaning against the bath. I shook my head. 'Great,' he mumbled. 'Fucking great. Fucking brilliant.'

'I thought you were going to be back earlier. I was going to go to the shop when you got back, and now it's shut. You should have come back earlier, Dan.'

'It was just a quick drink with the lads. Jesus, Clover. I can't get anything right now, can I?'

'Why are you drinking when we can't afford to put the heating on?' My voice was thin and high-pitched. I was becoming the person I'd dreaded: I was a nag.

Dan buried his head in his hands, but I couldn't stop there. It was both our faults, what happened next.

'I wanted you to come home and help me put the kids to bed. I just thought we could put the children to bed together and then have a drink here. Not in the pub. You're always in the pub. You're never here. Or if you are here, you're wanting to be in the pub.'

'Is it surprising, with you on at me like that? It was only a couple of pints.' Dan didn't look at me as he spoke. He was fumbling with a packet of Golden Virginia and a Rizla, the tobacco falling onto the bathroom lino, so he had to start again with a pile of brown tobacco dust lying at his feet.

'A couple of pints?' I hissed, arms folded across my chest, my face hard and twisted. I looked angry and ugly, but right then I didn't care. When I'd first met Dan, I'd wanted him to love me completely. I'd tried always to smile when I was looking at him, tried to keep my lips in a permanent irresistible pout he would want to kiss. Now, he looked up at me, winced, and dropped the tobacco again. I grabbed the packet from him, plucking deftly at a Rizla, and then handed him a rolled cigarette. 'You're too wasted even to roll a fag, Dan. You really expect me to believe that you had a *couple* of pints?'

He turned away from me. 'Look. I bought you these.' He proferred another peace offering in a plastic bag. In it was a box of chocolate profiteroles, the plastic dome dented so that the buns were squashed, cream smeared across the inside.

'It's a bit late for that now, though, isn't it? I put Jimmy and Dolly to bed on my own and made supper hours ago. Have you got any idea, Dan, what it's like spending a day with a baby and toddler alone and then spending the evening waiting and wishing you'd come back? Why can't you think of me for a moment, or at least of us together? I have been on my own all day and I only wanted to spend the evening with you, and now look. It's too late, Dan. I didn't want the evening to be like this, I didn't want *anything* to be like this. It's too late now, Dan, it's too late for anything, can't you see that or are you blind? No – you are *drunk*.' I wiped the back of my hand across my mouth to remove the spittle. Dan dropped the box of profiteroles and shook his head.

'Jesus fucking Christ, Clover. Just shut the fuck up, will you? Shut the fuck up, you little tart.'

'Don't tell me to shut up. Don't swear at me. Do not swear at me, Dan!' I shouted. And then I made a big mistake: I leant forward and pushed him, very hard, in the chest with the flat of both my hands. Suddenly he was above me, leaning into me, his face exploded with anger.

'Don't you fucking touch me, Clover. Why should I want to come back to you when all you do is bitch and moan and complain about how useless I am? Look at yourself! You stupid fucking cow. You've got no fucking idea about what it is like to do a day's work in your life, you spoiled little bitch, you fucking bitch!'

I shouldn't have pushed him. I shouldn't have tried to fight back. I should have known that from all the evenings I'd spent at Al-Anon. The thing all those people with drunk mothers and husbands and children and fathers and lovers had said was, 'Do not try to engage with the alcoholic when they have been drinking.'

But engaging is what I love to do, so trying not to engage with the alcoholic in my life was just not an option. This was the way it always went between us. We batted the insults backwards and forwards between us like ping-pong balls: You're a drunk. You're spoilt. You're always pissed. You're a nag. Backwards and forwards they pinged, and sometimes they just slipped underneath the sofa or behind the television and were forgotten about for days or even weeks. But we loved the game, really, and I don't know how but there was always an inexhaustible supply of those shiny white insults to lob at each other.

Dan was raging and crazy. I had pushed him against the wall and I could see his body quivering. For a moment I wanted him to hit me in the face. I wanted him to hit me really hard and to feel the slap of his hand across my face. I needed some visible sign of what was happening between us.

But he didn't hit me. Instead he threw me back across the room towards the sink then he ripped open the box of profiteroles, throwing a handful of chocolate and cream pastry at me.

'Here's your fucking pudding, you miserable little bitch,' he said, scooping a profiterole out of the plastic box and hurling it across the room. 'And these too. You bitch. You stupid little cow.'

The balls of pastry glued to the wall behind me, the brown chocolate and white cream mixing together and running down the ivory bathroom walls. Then Dan picked up the flowers by the bath, flinging them across the room at me too so that the petals fluttered down, mixing with the mess of pastry and chocolate.

He turned around, wild in his eyes at the energy unleashed between us. As he turned to leave the room his shoulder knocked the plain wooden mirror hanging above the sink. It had been a wedding present but now it slipped from the wall, hitting the bulb over the sink, plunging the room into the darkness. The bulb shattered all around and I felt something cold against my cheek as the mirror clattered to the ground. In the gloom, I saw purple petals and chocolate sauce and whipped cream cut through with jagged shards of broken glass. And blood too. There was blood in the cream and a funny taste in my mouth, like cold metal, and wet drops of red were dripping onto the white floorboards.

It took over a year to completely separate from each other, but we are friends now, and neither Dan nor I have looked back.

CHAPTER 7

On Dragon Hill the night is so dark I can barely see the outline of Jimmy beside me. It isn't actually raining but the air is cold and wet, a fine drizzle of mist covering my face. Jimmy stamps, pushing his hands into his coat pockets, stifling a sigh.

'What are we doing here again, Mum?'

I'd woken Jimmy at half past one, a time the house was so quiet, it seemed to be secretly watching me. I'd knelt by my son's bed, shaking his shoulder gently as he shrugged me off, heavy with the deep sleep of a fifteen-year-old.

'Jimmy? Remember our plan?' I'd whispered. 'It's the solstice. We're going onto the hill, remember?'

Rubbing his eyes, he'd unfolded himself from the duvet, pulling on jeans and trainers and following me from the house into the car, headlights illuminating black hedges on empty roads as we drive up to Dragon Hill.

It is midsummer's eve, the shortest night of the year, when the Ridgeway hums with magic. On Salisbury Plain, Stonehenge will have played pilgrimage to thousands of partygoers and druids, chasing the mystical, and the stone circle at Avebury will also be busy. The magic of the Ridgeway and White Horse Hill on this night is more secret. I've been up here a handful of times on 21 June, and rarely seen more than a lone druid on a personal pilgrimage. Now, Jimmy yawns, looking around at the blank darkness I've pulled him from his warm bed to witness.

'It's cold,' he says, following directly behind me as I walk in silence from the car park towards the dark sides of the hill. 'Mum, I'm cold.' He pauses and sighs again. 'Is there any bacon at home?'

'Come on,' I say, putting my arm through his. 'Let's walk faster.'

We walk up the hill in silence until the ramparts of Uffington Castle are rising ahead. In the darkness I can make out another figure, just one, on the far side of the castle.

'Look, Mum, a hippy like you,' whispers Jimmy, sniggering at my shoulder and making me giggle as the figure comes into focus, a drum hooked into the crook of his arm, gently beating out a rhythm that's lost into the night. Without the huge spread of the landscape of the valley to focus on, I feel pulled tight into the hill, as though the presence of the White Horse and all the spirits around it are just beside us. If I was alone, I'd find this spooky, but with Jimmy beside me, his shoulder touching mine as he's getting so tall, I'm not scared. The drummer has made his way to the middle of the castle, and I can see the looming shapes of other figures now too, although the darkness makes it hard to judge quite how close they really are.

I feel tangible impatience from Jimmy as we stop at the highest point above the horse, waiting for the darkness to thin out into dawn and the first light of the new day. Mist drizzles my face and soon my hair feels sodden. There are no stars, no streaky, stunning dawn, just the feeling of a wet green England slowly waking as light unfurls around us.

Amid the fading darkness, very high up in the air, a skylark starts singing. I feel something close to melancholy lurching inside me, and hold my breath. Our presence here together in the dark on the hill seems so fragile. I want to hold the moment in the darkness, before it gets light, with a skylark singing high above my son and me. I never want to lose it. But the darkness cracks and the yellow light of dawn smudges across everything. And now another skylark starts singing, piercing the sky as yet another joins in, like points on a compass drawn in an arc across the emerging horizon. I breathe out. The light thickens. The hill is singing.

*

We have been here before, Jimmy and me, up on the Ridgeway on the shortest night of the year. I remind him of it, half an hour later, as we walk back down the hill through naked new-morning light. I brought him and Dolly camping at Britchcombe Farm above Uffington several times when they were very young. That summer, the summer I was first alone as a single mother with them, was like a gift I unwrapped again and again. I was entirely delighted at the glittering novelty of this new freedom with my children as I walked away from my marriage. Managing the present and contemplating the future was terrifying and wonderful, because all the worry in it was only mine. I no longer had someone else's addiction and the demons that exist in that darkness to fight with. I was twenty-eight, completely responsible for two very small children, but that was a joy and a gift after what I'd been wrestling with for the previous four years.

My stepmother Alexandra gave me the best advice in those early days, when she told me, firmly, that I must make sure I never needed to turn to anyone else for money. 'Do not ask him for anything,' she said simply, leaning up against the sink as we stood in the kitchen in the house in Oxford. She and Rick visited often after my divorce and I depended on the camaraderie of those visits. 'Do not depend on his contribution in any way at all. Know that you and you alone can provide for the children. Find the skills to do that.' A small gold brooch shaped like a stork with ruby eyes glinted on the lapel of her black silk jacket.

Our divorce had been straightforward, since we had no possessions or money to divide, and the children and I continued living in the little house in Oxford where Nell and I had lived as students. Dan and I might have fallen apart, but he saw the children a lot. He'd take them for tea after school, or for long weekends and holidays with his family in Hereford. They'd return with stories of fishing trips and picnics, and I always knew the times they spent with Dan and his family were very precious.

I had been making my living as a freelance journalist for less than four years, and financially I still staggered from one side of the month to another. I wrote in pockets of time I found stuffed down the back of the sofa beside biscuit wrappers left by Jimmy, or hidden under Dolly's nighties that hung along the radiator. I wrote last thing at night, when the children slept, or early in the morning at the kitchen table before they woke up. It was haphazard, piecemeal work, but it meant I could be at home with the children, at least for as long as I could stand the complete insecurity of having no idea where the cash for my next supermarket shop was coming from. That feeling, anyway, was hardly new.

When he was small, Jimmy was a blond streak of mercurial energy that I couldn't contain, darting up the walls and almost literally finding its way up along the curtains. I worried he might be hyperactive. The sofa was his climbing frame and when I emptied his trouser pockets out beside the washing machine they'd release confetti of screwed-up metallic sweet papers. He only liked white food – pasta, bread, milk – and refused to play team sports. I'd thought I had to make him play team sports as it was something boys should do, even though I'd always hated them at school myself. But he hated them just as much as I had, and seemed to know that, without me ever telling him.

Dolly was a different creature, more watchful, who took life at her own pace and seemed to know exactly what she was doing, even when she was very small. She was a tiny, beautiful baby who grew into a little girl who barely spoke or walked until she was two, when she stood up and determinedly told me she wanted to join in. I'd thought that having a daughter would be like seeing a version of myself but Dolly surprised me, because even at three she seemed to have a confidence and self-belief I still can't call my own.

When Jimmy and Dolly were seven and four I took them to see a cartoon called *The Incredibles*, and suddenly Jimmy was on the screen in front of us in the dark: represented in a small blond boy called Dash, who darted around with endless energy and kept his mother running. For a few months after that Jimmy liked being called Dash and my bedroom floor was littered with plastic *Incredibles* toys.

'It's because me and Jimmy and you are actually *The Incredibles*, isn't it, Mum?' Dolly asked me, lying on my bed after I'd finished reading to her, and I nodded. For a while after that we had a black-and-white pony I'd bought from a rescue centre in Gloucestershire. She was called Queenie, which might have suited a glossy bay mare with a plaited mane, but she had a scraggy coat and a hangdog expression. The children wanted to rename her, so the pony Queenie became Dash.

Dash came from Dartmoor and looked like a small rocking horse, with a velvet nose and jigsaw markings. She cost £100, which I didn't really have to spare, but it was an investment worth making since she absolved me from another afternoon in the park. Standing behind a swing or poised at the bottom of a wet slide among empty crisp wrappers gave me the same hopeless feeling of despair that team sports had left me with.

Near our home in Oxford were some allotments, set in a watery meadow covered with dots of Canada geese. Dash's grazing there cost a fiver a week and I didn't bother with a blacksmith so the children rode Dash unshod. She was practically free to keep and while the army of worries still marched on, there was relief in knowing I'd felled some of them by providing the children with a pony, even if we were living in the middle of a city. *Jimmy might be hyperactive*, I told myself, *but at least he can ride. Dolly might not be able to hold a pencil, but she knows how to put a head-collar on*. The red-and-blue plaited velvet browband and hard silver bit on the bridle hanging by the schoolbags in the hall felt familiar too.

In between I was learning how to be a mother as the children grew, smoothing their moods when they flared up, teaching them to read, pushing them on the swings in the rain, slicing crusts off packed-lunch sandwiches, taking them to the meadow near school to cook sausages on a fire and play hide-and-seek until it got dark. They rode Dash bareback to the corner shop for sweets and learned how to do up a bridle.

If this sounds romantic, that is because it was. With Jimmy and Dolly beside me, there was no grind, no true hardship, just a developing love story between us that seemed to get thicker and more luxurious with time. We were a band of three together and nothing could ever break us. I was a single mother, although that's not right since there's nothing 'single' about parenting children on your own. I wasn't a single parent but a triple or quadruple parent since that's what bringing up children alone feels like. I felt as if motherhood had made me into a warrior. Once, another friend split from her husband and I thought she was pathetic when she said she wanted a knight in shining armour to come and rescue her. You cannot wait to be saved. You have to be the knight.

This didn't mean that I didn't cry and I wasn't afraid. Nightmares of Mum still pounced on me at 3 a.m., or crouched on me, breathing into my chest, at dawn. When I allowed my mind to think about what had happened to Mum, or imagine an alternative Friday afternoon, when I might be driving to see her with the children for a weekend with Granny, I still found myself reeling with disbelief and desire. The ongoing horror of Mum's daily life made really letting go of the past almost impossible. Emotional pain became a refuge because it was familiar. Scaring myself into silence by chasing the galloping anxiety that pounded through me, encouraging it to run on unchecked rather than reining it under control, was sometimes addictive.

And hurting myself felt good, shut tight in a box in the darkness, when I wanted to be close to the memory of Mum. What I had with the children was so sweet and soft, but I also needed a space that was separate from them in its darkness, where I could scare myself in order to feel alive. I craved strong emotion and the sensation of fright. Racehorses, with their thunderous gallop pounding over the hills, were what I went back to as a way of feeling that fright. Sex too became a strange sort of punishment. I didn't like it when one of the men I was sleeping with said, 'I want to make love to you.' Then I'd walk away, because what I wanted wasn't loving but a special sort of violence I could hide in, far away from the rest of my life. Sex was a way of becoming an object, rather than a person who feels pain and loss and despair. I wanted no respect from the men I fucked and who fucked me, and I gave them none, either. I felt like my life was in boxes.

Mum was alive but always beyond reach. My longing for her and my desire to return to the space called home that she had created for me was infantalising; it made me feel like a baby, crying unheard by a mother who does not arrive, lying alone in a cot as it reaches for a mobile hanging above its head it can never touch. Sitting beside Mum in her nursing home, and holding her hand as I talked to her about Dolly's second birthday, or Jimmy's first day at school, made me feel violently cut off from the person she had been. Sometimes, friends would ask if there was some part of her that was still familiar, some essential, internal jewel of the mother and woman she had been. Mum's nurses saw it, they said, but I think my siblings and I struggled with it.

'I know you're not supposed to say this, but Charlotte is our favourite,' one of the nurses told me, echoing a sentiment many of them had said across the years, in the different homes she moved to. After the nursing home in Norfolk closed down, we moved her to a home in Oxfordshire. 'She loves a joke and she will often squeeze my hand when I'm making her bed or changing her pad. She's a real sweetheart.' Somehow, in her damaged state, Mum reached out to those angels who looked after her. None of them had ever known the person she had been, but all of them saw something light and loving in her that had been there before.

From us, though, it was often hidden. Sometimes she completely blanked me, like I was invisible, as I sat down beside her. At other times, she'd pull at my shirt like she might rip it, or squeeze my hand so hard it would hurt, but she would never use that same strength to embrace me. She would never kiss me when I lowered my face down to kiss her, and she'd usually push away the cards Jimmy and Dolly had made for her, or the photographs I'd taken to show her, moaning and choking or just staring at me with her half-closed eyes. When friends asked me what she was like, it was hard and always painful to describe the different versions of the person I was meeting every time I walked into her nursing home. Apart from the loving connection she had with the nurses, everything about her had changed, and the thought of Mum making a new life for herself in her much-altered state still makes my heart ache.

Severely brain-damaged patients are sometimes referred to as 'vegetables' but this term absolutely did not apply to Mum. It was often clear she had some memory and strong awareness of what had happened, but since she was unable to communicate at all, even through the most basic sign language, it was impossible to get a real sense of what she was thinking or feeling. I don't know if my mother recognised me as Clover, her youngest daughter, ever again after the day of the accident. I cannot tell whether she really knew who anyone was ever again. I have no idea if she liked me or loved me when she saw me, and it's possible that the reason she looked away so often when she saw one of us was that we all represented too much sadness for her.

It was often easiest just to sit beside her without saying anything. I liked taking the children in when they were babies and then toddlers, as they brought so much pleasure to the other elderly people Mum shared her home with. But usually I left feeling completely devastated and defeated, having failed to connect with Mum, and I truly hated myself for that. But many times I also hated the woman who sat in the nursing home, choking and moaning, tapping her feet as she elaborately slurped a cup of tea, sucking her toothless mouth in a macabre imitation of my mother that she had taken away.

About ten years after the accident, I stopped believing that if I prayed hard enough Mum would get better, and started wanting her to die. Driving to her nursing home made me grip the steering wheel, my breath quickening and heart pounding. I wanted to be a murderer and make her life end. My mind boggled with slow-motion grief when I imagined another five, ten, twenty, thirty, even forty years of sitting beside Mum in a nursing home while living behind the smashed mirror of what had happened. She was only fifty-two when she was lost in the accident and longevity is a family trait. Her aunt, who was still driving her Shetland pony and cart the year of her death, died at one hundred and four, while my grandmother died at ninety-seven. Thinking of Mum sometimes made me clasp my fingers over my eyes like I was watching a horror movie, but when I did look out I saw the decades ahead taking her further and further away into her strange world, while seeping trauma oozed across all our lives, like spilled black ink ruining clean blotting paper.

It often felt like we were all frozen in time at that moment on 25 November 1991 when Mum had fallen off her horse. I saw myself and my sisters and brother pressed up against a thick pane of glass, unable to move but leaning with all our might into it, wanting to get beyond that moment.

I knew it now: death would have been better. Her pain would have been over in an instant, instead of permanently paused, unending, thickening and growing more complex as one year passed on into yet another year.

She didn't look like my mother any more but when I saw her, I felt so sorry for her: a woman in deep pain, terribly damaged, who had no pleasures in life. Her medical notes detailed one physical and emotional catastrophe after another. She couldn't smile or laugh, except in a strange, choking imitation of the sound. The noises she made were like someone who is very distressed and reminded me of the way I felt, the sounds I wanted to make, when I thought of her or spent an afternoon with her. There were calls from her nurses every week with news of a urinary tract infection that was giving her anxiety, insomnia that had meant she'd had a fall in the night, an epileptic fit that had put her in hospital. When her GP called to explain calmly that she'd developed eczema all over her body, bloody and raw where it had become infected due to her incontinence, I put the phone down and screamed into the silence of the room around me.

My God, hasn't she suffered enough?

The past life Mum had made for us was not just gone but smashed into pieces, ripped apart, broken and ruined. Mum's accident didn't happen and end, but went on, unceasing across decades. It crucified my heart.

As much as possible I tried not to show the children the scars inside me, although sometimes the blood welled up and I couldn't hide it. Snatches of a certain song, the words from a childhood book she had read me, even the sudden flash of yellow kingcups in a ditch or a blanket of bluebells in woodland could make me cry. Then Jimmy would hug me, burying his head that always smelt of digestive biscuits into my neck, hugging me closer with his warm, pudgy hands. 'It's OK, Mum, to be sad, because of your mum. It's OK.' He was four years old and he understood it all.

The rest of the time, my life in Oxford with the children was warm and sweet. That first summer together, when it was just us three, I bought a camper van for £1,000 on eBay. It had a tiny Formica-topped kitchen and dark-blue plastic seats that folded out into a lumpy mattress. The steering wheel was big as a cartwheel and it was safer to park on a hill since the starter motor didn't work that well. We drove to Cornwall in the rain, staying with a friend who had rented a pink house on the beach. Dolly was only one and wasn't walking, so I carried her into the surf on my hip as Jimmy ran in and out of the water, his hair plastered to his face, beaming.

The children and I wrote love letters to each other in the sand, ate crab sandwiches and fished for mackerel, which we'd cook on a throwaway barbeque on the beach at dusk. We drove back up the coast through Devon, stopping at campsites and eating fish and chips on beaches. At night we slept cocooned together, my band of three, on the mattress in the back of the van, as Dolly lay in the

crook of my arm and Jimmy asked me a never-ending series of
questions about the world changing around him.

'Why do dogs wear leads?'

'Do you think a flea is bigger than a nit?'

'Why can't you see farts?'

'Do you actually believe, Mum, that every single snowflake is
different? How can anyone test that? And, Mum, when can we get
a pet ghost?'

When I got back to Oxford and the holidays were over, I wrote.
I worked for cheap trade journals and financial websites, baby
magazines and the occasional national weekly. I developed writing
voices I could use for different magazines and realised that by
manipulating that voice, I could be commissioned by the *Financial
News* one week to write a report on Credit Suisse, and the following
week write a saucy piece on how to fake an orgasm for the style
section of a national newspaper. Occasionally, I was asked to write
travel articles, and was almost speechless with disbelief at the extraordinary luxury of being paid to take the children to stay in a log
cabin in Norway, or to sample a new spa in Estonia.

There were other travel commissions that took me away from
the children every four or five months for a week at a time, but
until I met Zour, my desire to step outside my home life was really
nothing more than an occasional holiday masquerading as paid
work.

When Zour came into my life, that changed. He was on a horse
the first time I saw him. Of course he was on a horse! A rippling,
muscular chestnut horse with a flaxen mane, cantering in an endless
circle with a man standing on its back. I stood in the door of the
barn, watching, and for a moment the man glanced sideways, catching
my eye, then he quickly looked back to the horse and the sand
circle it galloped in, its hooves beating the ground hypnotically.

Zour was part of a Cossack troop Nell had brought over from
Russia for her circus that summer. The travelling show she and her
husband Toti had started after the Millennium in the summer Jimmy
was born had grown to a company of thirty or forty performing

artists, musicians and tent boys who travelled in showman's wagons across the south of England every summer.

It isn't surprising to me Nell started a circus, although it's something that astonishes people when they ask me about her: 'She has her very own circus? A real live circus?' She was the child who suggested we dress our cats up in dolls' clothes then push them around in prams. While I was the child playing with a baby at every grown-up lunch party, Nell was the one directing the seven-year-olds to put on a play. When a neighbour asked her to organise their daughter's birthday party, Nell set up a circus party. The galloping danger of horses had been my solace after Mum's accident, but I think Nell found a similar consolation in celebrating the power of horses when they perform in a ring.

I'd always spent a lot of time with Nell at the circus, but that summer of 2005 turned it into a full-time job, running a chaotic backstage café, flipping bacon and making cheese sandwiches and cups of tea for the artists. Jimmy was only four and Dolly wasn't even two, so leaving Oxford was easy. I wrote a weekly newspaper column about life on the road with a travelling circus, and the summer whirled by like a carousel. Zour often invited me into his caravan, making pots of chicken-and-parsley soup or cumin rice called *plov*, laying out plates of sweets for the children and lining up shot glasses of vodka for the many performers who crammed inside. Sometimes I saw him watching me, and late after the opening show he pulled me into his caravan when all the other artists had left, and I spent the rest of the summer there.

Throwing himself off a horse in the ring, dressed in furs and shouting words in Russian at two other Cossacks, was all part of his act, but he also told me about his home in Ossetia, the mountain lands beside Chechnya that are sometimes compared to the Garden of Eden.

'In Ossetia everyone knows about war and everyone prays for peace,' he said, a jagged scar running like a bolt between his eyes. He told me about growing up during the break-up of the Soviet Union and witnessing the fallout of the war in Chechnya. 'Very very criminal time,' he said, pronouncing it 'creeemeeeenaaaal' so that it sounded like an expensive face cream. We spoke English so broken that sometimes I wondered if we were talking about the same thing. Having trained as an athlete when he was younger, circus had been Zour's passport out of criminal life. 'I go to circus or Interpol,' he explained, cheerfully.

I didn't stand a chance. It was impossible not to fall in love with him, even though we spoke a different language, even though he had a wife in Ossetia, even though he consumed vodka faster than even Dan had done. That summer none of this mattered because I was living time out of mind and the only world that existed was inside the ring of circus wagons.

'Time pass very quickly. When I leave, you come to me,' he said to me one night as we lay in the slice of bed in his caravan. 'Come to my country. Promise. You come to the mountains. We will take horses and ride in mountains. Promise me when I am gone from England, Clover, you come to me.' It was honey and syrup dripping from the inside of an orchid. Of course I would follow him.

Vladikavkaz, the capital of Ossetia, means 'ruler of the Caucasus', but after the mountains themselves, Zour was obsessed by Ossetian traditions. He showed me photographs of the city, studded with the golden onion domes of the Russian Orthodox Church, but the rituals he described around his life spoke of a pagan tradition reminding me of the standing stones of the Ridgeway. Bare-chested at the stove in his caravan in England, slicing herbs for chicken soup, he told me legends about the Nart saga heroes and Uastyrdzhi, the Indo-Iranian warrior god Ossetians revere as St George. He described a life where feasting and food were the lynchpin of a culture revolving around the thick blood ties that bind family to family, friend to friend, brother to brother. When he asked me about English customs, I could only think of fish and chips or Morris dancers, but was silenced when he showed me videos of Ossetian national dancing, where men wore the belted black robes of warriors, twirling around with pointed knives, strange, violent and beautiful.

Casting around for anything of Old England to show him, I took him to White Horse Hill. It was late August, so hot and still that dandelion fluff hung motionless in the evening light and the sound of the church bells in the valley below floated up the hill. Zour wanted me to tell him everything I knew about King Arthur, who he saw as England's greatest king.

'There's a legend saying Arthur isn't dead, just sleeping,' I said as we walked up the hill, the landscape yellow and exhausted in the flat heat of August. 'When England really needs him, he'll rise up to fight again for us. And when that happens, the legend says the White Horse will rise out of the grass and stand on Dragon Hill.'

Zour stopped just above the horse. 'Arthur,' he murmured, pronouncing it 'Ar-tour'. In the gathering dusk he told me about the Alani, the nomadic horseback warriors who raided the steppes to the east of the Black Sea. They were ferocious and unbeatable – until they met the Romans in AD 175, who, recognising their unparalleled skills as warriors on horseback, sent an Alani cavalry unit to Britain. In Northumberland their leader, Artoris, became a local legend and Zour believed Artoris was actually King Arthur.

'King Arthur was our brother and he was your king. Arthur was Ossetian, Clover. He was Artoris, from Alania,' he said, suddenly grabbing my wrist and pulling my sleeve back, turning his own wrist over so our arms revealed their tracks of veins. 'You don't know? You and me, we share the same history. We share the same blood.'

He dropped my wrist, reaching for his pocket and flicking open a pocket knife, slicing a thin slash across his thumb so that crimson blood jumped out, then he took my hand and before I could protest quickly sliced into my thumb too, squashing our skin together so that our blood mixed. 'You see? We are very bad. You and me, we are very the same.'

Zour's declarations excited me, of course they did, but following him to Ossetia as I had promised wouldn't be easy. The war with Chechnya may have been over, but kidnappings and random bomb-ings throughout the Caucasus were common. The summer before I met Zour, Beslan, a suburb of Vladikavkaz, was struck by a horrific Chechen separatist terrorist attack on a primary school, in which 1,100 teachers and children were taken hostage, leaving 385 of them dead. The Foreign Office recommended 'only the most essential travel' to North Ossetia, and it was clear that the 'turbulent north Caucasus' – as I increasingly heard it referred to on the news – wasn't a tourist destination.

I ignored this advice and anyone who told me not to go, since as I saw this, my pounding desire to go there really was 'the most essential travel'. I knew there was risk involved, but that only made me more determined. Zour was offering me large-scale adventure, and nothing was going to stop me. I packed frothy underwear and some tight, new mini-skirts and high-heeled leather boots. Jimmy and Dolly shared my excitement, though theirs was at the prospect of a holiday with Dan and his family.

I felt no compunction at putting myself in potential danger. I saw myself as indestructible, and believed nothing as bad as what had happened to my mother would be revisited on my children.

Lightning, I told myself, doesn't strike twice in the same place.

Zour met me in Moscow, embracing me elaborately at Domodedovo airport as if it was me, not him, who was returning from a near warzone. We stayed up all night in a hotel room, laughing at everything the other said, hungry, relishing each stolen second we had together. I'd paid for the trip by selling a travel article to a newspaper, but after hours of being a tourist at the Kremlin and Red Square, I wanted to see a different side of the city, where people lived normal lives. Zour shrugged, kissing me hard.

'All you want, I bring you.'

We caught the metro to the furthest station north where we waited in the snow, smoking, until a blacked-out car arrived and Zour bundled me inside. There was a Kalashnikov on the floor and four men in black coats, who greeted Zour like their brother. The eldest, Aslan, in his fifties, pulled Zour into the passenger seat as I squashed into the back between two men, the only heat in the car coming from the end of their cigarettes; my toes in high-heeled leather boots became like blocks of ice. Russian voices jabbered away beside me, an intense male energy filling every inch of the car, until Zour caught my eye in the rear-view mirror.

'Am I being kidnapped, Zour? So soon?' I said, and he laughed, translating, so they all laughed. They looked like one another, with cropped dark hair and weathered skin pulled tight over Slavic cheekbones. Suddenly, the man beside me opened his gloved hand. He was holding a small silver disk, stamped with a familiar horseman and a dragon.

'Take it, Clover,' Zour said, watching me in the mirror. '*Sainta Georgia*. For safe travel. Take it. Tomorrow we take train to Ossetia, but now we stay beside Moscow.'

We drove for another hour, grey tower blocks covered in snow giving way to an emptier landscape until village houses dotted the streets. At some point the men lit a joint, filling the car with a soporific smell of herbs so that I leant against the shoulder of the man who had given me the silver charm, and slept.

When I woke we were parked beside a kiosk with a metal grille where Zour bought cigarettes and a bottle of Coke. The previous week, there had been a fight outside the shop and a man had had his hand chopped off with the end of a shovel, Zour told me, brightly, as finally the car pulled up outside a small house. A woman with long red hair opened the door, the warmth from her kitchen melting the snow on her doorstep.

'Wife, Zina,' explained Aslan as the woman embraced me, her mother standing behind her, rocking a tiny baby no more than a month old. Zour explained they were Chechen and had left Grozny during the war. A television blared out news I couldn't understand as Zour and Aslan said elaborate toasts for his arrival at a table spread with bowls of grated carrot, sliced sausage, pickled cucumbers and squares of honey cake.

For what felt like hours, we sat at the table, eating plates of food, drinking and toasting until I felt flushed and exhausted. Then Zour took me outside and we walked through a pine wood near the house. Snow crunched underfoot but the air smelt green and sharp. In a clearing we stopped beside a tree with yellow apples the size of small plums. They tasted cold and clean after the heat of Zina's kitchen. Zour stood very still beside me, snow catching in his black hair as the crystals fell silently around us. Through the twilight, a child suddenly appeared from nowhere, then stood quite still, watching us.

'Everything in Russia, it is strange and hard,' said Zour, his fingers holding my chin as he turned my face up to his, but he didn't kiss me. I turned, walking into the clearing and away from the intensity of Zour, because the snow felt constant and reassuring. When I turned back, the child had vanished. Everything about that moment was intoxication and I remember it like a white dream.

Back at the house the men sat hunched in one corner, their voices filling the space in the room as Zina and I stumbled through a conversation in sign language. From the men there were a handful of words I understood, like *Perestroika*, Gorbachev, Moscow, but mostly those voices were just the low, throbbing hum that I could still hear as I slept in an upstairs room, on a mattress on the floor beside Zina, her mother and the baby. Downstairs, the voices didn't seem to quieten and the television stayed on all night. Night and day melted into one another so that I was dizzy, drugged with sleep and the heat of the house.

Sometime later, when the light arrived, Zina made more food, covering the table again with fried rice with dates, clear soup bobbing with dumplings, and pork patties. The women didn't leave the house, uncomplaining as Aslan and Zour suddenly vanished in a flurry in the car, as if something urgent had happened, returning two hours later, when Zour told me to pack very quickly. 'We leave now for the train for Caucasus. But first I will show you horses.'

Zour took me to meet the Cossack troupe at the Moscow State Circus, where he'd worked almost two decades before, in his twenties. He led me by the hand through a warren of corridors lined with dressing rooms, squashing past girls in fishnets who eyed me glassily, their lips greased with crimson lipstick. Zour knew most of them, shouting greetings into dressing rooms where lithe figures pulled on sequinned pants, shrieking greetings in return when they saw him, blowing kisses, squeezing his outstretched hand.

The last room off the corridor was the Cossacks' changing room. Here there were no lipsticks or sequins, but a whole wall covered with icons of St George, in front of which a dozen men were pulling on fur gilets and leather boots, just like they were going to war. As in Zina's kitchen, a makeshift table in one corner was covered with plates of sliced meat, pickles and piles of herbs, and upon seeing Zour the men pulled up stools and crates at the table.

'Little party,' explained Zour, passing me a glass of vodka. The men sat draped around one another and when Zour saw me looking surprised, he explained.

'We call each other brothers,' he said, 'because we share the same life, the same dreams.'

Afterwards, Zour took me downstairs to a backstage rehearsal ring, where a man was standing bang in the middle of it, surrounded by six muscular bay horses who were cantering around the ring.

'Beautiful horses, no?' said Zour, motioning to the animals. I nodded, resisting the urge to lean into the ring and touch one of the glossy animals as they cantered on. 'This circus was second home. I perform here, doing repetition again and again in Cossack troupe.'

I wanted to stay and see the show starting in an hour, but there was no time for that. There was a train to catch.

The quickest way to get from Moscow to Vladikavkaz is to fly, but Zour had told me about the train that snaked down the western edge of Russia beside Ukraine, stopping at Rostov-on-Don and rattling across the steppe for two nights and three days, travelling 3,000 kilometres south into the mountains. We left the train only briefly in those days but lived inside the cabin, stretched out on the red velvet seats of the bunks playing cards, a blue glass vase with a fake rose between us. It was hypnotic, the movement of the train and the heat of the cabin and the certainty of Zour close to only me. He left the train reluctantly, jumping down at tiny stations to exchange handfuls of roubles for beetroot salad and bottled tomatoes, hot cherry pastries and plastic cups of soured yogurt. We bought glasses of steaming coffee from the *provodnitsa,* the middle-aged lady in a pale-blue-and-gold uniform who rattled her keys up and down each carriage, and who was not to be crossed. Zour charmed her, of course, persuading her to ignore the vodka bottles he brought in and that, of course, we must be allowed to smoke in our cabin.

Sometimes the platforms were empty; at other stations, men walked through thick snow carrying sticks strung with smoked fish, shouting, '*Ryba, ryba, ryba!*' Between most stations traders boarded, selling local honey, finely woven goat-hair shawls, gold bracelets, cashmere or bags of coloured soft toys, which Zour bought by the armful for my children.

The train snaked along the edge of the River Don, down to Rostov, and Zour explained that if Kiev was the mother of the mafia, then Rostov was the father. At Rostov station, a regiment of Russian soldiers in camouflage, en route for Grozny, were boarding the train. On the far side of the platform, I watched a girl in a tight leopardskin coat leaning in to a man in a blue uniform, whispering into his ear.

'Very criminal area we in now,' said Zour, watching me. I told him I wasn't afraid, and that the closer we got to his home, the safer I felt. He smiled. 'You want me to show you real life of the Kavkaz? The real people? Sometimes they criminal, very, very criminal, but I show you all.'

I shivered, clenching and unclenching the tension in my wrist.

Before we arrived in Vladikavkaz, Zour put his hands flat on the table because he had to tell me something.

'Two times, I lie, Clover,' he said, his smile smudged from his face.

One night at the circus in England, a tall, angular girl in tight black trousers and red lace had arrived to see Zour. He'd said she was his cousin, but now he told me she was a girlfriend. Also, he had slept with his wife before he came to meet me. He told me these facts solemnly, as if they might come as a shock to me.

I looked away to the steppe, which flashed past, seemingly unending. I had my eyes wide open. We only had these moments together and I couldn't be hurt by him. If I was to be hurt, it was a pain I craved. As the train slowed at a deserted station, I watched a man working his way along the platform, sweeping snow into bigger and bigger piles.

'Zour, these things, they don't hurt me. I'm not your wife and I'm not yours. I'm here just for now. Just for today. You know that?'

He narrowed his eyes, nodding at me, but I knew the spaces between us were too great for either of us to really understand.

Zour didn't live with his wife – she had a home with their two-year-old twins outside Vladikavkaz – but she needed an explanation, so he told her I was a journalist who required local protection, which wasn't a lie. At that time, I was good at breaking my life into pieces. I knew how to look closely at things I wanted to see, and push other things out of focus. In Russia, for a man to be sleeping with a woman who isn't his wife is normal, so I ignored the fact he was married with children as young as my own. I was no threat to her, nor she to me.

Instead of seeing his wife, Zour took me straight to the flat where he'd grown up and lived all his adult life. Balancing an orange-and-white enamel kettle on a Communist-era cooker, he started preparing food as soon as we arrived, stripping out of the black jacket he'd worn for travelling into the blue sports trousers I'd known him in all summer. He told me again about the mountains we'd visit, the horses we'd ride, the high times we'd have together, and then he poured two glasses of vodka, making me drink to safe arrival, before he pulled me towards him, pressing me against the table so that I was lost because he was all around me and inside me too.

When I think back, what I remember is that there were always horses around us in Ossetia. We drove three hours from the city into the mountains, the car filled with cigarette smoke and folk-tronica music as we flashed through villages, dogs barking and the streets dotted with elderly ladies dressed in black. The landscape was bright emerald green until we reached the higher levels of the mountains, where the air was cold like iron and snow flurried across the road. When the tarmac ran out we followed a stony track patched with snow to a wooden house painted with a black-and-red geometric pattern. Zour pulled up, leaving the doors flung open, music and engine blaring, shouting until a man with cropped grey hair and crooked eyes emerged, raising his arm in greeting.

Hasan kept a herd of horses in some paddocks running up the mountain's edge behind his house. He and Zour talked without stopping, ignoring me, as they threw heavy saddles onto two ponies. Then Zour legged me up and vaulted neatly onto the back of Hasan's horse, sitting beside the saddle. They continued talking as we rode into the snow, passing two children in felt hats dragging a donkey on a string rope, who didn't look up or seem to see us at all.

'I take you to sacred place, for *Sainta Georgia*,' Zour explained, twisting around behind the saddle to me and grinning. 'Because you are forever, Clover. Forever.'

The track ran to a clearing where the slopes flattened out, revealing a stone hut surrounded by clumps of trees. Leaning down, Zour caught my horse's bridle, instructing me to jump down, tying both horses to a nearby fence. Inside the hut was a long table running down the middle of the room; three walls were covered with faded paintings of Saint George. A central wooden pillar was tied with frayed, old ribbons, but the hut felt alive, as if we'd just disturbed a party there. Hunks of Ossetian bread were strewn across the table and grains of salt spilled across the wood, with half-empty vodka bottles and a handful of shot glasses scattered across the table too.

Zour poured three glasses, handing them to Hasan and me as he said a toast to Saint George. The vodka was clear and pure, sending a jolt of adrenalin into my bloodstream. Zour had a small bag slung across his chest and now pulled a pointed silver knife, some cooked steaks and a new bottle of vodka from it. He sliced the meat, handing Hasan and me hunks to dip in the salt. The bottle of vodka would be left on the table, as an offering for Saint George, and for the next visitors.

Beyond the hut was a waterfall with thundering white water pounding the black stones below. The men shouted to one another to be heard as Hasan pulled a pistol from his belt, taking aim, casually, into the rocks behind the waterfall. The shot cracked through the valley, echoing onwards as Hasan handed me the pistol, motioning me to fire too. It felt heavy in my hand, and as cold as the water blown off the waterfall. When I fired, the same crack bounced between the peaks around us as the pistol kicked backwards in my hand. It felt too hard, like the coldest destruction I could imagine, and I handed the pistol back to Hasan, shaking my head when he motioned to me to fire again.

It was dark by the time we rode back down the mountain to Hasan's house. We stayed that night in a wooden hut, the rooms empty apart from a bed in one corner. Zour lit a fire in the stove, and when it was hot he unzipped his top, pulling at my body so hard he hurt me as he turned me over.

That night I dreamt separately of my mother and then the children, hearing Jimmy's voice saying to me, 'What are you doing there, Mum?' and woke heavy with a guilt I wanted to forget.

If I didn't think too much about my life in England, the days I spent with Zour felt like an intoxicating party. When we walked into a restaurant the music would be turned up and tables pushed back. Everywhere we went, tables were laid up with plates of food, bottles of vodka were pulled out and impromptu feasting would begin. He carried with him a special sort of excitement so that even bumping into a friend in the street was a reason to celebrate. Quiet days didn't exist and I began to understand the Ossetian mountain spirit that reveres hospitality above almost everything else. Even stopping at a garage to change a blown tyre turned into a party, where a woman with short brown hair called Malika fried spicy sausages and sliced onions on a single gas ring at the back of the mechanics shop, and Zour toasted our good fortune with shots of spirit.

Many of Zour's friends were very poor, struggling to find work, and sometimes a whole family was living in two or three small rooms, but they were brave and never self-pitying. The patterns of their lives were often broken and usually fractured by trauma but they had an energy for being alive and a quiet dignity in the face of tragedy I found compelling. Irina lived with her two teenage sons and worked in a local beauty salon. She'd loved her job but painting nails paid her twice her teaching salary. She was bringing up her sons alone, since her husband was in prison for murder. Once in a restaurant we met a man who wore a black suit and cream wool tank top. He'd served fifteen years in Chechnya, he said, as Zour translated, telling me that was like thirty years anywhere else. He smiled as we played cards, utterly charming, until he tried to show me an execution video on his phone.

'Zour's god is horses, you know this?' he said later, looking sideways at me as he shuffled the cards. 'My god is guns.'

One night Zour took me to a tower block, mounting the steps three at a time until he hammered on a plain wooden door and a man with eyes like black pools opened up. The flat was very sparse, with no carpet and bare light bulbs glaring from the ceilings, curtain-less windows high up on the wall so no natural light came in. Yet from inside came the sound of feasting and celebrations, chairs pushed back from the long table as Zour appeared. Twenty or thirty men sat around the table, which as usual was covered with plates of food and bottles of vodka. The men hugged Zour, stepping back to shake my hand as he pulled me to the top of the table. Sharp knives like daggers or large penknives covered any spare space, and in one corner of the room a collection of rifles and a Kalashnikov were propped beneath a shelf lined with pistols.

Zour translated their questions, as they wanted to know why I had come to Vladikavkaz, when I was coming back and who my gods were. They talked about King Arthur and the Alani as if they were still part of that warrior breed, and always the conversation returned to ethnicity. Over a long evening, Zour explained the men had just come back from making a sacrifice to Saint George at a chapel in the mountains. I smoked as he talked, glancing at the pools of water on the concrete floor where the snow from their boots had melted, and noticed it was marbled in places with blots of blood that streaked their dirty green camouflage trousers. I ground my cigarette into an ashtray, suddenly uncertain, until Zour laughed loudly, slapping his thigh as he handed me another lit cigarette.

'Sacrifice of sheep, Clover, not man. They cut the throat of sheep to make sacrifice for Saint George.' He laughed again, reaching for another bottle. 'Watch, Clover. Watch what I show you next.'

I never knew, from one moment to another, what he would show me next. I don't speak Russian, and even if I had done, Zour could have slipped into Ossetian to confuse me. I could recite whole toasts to homecoming, Saint George and the warrior life off by heart by the end of my trip, but had no idea how to ask where the station was or order a meal. Most of the time, though, Russian wasn't a language but the background hum and music to everything we were doing.

Zour was mercurial and I never really knew where we were going or what was about to happen next. I would spend hours with dark-eyed men, standing around in the snow as plans were made, discussed, changed and changed again. I was familiar with the feeling of being disorientated, moving suddenly from a hot kitchen to a cold car to be driven to a car park where Zour would stand in the snow, smoking, with men in black coats, always looking sideways. They'd talk urgently on their mobiles and when credit ran out would all swap SIM cards. Their language sounded intense and urgent, sometimes angry but never frivolous. There was so much urgency, and yet for so much of the time, nothing happened.

If I had not been so fascinated by the people and their lives, my lack of autonomy might have been frustrating. Over the course of two years I visited several times. I knew the journey but was never bored, although Zour often made me angry so that I'd shout at him, protesting that surely we didn't need to leave the house so suddenly, at 3 a.m., for another mystery assignation. But, more than anything, he made the time we spent together seem like a shimmering adventure. He made my heart pound, and even when we'd been up all night, drinking and talking until dawn, I'd often find myself unable to sleep, lying beside his naked body as adrenalin and a terrified, delighted sleeplessness coursed through me.

I was fascinated by the intensity with which he and his friends communicated, and now I wish I had known what they were talking about. At the time, it was part of the game. Knowing nothing and being powerless was part of the reason I wanted to be there and why I kept putting myself through the inconvenience of going back to Ossetia, back to Zour. I craved the weeks when I could leave the control of my own life behind. In England, I was always the driver and I was always the one on the end of a mobile phone, fixing plans, making life happen. Dan saw the children after school once a week, but every decision was down to me. It was up to me to make the money for every school lunch or karate lesson, and it was up to me to be there at every sharing assembly and parents evening.

In Russia, it was completely different. I'd hand Zour my passport and become a passenger in his life. Giving up control was part of the elaborate fantasy I was taking part in, since I was Zour's fantasy just as much as he was mine. I allowed him, wanted him, to control me. Without saying anything, I played the role of his moll.

I went back out to Ossetia the following spring after selling an article about the food of the Caucasus mountains to cover a story on sacrificial animal slaughter, which plays a key role in Ossetian feasting. We drove into the mountains in a convoy with Zour's friends, stopping high on the horizon where the air got cold to meet a family who lived in a one-room house built into the rock face. An embroidery of a mountain scene covering one wall and beds and tables constructed from planks and plastic crates were pushed into one corner. The rock face above their house was mottled with bullet holes. They were very old, Zour told us, sniper bullets Ghengis Khan met from the Alanni defending this very spot. One of Zour's friends bought a sheep from the family, thrusting it by its horns into the back of his truck as we crested a hill and the ground evened out to reveal a clearing and a stone building which I recognised as another chapel to Saint George. The sacrifice was fast, toasts and rituals repeated for Saint George as the sheep's neck was quickly sliced open, crimson suddenly seeping into the ground around it as a distant look flooded across its face and it collapsed. Afterwards, the men butchered the carcass, moving swiftly over the meat, their knives flashing in the evening light.

'Ossetian men very good with knives,' Zour said, watching his friends butchering the carcass, the blades of their knives zig-zagging across the dead sheep. They roasted the sheep on a fire, and there was a feast later with a platter of grilled mutton, bowls of grapes, sliced tomatoes, pickled garlic and grated carrots that we ate in the chapel. It was utterly foreign and strange and it delighted and horrified me at the same time, because it was the strong motion I was craving, allowing me to step far out of myself and beyond my own life.

I returned from each trip to Ossetia with my suitcase heavy with knives. Zour's friend had a habit of swapping possessions like knives or neckchains and even their clothes as a tangible sign of their shared bonds. Once I was given a watch by a man with grey eyes like flint who we picked up on a high road in the mountains. He told Zour he'd been in the Beslan siege, and he didn't blink as he recounted pulling children from the flames, looking away. He insisted we visit the school together.

It still stands as it was left after the attack. Burned-out rafters held up a skeleton of the building, walls were covered with bullet holes, and blood smeared across the wall in the science lab where, the man told us, a female suicide bomber blew herself up. Photographs of the hundreds of victims lined the walls of the gym, and bottles of water had been placed below them as offerings, signifying the water that the terrorists denied their victims for the three days they held them before they blew up the school.

Afterwards we walked to the graveyard created for the victims. Marble headstones sat in lines across the windswept plot, and elderly women, openly weeping, tended the graves. Colourful toys or dolls with glassy eyes and bright yellow toy trucks had been left as offerings to the dead children, and a huge statue of three mothers holding up twelve angels towered above the graveyard. Doves were released when the statue was first unveiled, Zour told me.

'They would not leave the graves,' he said, turning away from the statue, stuffing his hands into his pockets, because it was suddenly cold. 'The birds were like the children, staying close to their mothers, their homes.'

Over the course of my second year of trips to Ossetia, however, the lightness and celebratory spirit with which they had always been imbued before subtly changed. And then, in 2007, came a trip that I paid for by writing a piece about Sochi, the Black Sea resort which had been Stalin's playground, but which was now a building site, gearing up for the 2014 Winter Olympics.

It was steaming hot so that my hair frizzed, and mosquitos scarred my legs in the near-tropical climate. We had been due to meet at the airport, but Zour was late, arriving five hours after the scheduled time, when I'd already left for the hotel. He wore dark glasses clamped to his head, vodka seeping from his skin, a purple black eye bulging from behind his shades after a fight on the train.

I was writing about a glossy new hotel being built for the Olympics, staying in a room with a revolving glass wall and a massive, padded, black-leather bedhead behind acres of Egyptian cotton. I was struggling for money at home, and Zour had nothing, having spent everything he'd brought with him on a crate of vodka for the train from Vladikavkaz.

'Not a single rouble and not one kopeck,' he said, laughing as he turned out his pockets, and a bead of sweat ran down my back. For the first time, I was bored with Zour, and angry too, penned in by the revolting luxury of the hotel and the heat and humidity. We fought for three days in Sochi, then boarded a train for two days, travelling into Ossetia. I was restless and the train seemed uncomfortable, Zour's hand on me suddenly too insistent and strong.

Standing between compartments, smoking, I shouted to him over the roar of the train, telling him something I never thought I'd say, that this might be my last trip to Vladikavkaz. I could smell coal smoke in the air as Zour looked quickly towards me, his chin tipped downwards.

'Never say that, Clover. Never say this end,' he mumbled, turning away as he lifted his fist and smashed it through the thick glass window separating the carriages. I lurched, glass crunching beneath my shoes, but he had turned on his heel, walking quickly down the carriage as crimson tears of blood spilled from his knuckles.

As he passed them, half a dozen women in another carriage reached into their bags and pockets, passing bottles of yellow iodine and packets of bandages towards him. When the train stopped at the next station, he was ushered to a medical room, where a nurse in a pale-blue uniform quickly stitched his skin together, her long brown ponytail bouncing as she giggled at Zour's jokes.

It wasn't until afterwards, when we were in Vladikavkaz and the heat and fights of Sochi were behind us, that I registered how strange it was that there had been a medical room at the station, and that so many women had been carrying first-aid kits, ready to doctor their wounded men.

In Ossetia I was always surrounded by men, in thrall to their lives of rich adventure, chasing romance and warrior memories in the high Caucasus. Their women, though, lived trapped indoors. All of the wives of Zour's friends existed behind glass, looking out from tower blocks or mountain shacks, rocking children on their shoulders as they waited for the men to come back, never quite sure of how they would return, penned in by the effects of machismo and alcohol.

Over the two years I spent there, I started to see Ossetia as a place obsessed by death and tragedy, which the men drank like strong alcohol. The men toasted peace as if breaking their hearts for it, while talking, unendingly, about the beauty of fighting. They were obsessed by blood. In Ossetia, tragedy was part of the everyday dialogue and currency of life, for the men who lived by it and the women who felt the effects of it.

As a result, the wounds I could feel inside me hurt less when I was there. Among Zour's people, I was no longer a stranger, since they all knew what trauma felt like, and sometimes when I was there I became accustomed to the idea that blood feuds might be a normal part of life.

Another day, to answer my endless questions about how his society really worked, Zour drove me towards the border with Ingushetia, the republic bordering Ossetia that had witnessed generations of bloody overspill from Chechnya.

The houses thinned out along the gravel track as Zour drove with his arm over the window, chain-smoking as he explained that this had been an area of vibrant villages until the war in the early nineties. An hour beyond the last village, he pulled over in the twisted remains of building plots, and we walked across the broken ground as Zour pointed out the lost foundations of a whole village.

From a distant mountain peak came the echoing rattle of a gun. A shrieking memory of pain hung around this village that was no longer there. Burned-out cans littered the ground and strands of barbed wire wrapped around a broken buggy. Rubbish, charred black, shifted gently in the afternoon wind. Imagining the lives that this space had held, and the death that had seeped in here, I felt completely disgusted by myself, tourist to tragedy, and for the first time suddenly afraid of where Zour would take me next.

'You want me to show you real life here. This is very criminal area, very dangerous area,' Zour said, his back towards me. 'Terrorists here too, snipers and so on, you see, Clover. Even though the police poisoned the water, there are terrorists living in these forests. This is what you want me to show you, and I show you.'

His voice echoed around the dirty earth, vanishing into the forest in the distance, where I imagined eyes looking out, tracking us. The hard, metallic music of Deep Purple blared from the car stereo, and at that moment I could not trust him. I knew I'd taken myself to a place that was too dark. I turned away from Zour, craving the light.

On the last night we spent together we rode into the mountains. It was warm, heat gathering between the pine trees as our two horses picked their way across the stony track. Midges danced in the dusk and the mountains felt unending. We rode for two hours, daisies touching the horses' bellies as we cantered through valleys, before the slopes rose ahead and we slowed to a walk, the only sound our own voices, muffled in the bowl of the mountains. We stopped in a clearing between the trees, tying the horses to a pine tree as we walked the last 100 yards to a riverbank, where Zour pulled off his T-shirt and scooped handfuls of crystal water over his head, laughing about how hot and still and perfect the evening was.

I stood apart from him, pulling my hair back from my face as I turned around, the mountains spinning above me. Zour walked towards me from the bank, making the motion of snapping an imaginary camera, taking a photograph, his black hair spiky with river water.

'I keep this for me, this image I take of you, when you not here,' he said, running his thumb down my cheekbone, then down my neck, then reaching into my shirt and pushing me hard down into the grass.

It rained, later, drenching my hair and disguising the tears that were suddenly there on my cheeks. I was grateful for it, not wanting him to know I was crying. We galloped the horses back across the last field as, breathless, Zour twisted around in the saddle, leaning across to me, grabbing my hand.

'For your coming back, Clover. Promise me, promise me. You come back to me.'

I nodded, biting my lip so hard I felt a dot of blood in my mouth. I knew, at that moment, that it was the last day we would spend together.

Back in England, I thought of Zour, and my strange longing for the hardship of his life, and felt the weight of my guilt and confusion heavy on me. For the first time in ages, a pain I was carrying seemed unmanageable. I started seeing a Jungian therapist who was finishing her training, so she charged only £10 a session. I visited her weekly at her tall, redbrick house in north Oxford, where children's coats hung in the hall and schoolbags were splayed on the sitting-room table.

'I don't understand what makes me want to go back to Ossetia,' I told her. 'It's dangerous and frightening, but when I'm there I feel alive. I want to be with my children but I don't understand this darkness I find in Ossetia that makes me feel complete.'

I told her about the guns and knives in Ossetia, and how the sense of casual violence seemed comforting compared to the suffocation and dread I felt at the school gate in Oxford. I confessed to her that I was hardly seeing Mum, but at night dreamed about being hunted or locked in cupboards, hiding to escape an unending mortal danger. I sat in her sitting room and cried, observing, despite my tears, the contents of her shelves, which were filled with musical instruments and schoolbooks: the props of her happy, functional family life. It was like a foreign land.

'How do I get this darkness out of myself? I feel like I need to cut it out of me,' I told her. 'I need to get rid of it.'

She paused, and then looked straight at me. 'You're the sort of person who needs some kind of darkness. There is nothing wrong with that. It's not a sign of anything bad, it is just a part of your psyche,' she explained, her voice calm and even. 'You cannot cut it out of you. It will always be there and if you try to get rid of it, it will find itself another place in you.'

'Can't I get rid of it? Get better from it?' I implored, but she shook her head.

'It's part of you. It will always be there, but you can learn how to make that darkness yours.'

CHAPTER 8

There are only stones and trees and emptiness around us. It's so high up here on the hill that I feel my head and my heart expanding, as if they are being opened up to something completely new. It's not as if the Ridgeway ever goes away, but it's taken so much to get up here, just us two alone.

The Ridgeway is always there on the horizon above the house. I glimpse it, first thing, from my bedroom window, rubbing sleep from my eyes as I pull on black jeans and a T-shirt as soon as I get up, and I watch it, half an hour later, as Dash and Evangeline pull at my jeans while I stand in the kitchen, making tuna sandwiches for Dolly and Jimmy's packed lunches. I track it as I drive to Faringdon, and it seems to watch me, later in the afternoon, as I walk down the green with Dolly and Evangeline after school to check on the ponies in their field. Its presence is reassuring, but tantalising too. I crave it, and sometimes weeks pass before I get up there.

Now we are here, alone, and we leave the high curve of the hill and walk west along the strip of Ridgeway that cuts across the wheat field to Wayland's Smithy. I take his hand but we don't talk until we're far from the road, walking through the afternoon together because that's the only place we want to be. I can hear his breathing beside me, the soft fall of his trainers on the ground as he squeezes my hand. Something makes us both stop and turn to face each other.

'Do you want to? Here? Right now?' One of us says it.

'Against this stone? Because that will be there for ever and we're only here now.'

His neck smells of man and sweat and the skin I want all round me. A wood pigeon coos in the tree above us, then rises from the branches and is gone. I want to feel urgency and that complete loss of myself. I am impatient and hungry, pulling him closer to me and needing every part of him. Bramble thorns scratch my leg and I slap a mosquito on the back of my thigh. I'm distracted by every snap of twig around us and only just get there.

'Come on. Someone's going to see us,' I giggle, kneeling as I buckle my jeans back up again.

'But there's no one here,' he says. 'Only you and me.'

The ancient earth is jagged against my back and I feel wetness against my shirt when I press my hand to the small of my back. There's a spot of blood. I lie back, green beech branches spreading and spinning above as I press into a bed of damp leaves. The earth is warmer and softer than the rock, and when I lie back the sky pixelates into millions of giddy pieces of atom and light above me. When I put my ear to the earth, I can hear the gallop of a thousand hooves. It's blood, rushing in my head, but it sounds prehistoric, like the earth and I are breathing in time.

*

I am dazzled by sunlight all that first summer in Baulking. The children run straight from the kitchen out onto the tufted lawn in front of the house, the door always open. Light and space surrounds us.

Dolly and Evangeline spend much of the summer playing with the Shetland Holly. My cousin Chloe lends me a basket saddle that fits Trigger. I sense forgotten memories of riding with Candida when I was very young, perhaps before I could even talk. Just one, Dash doesn't have the balance to sit on a pony, but in the basket saddle he rocks around on top of Trigger, looking delighted by himself, like a fat emperor being carried on his litter. I buy a packet of brightly coloured rosettes on the internet to play gymkhanas and Dolly sets up trotting poles from old logs in the paddock and a line of flags to weave the ponies through. Almost every day, she and I lead Holly and Trigger with Dash and Evangeline up and down the long village green in Baulking. There's no shop, school or pub here, and the unmarked, potholed road running down the edge of the green goes nowhere except to the farm at the end, so the few cars that pass are all local people who live in some of the dozen houses around the western edge of the green, and who all raise a hand of greeting to us.

I buy a painted wagon to use as an office. It's emerald green with ornate paintings of lakeside scenes all over it and roses painted across the chassis. Inside, it's big enough for my desk and a double bed, so it becomes a spare room when friends stay. I work there every morning while Dash and Evangeline play in the garden with their au pair David, who has dark eyes and a languorous expression. I can hear them from the wagon, where I light the stove in the corner to work at my desk until four every afternoon, when Jimmy and Dolly peel off the school bus that stops outside our house, signalling to me that it's time to leave the wagon.

Dash starts walking, and Evangeline runs ahead of him. I breathe out. It's the first time in over two decades the cracked pieces join up and I feel them make a new whole.

My craving for strong motion, that had taken me to Ossetia and further than I should have gone into Zour's world, wasn't something I could easily abandon. My therapist had been right: I couldn't just cut it out and throw it away. I had to find a way to live with it.

I tried. I buried myself in my work, churning out several articles a week and writing on anything an editor set me, giving everything that was left of me to the children. Jimmy and Dolly were growing up as their years six, seven, eight slid past, and were completely occupying, so I wasn't lonely because I had them with me, but I felt alone quite often when they were small. Because I'd had them both in my mid-twenties, sharing motherhood with close girlfriends wasn't something that really happened. Most of my closest friends wouldn't have children for at least another five or six years after that, by which time Jimmy and Dolly were six and seven and I'd passed the maelstrom of those early years with toddlers, when it's easy to feel you're caught in a vortex of tiny, mismatched socks, ripped picture books and constant, low-level concussion.

Instead, the people I spent most time with were the au pairs who lived with us in those first few years of single parenthood. I couldn't afford a nursery or even a childminder for two children, so instead found foreign students who wanted to swap a few hours' daily childcare for board and lodgings. Our house was tiny, with two proper rooms and a boxroom that I used as an office. The children willingly gave up their shared room for the au pair, clambering into bed with me each night, and our house was filled with a line of foreign students. They brought so much to our lives: Dede, the PhD student from Congo; Peter, from Slovakia, who stayed with us for eighteen months; Giovanni, from the Paris suburbs, who wore skinny jeans, a skinny tie and wanted to work in fashion; Edina, beautiful and quirky, like a younger, funnier version of Mary Poppins who the children adored; and Kristina, from Hungary, who was almost a second mother to the children, living with us for over two years at a time when I was away at least twice a week in London.

I was lucky, as I was still living in the terraced house bought in Mum's name two years after the accident, the house Nell and I had lived in as students. It was purchased back when we were still blind and optimistic, believing Mum would get better; Rick had bought the house after Minety was sold as a place she might be able to live.

The house gave me my freedom, even though it reminded me how tightly I was still bound to Mum. After Dan and I split up, I behaved exactly as people say divorcees do. First I cut my hair short and bought an entirely new wardrobe. Then I repainted the house, covering the bright primary colours of my marriage with chalky pink paint I mixed myself. I bought curtains in a charity shop covered with a mass of roses and a throw covered with more roses for the bed I shared with the children. I thought I could tether our lives to the same things Mum had shown me as a way to love and set about recreating them. I had a big kitchen table that had once been Rick's desk, and covered it with a brightly coloured oilcloth; I grew rows of marigolds in the garden. The children attended a primary school behind the house and after school we rode the black-and-white pony Dash round the streets nearby, tying her up outside the corner shop so that Jimmy could run inside for Refreshers and salt-and-vinegar crisps.

I wanted that house to feel like home more than I wanted almost anything else in the world, but then nightmares of darkness and being trapped in perilous situations were replaced by more urgent dreams about finding and losing a home. Minety, or a strange imitation of a house that might have been Minety, was usually at the centre of these dreams.

I dreamed of losing all Mum's possessions too, and would wake feeling cold, despite Jimmy and Dolly's hot little bodies pressed against me. Then the murky grey arrival of dawn warned me that I couldn't roll over and forget it all. Instead I lay awake, worrying about what had happened to the noisy bell Mum had used to ring when we were outside riding in the paddock and she wanted us to come in for supper, or the embroidered cushions she'd kept for the drawing-room sofa. Minety had been such a monumental home and I still struggled to understand how it could all have disappeared into nothing, taking the life and the family we had with it too.

Mum was cared for beautifully by the nurses, but by her mid-sixties had started getting ill more regularly. Monitoring the cocktail of drugs she existed on was complex, since a drug she'd be prescribed for pain relief might have a side effect of making her urinary tract infections flare up. When she'd started waking at night, lying in bed shredding her sheets into ribbons with her nails, she was prescribed sleeping pills, which gave her more peaceful nights, but made her sick, while an anti-convulsant prescribed to manage a bad period of epilepsy dried her skin out so badly her eczema flared up again.

'We're not really moving forward, just back-pedalling to stand still,' her nurse, Kim, said, spooning pureed food into Mum's mouth and smiling at her with the special kind of warmth I reserved for my children.

There were music afternoons at the home and I'd arrive to find Mum tapping a tambourine with one hand; at the Diamond Jubilee the nurses made cream teas and the residents sang songs from the Second World War. Music was only one aspect of the therapy there; art was another. Mum would paint colours onto a sheet of paper if a brush was put in front of her, making a semblance of sense, but would then try to eat the end of the brush or drink her murky paint water. She was becoming institutionalised too, so that she stood up on her own less and less and sometimes her nurses had to use a winch to get her out of her chair.

Just as she was moving to a new home in Oxfordshire, the NHS suddenly reduced her funding, claiming her needs, which had only grown more complex with the years, were no longer intense enough to justify the high level of nursing she'd always had. I was so angry that I took the NHS on, watching countless assessments by social workers who were determined to prove Mum was mentally competent and in control of her life, and that her nursing needs, managed with such sensitivity and care by women like Kim, were not as challenging as they really seemed. They'd sit shuffling forms, stuffing custard creams into their red mouths, wholly focused on proving that Mum didn't actually need the twenty-four-hour care she was currently receiving. They'd put picture cards in front of her, or ask her basic questions, and she'd stare glassily back at them, nodding to every question, which they'd seize on as proof she understood, even when I asked her if I was her son, and she continued nodding.

Having spent years and years trying to break through to Mum, and failing, I became increasingly enraged by the social workers. Though the bureaucratic machine of the NHS was a terrifying enemy, I pored over Mum's notes, reading up on similar cases, forcing myself to become a legal and medical expert on the physical and mental health needs of severely brain-damaged patients. Winning the case obsessed me, not just because of the ethics of removing care from severely disabled patients, and because I was enraged by the way the NHS were now portraying Mum in order to remove her rights, but also because it was a way I could return to the battle of the accident. I felt that if the NHS won, then the accident would destroy me. I argued Mum's case before countless medical tribunals for four years. Jimmy and Dolly were still very small then, and sometimes my friend Claudia would cook supper for them so I could spend the evening or whole weekend combing through Mum's notes with a fine-tooth comb, trying to understand her unreadable mind and body a bit better. Fighting the NHS is very difficult, since at tribunals it appoints its own judge and jury, so the odds are heavily stacked against individuals, whose will tends to break over time. I categorically refused to accept the lies they pedalled. I wrote about the case several times in national newspapers, and the story was picked up by a television producer, who asked me to present a documentary on end-of-life care for severely ill people. I fought and won against the NHS, twice, once for a period of four years, and then again, when they came back at me, with even greater force, a decade later.

'You're our very own Erin Brockovich,' said Jessie, the features editor on a newspaper who had become a close friend, and that was consoling at a time when I felt trapped. The house in Oxford, which had offered me freedom in my divorce, had become my own metaphorical prison, since it was technically Mum's and bound up with her. This was a new haunting. I'd spent a part of every day since the accident wanting Mum and wanting to know what she might have thought of the path I was taking through life. But this longing also felt like ties that bound me very tightly to the past;

ties that I looped round myself as I tried to emulate her skilled motherhood. Sometimes they felt like they were strangling me.

And so, against the backdrop of my campaign for Mum, I had to fight for myself too, and creating my own home for Jimmy and Dolly became my new goal. I started pushing away from the hypnotic lure of the past, trying to create something completely separate for the children and me. I consciously created a home that was very very different to Minety.

With no rent to pay on Mum's house, I was able to save up for a deposit, and we bought an ugly, 1960s townhouse on the edge of a housing estate, with a sitting room and kitchen on the first floor and bedrooms for all three of us. None of the people I knew in Oxford lived anywhere near it, preferring to tuck themselves into rows of socially acceptable Victorian terraces on the other side of town. Once, a divorcing friend in the midst of chasing her ex-husband for maintenance payments came to visit. She stepped through the big plastic front door, settling herself at my kitchen table to share her woes.

'I mean, if I don't get a proper settlement, I might end up living somewhere like this,' she said, looking properly horrified.

I thought she was stupid and blind, because if you looked beyond the plain pebbledash houses and the pub with broken windows on the corner, you could find water meadows that were like a special secret stretching out to the ring road.

The house was on the far side of Oxford, taking us further than a bike ride from the yard where we kept the black-and-white pony, Dash. With a mortgage to pay that kept me writing long days, I no longer had time for mucking out or leading the children up and down to the corner shop. Jimmy was not that interested in horses anyway, and I knew Dolly could ride with Nell when we saw her at the weekends. Remembering Brad's clarity about not being sentimental about horses, I sold Dash, and my £100 purchase turned into £1,200. I was privately thrilled that city life hadn't softened my dealer's touch. And when Dash was gone, I consciously turned away from horses. I stopped visiting the racing yards where

I'd ridden thoroughbreds when the children were small, and packed the browbands and bridles into the attic.

In many ways it felt like a betrayal, as though I was rejecting the talismans Mum had planted in my childhood. But the tension I felt between past and present was sometimes unbearable. Whatever I did today seemed to be in competition with the way Mum had shown me to live as a child, and that was, eventually, suffocating.

My work too was another way I could be different to her, because she'd never had a career, so although it was entirely necessary to be committed to my job, as working provided my only income, it also sometimes felt like an act of defiance. I bought black clothes with gold buckles from Zara, the kind that look ridiculous in a stable yard but are made for meetings in London.

Without the horses, the children and I now had different adventures. We spent a lot of time driving up and down the A303 to Devon or Cornwall to go camping, and we did a road trip down the Pembrokeshire coast, sleeping in campsites on white-sand beaches.

Motherhood was entirely occupying. Jimmy and Dolly were growing up and were no longer the dots and scribbles they'd been as toddlers, but were becoming people. I worked a lot and travelled occasionally. I felt completely urban, and that was safe and liberating. I was very happy even though I was as far removed from horses as I knew how to be.

But, as my therapist had warned me, my inner darkness could not be cut from me; that visceral thrill that both freed me and held me captive at the same time. There were still nights when I vanished into escape, when the pounding high of drugs in my brain and the thrill of sex with anyone, as long as they were a stranger I could walk away from afterwards, blanked everything else out. These men never really saw inside my life, and certainly none of them met the children.

Every divorcing woman needs a sister in crime and for a few years mine was Anna. She'd walked away from her bad marriage the year before I had and she was the complete antithesis of the Oxford married couples surrounding me, who offered pity and disapproval when I wanted them least. I fell into Anna, who was usually in the middle of a personal crisis even more acute than my own, but that never stopped her being anything less than dazzling. She would always open her door to me in the middle of the night after I'd left a dinner party where I was a lone domino among a table of pairs. We'd sit at her kitchen table in pyjamas, swallowing vodka and drinking to the cult of single motherhood. For a while her two sons were at a school close to the one my children went to, and in midwinter we would walk across the meadow near her house, drinking from a silver hip flask full of brandy while laughing without once drawing breath. We took the children camping in a sodden field in Yorkshire, making whiskey coffee around a campfire while our four children ran wild. Those days are imprinted on me as muscle memory of the sweetest kind. A bit later she left Oxford to move back to London and into the arms of a proper boyfriend, but until then she was my brightest light in those first five years after I left my marriage when I would have done anything for Anna.

There were men too, but when I tried to be good, it always went wrong. I slept with a man I met walking in the playing field near the house, who seemed like a rough diamond, until he told me he robbed houses for a living, and I realised there was no diamond there. The trumpet player who invited me to his flat in Brixton turned out to be a violent drug dealer. The accountant, who seemed so kind and sensible, was actually in the SAS and suddenly vanished, just at the point I thought we were actually getting somewhere, to the jungle in Borneo.

All around me, friends started having children. Casual couples became marriages, then families, and I felt on the outside. I hated the pity that can come with single motherhood, especially as I felt my life was much more interesting than those of the safe, married couples around me. That pity, and disapproval, only made me wear my skirts shorter and my heels higher to wake up with another man I didn't know, but who I was sure I'd never meet again.

None of this really hurt because Jimmy and Dolly were a life force so powerful I felt wrapped in the special love we shared together. Jimmy had started the violin and, while I cooked supper, Dolly would watch him practising, her fingers stuffed into her ears and her face contorted in pain. He did karate lessons once a week in a community hall too, his frenetic, childish energy channelled into the intense elegance of *kata*. Dolly had a way of surprising and charming any adult she met. She was very funny, her singular and eccentric mind developing along paths I could never have predicted.

I loved sitting on the edge of Jimmy's bed as he solemnly talked me through his Lego collection, or returning from a charity shop with Dolly with a haul of brightly coloured china we'd stack between books on the shelves in the kitchen. I covered the walls of the sitting room with country-music posters I bought on a trip to America with my sister Emma, and hung a huge mirror above the kitchen table so that it reflected the window, which looked out onto the spreading weeping willow, flooding the house with light.

Nonetheless, the memory of the Caucasus occasionally pulled at my heart when I was feeling alone. Then I'd listen to Ossetian music, turning it up really loud if I was driving on my own, so that the car and my head were entirely filled with a strange folk music mixed with a hard techno beat which combined all the worlds I wanted. Sometimes, late at night, I'd stand in the kitchen alone, swallowing shots of ice-cold vodka and eating salted cucumbers because they reminded me of nights sitting around a table with Zour, talking about Ossetian ethnicity and Chechnya.

I was forcing my life forward but often memory and desire disturbed me. Mum's accident had opened a well of longing inside me that could suck me in with startling ferocity at any moment. It was signalled by a sudden shortness of breath or a pain in my chest that told me I was about to cry for no reason. With it came a longing to be taken somewhere different. Once, I was sitting at the kitchen table, lost in work, when Dolly appeared beside me, dropping her school rucksack next to the table as she kissed me, then opened the fridge to pull out a bottle of milk and reach for a packet of digestive biscuits on the shelf above. I was happy, right there in the moment, very close to her, until she started humming a tune in her soft, girlish voice that sent me spiralling, dizzy, backwards. I looked up quickly, invisible elastic pulling me towards her.

'What is that? That tune you are humming?' I asked, as the pixels of the past that always hung around me suddenly sharpened into focus. 'What's that tune?' I said quietly. 'I recognise it. What is it, Dolly?'

'We're learning it at school. It's a hymn,' Dolly replied, then started singing so that her clear, sweet voice rang around the kitchen.

> When a knight won his spurs, in the stories of old
> He was gentle and brave, he was gallant and bold
> With a shield on his arm and a lance in his hand
> For God and for valour he rode through the land
>
> No charger have I, and no sword by my side
> Yet still to adventure and battle I ride
> Though back into storyland giants have fled
> And the knights are no more and the dragons are dead
>
> Let faith be my shield and let joy be my steed
> 'Gainst the dragons of anger the ogres of greed
> And let me set free with the sword of my youth
> From the castle of darkness the power of truth.

The tune wove through the castles of darkness of the immediate past, whirring backwards in time to Mum, to her singing the same tune when I was Dolly's age. Oblivious to the lure of that past, Dolly walked easily around the kitchen, stopping to pour herself another glass of milk, but memory clawed at me and I felt that familiar longing to be back in the past with Mum, or, listening to the lyrics, to be carried away into the fantasy of Zour and his dark knights.

I squeezed my eyes tightly shut, forcing back the pain in my throat that told me I was going to cry, quickly lifting my flat palms to my face to wipe away the tears before Dolly could see them. As she wandered around the kitchen I wound the cord of my laptop up, putting it away so that Dolly could spread her homework on the kitchen table, then I moved to the sink to run a pan of water for pasta for the children's tea. The pan overfilled into the sink and time passed onwards.

I'd imagined life would go on just like that. I would work, and travel when I could, and the children would get bigger. My life would be all about the children and me. Trying to fit a boyfriend into this wouldn't work.

'You don't always have to see yourself as so independent,' a friend of my sister said. 'You don't have to see yourself as a unit.'

Oh but I did. As a unit I could keep the children and me safe, together, as we went off to spend another weekend with Emma and her family, or to stay with Nell at the circus.

But my unit changed the winter it snowed very hard for the first time in ages. It was Christmas 2009, and the digital clarity of the approaching year, 2010, looked neat on my computer screen. Jimmy was almost a decade old, growing up from the darting shot of mercury he'd been as a little boy. He'd started bending away from me, thinking about secondary school and his own concerns. Dolly was six, a skinny bean with thick brown hair, clopping around in pink cowboy boots and a denim skirt, always doing her own thing.

I was busy, working that night, and almost didn't bother answering the text message that arrived, asking if I wanted to meet for a drink. I recognised his name as someone I'd known at university – but my only memory was vague, of being wasted at a party together just before finals. I remembered talking with him about his plans after university and he'd told me he was going to Cuba, with his girlfriend. 'Travel alone,' I'd urged him, 'the adventure will be better.' Later, I'd heard from a mutual friend that the girlfriend had become his wife so my advice had been wrong. A decade and a half later, I sat at my kitchen table and scrolled through his text. He'd moved back to Oxford, alone, was bored, needing distraction, and wanted to know if I was up for a drink.

I was on a deadline and it was snowing outside, thick whiteness
lying in the street. After it had got dark, the children had run into
the road behind the house. The uniformity of the snow was thrilling,
removing cars from the landscape so that the edges of the roads
and the double-yellow lines were all gone. Shrieking, just to make
a noise in the way children and mad people do, Jimmy and Dolly
lay down in the road and made snow angels. Afterwards they shivered, red-faced, in the bath together, and then the house was quiet,
the children in bed. Kristina, our au pair, was there. If I hurried I
could finish the article I was writing. *If nothing else*, I thought, *going
out into the silent muffle of the snow will be exciting.*

That evening I buttoned myself into a midnight-blue coat with
cold pearl buttons that fitted tight across my body, drawing a line
of black eyeliner across my lids and a slick of pink lipstick over my
mouth, because the snow outside felt like theatre I needed to dress
up for. I texted him back: I'd be there at eight, and could meet for
just an hour.

I wish I could step back and return to that pub in a corner of
Oxford, and watch myself walking into the bar and seeing Pete
again for the first time since we were both students. I wish I could
be thirty-four again, inside that coat, believing I knew exactly who
I was but actually on the brink of an entirely new life. Pete changed
my life, I know that now, and since then every planet inside me
and around me has shifted and realigned with his, but at that moment
he was simply a name from the past I'd be spending an hour with.
I wish I could go back now and see my face and my body as I
saw him for the first time. I'd like to feel again that moment when
Pete arrived.

It's not something I normally drink, but that evening I ordered
whisky and water without ice, and two or three times we left the
table to step outside to smoke Pete's cigarettes on the pavement.
My eyes must have left his that evening, of course they must, but
I feel like they were always on him as we talked, swapping confi-

dences about the route life had taken since we'd last seen each other. No doubt our paths had been different – Pete had been living in London and then Paris for most of that time – but there was a symmetry between us that felt familiar. We'd both married, unsuccessfully, very soon after university, and we both worked in the media and liked nothing more than other people's stories. We had a handful of friends in common and it seemed somehow surprising we'd not met since university. So there was a bond across time, but I know very well that within moments of sitting down with our drinks, I felt a tug of something much, much stronger than simple nostalgia for a few shared years at university.

I wanted to tell him about everything I was and I wanted to know everything of his, and three hours slid past without a seam. I felt he knew me, all the bad bits as well as everything else, and I told him about the things that scared me and what my nightmares were made of. It was as if his voice and what he was feeling was already inside me and part of me, just like it is now.

Pete has broad, beautiful, generous, blond features and very blue eyes, and that night I watched him talking, following the shape of his lips as they moved and the way he sometimes cast his eyes downwards with heavy lids. I wanted to be close to him and for a while I really wanted to touch his neck where the soft skin meets the hard collarbone, and I wanted to smell him and taste him. But it was getting late, much later than the single hour I'd expected to stay, so instead I bit my lip and looked away.

'I have to go, I have to be up early for my children . . .' I started, as the clock reflected in the mirror behind Pete's seat read past eleven.

'Don't go. Stay, please, and we can talk some more,' he replied.

It took nothing to persuade me, and it was after midnight before we stepped outside into the crunchy snow. He walked me back towards my car as we made plans to meet again, very soon, in a few days' time, and then from nowhere he said, 'You have to think about these things.' I breathed out and more than anything I wanted to put the palm of my hand flat against his heart and just rest it there and be still.

But I didn't, not that night, and I didn't touch his skin in the way I wanted to for another three months after that, although we met, frequently, to continue the conversation we'd started and test the feelings. I loved standing close to him so I could smell him and he always left me with a desire to bury myself in him and actually become a part of his skin. Whatever was happening, we both felt it, and it was very strong, despite the way we were quite consciously stepping around each other, like magnets, attracted but pushing back against that force.

One night, a few weeks after that first evening, we sat in a pub called the White Horse in Oxford, on our third or fourth date, and I told him about horses and riding and what they had been to me all through my life.

'I have a good seat,' I said, my legs in tight black jeans touching his under the table, wanting to catch the register of desire I saw sketch across his face. It was sort of pathetic, but I knew what it would do to him.

The week before, he'd come to a lunch party I'd given at my house for a lot of my friends, and he arrived two hours late, his shirt rumpled as if he'd been wearing it all night. I knew he was sleeping with someone else and I didn't want that.

'Can I just have a cup of black coffee?' he'd said, when I offered him a drink. I knew he'd come to my party from some other girl's room. I ignored him during lunch, annoyed since I'd organised it with him in mind, although of course I hadn't told him that. But when he said goodbye I pressed my body against his, reminding him.

He left his phone at my house after that lunch. I found it under the table, and that evening I devoured his text messages and emails. He wasn't just sleeping with one girl, but with lots of girls. I wanted to be all those girls.

There was something about Pete that made me feel both very safe and also tense with excitement. He made me think of a German phrase, *Mit jemandem Pferde stehlen konnen*, because that's exactly what he was becoming, a friend who I could steal horses with, because I felt I could trust him entirely and I wanted him, too. In our conversations over the previous weeks, I'd told him about the darkness I felt so strongly bound into me, that sometimes scared me with its ferocity, but he never looked away from that. I also hadn't known I could find so much happiness in one other person. Pete was cleverer and kinder and stronger than anyone I had ever met. I was in awe of him, and I felt as if in him I'd truly met my match. All those other men moving through my life – I knew very clearly they had meant nothing as soon as I met Pete.

I knew too from our conversation that evening in the White Horse pub that he'd never met a girl who rode horses. Now I wanted him to know how good my seat was, how strong my legs were, how determined I was. The risks I'd take.

'Cat among the pigeons, rose petals gone everywhere,' he emailed, a few weeks later, after we first kissed.

There were, though, other people still tangled around our lives. He was sleeping with other girls and there were short, final paths with other men I had to walk down too. For a while – at least two or three months, anyway – I resisted Pete because I didn't want to waste something big by simply sleeping with him, yet I also wanted to know this was the right decision for myself, and that meant for the children too. My romantic life was something I'd tried hard to keep separate from the rest of my life, and very few boyfriends had met the children at all. But I knew what was happening with Pete was unlike anything that came before. The thought of actually being connected to him was like turning round and facing every part of myself, all the darkness and light, love and loss, mixed up together like a drop of black paint diluting through a glass of clear water. That feeling inside me was precipitous and delirious. For the first time in my life I was showing someone who I really was; unafraid, now, of the scars under my skin. He saw all of me.

Three months after meeting, we stepped away from everyone else and really turned around to face each other. When we did, it was only ever us.

Pete and I had been together properly for less than a month when he took me to his hometown of Edinburgh. There was darkness and sex against a mirror in a hotel room, and I gave him that part of myself I hadn't known existed. Afterwards, we walked up Arthur's Seat and he told me he thought he was in love with me.

For me, there was no 'thought' about it. I knew.

Later I fell asleep in the car as we drove to his mother's house in the suburbs, and he told me he'd felt disappointed I'd just gone silent like that. He didn't know that being a passenger driven through rain in a hot car made me feel safer than anything else. I was going home again.

Bringing Pete into the children's lives was as natural as flinging open the windows on a dark house that's been shut up on a warm day. That summer I realised how tightly I'd been clasping them to me in order to survive. Pete helped me breathe out and feel a happiness that I'd thought was only something other people experienced.

Being with him was an adventure too. We talked, all the time, about where our lives would take us. In truth, I didn't mind where I was, as long as I was always close to him.

It's the same way I feel about him now. Pete is part of my heart and he's the rhythm of my body. When I'm scared, I imagine I can sit in his pocket close to his beating heart. I want every part of him for myself because he was the one who changed me by recognising the darkness I carried everywhere. He didn't try to make it go away. Instead he took the thing that beats inside me and helped me make it my own.

When I was sleeping with lots of different people, I always needed to know I could walk away because sex then was something that didn't really make me lose myself, and I didn't like to give away that secret part of me I'm both most ashamed of but closest to as well. He made me see that part of myself and not hate myself for it. He made me feel the darkness, and love that too. Because feeling the strongest desire, it turned out, meant letting the hurt come flooding right in. And the more I let go, the more powerful I felt, and then he wanted me more, too.

Sex is a refuge I've used in my life as a way of hurting myself, but actually choosing sex that hurts with the man you love most in the world is the ultimate act of trust. Then pain becomes balm; it empties your head and heals everything. Pete taught me that and I love him so much for it. He's never turned away from the darkness of my own personal trauma, but he helps me own it so that it's something raw and new, sweet and also sharp and sometimes even painful that happens just between us. I'm part of Pete even when he's not beside me. If I could sit inside the cavity of his chest I know I'd feel happy.

Of course, I took him to meet Mum as well. Her nurse was feeding her pureed food as we arrived, talking to her in a voice that was just louder than was comfortable.

'Charlotte, your daughter's here. It's Clover,' she said, flattening her vowels in the soft Wiltshire accent I'd first heard at the village school. Mum looked up and away as Pete and I sat down on the chairs on either side of her.

'I saw Nell last week, Mum, and went to the theatre with Emma the week before,' I said, tuning into the familiar running commentary of my life that had been going on from adolescence to now. In that monologue, whole lives had completely changed, but Mum never said anything. I'd hear my own voice as if I was listening at a distance, and sometimes I could almost switch off, but at other times the sounds of my voice relating my life made me feel as if I'd been struck and I wanted to hide from what was going on. But, with Pete there, I felt less horrified by myself, because he spoke to her with such kindness, gently taking her hand she was waving vaguely in the air when she saw him, so that she actually smiled at him, looking from him, to me, and back again. She looked happy.

Leaving the nursing home with Pete an hour later, I wanted to blow away the smell of boiled food and bleached sheets and cups of milky tea. We went to the Ridgeway. At Barbury Castle, looking down on Swindon and Purton, I felt the past jolt even further away, yet still so perilously close, as families chased kites and dogs bounded around after tennis balls. It was Easter weekend, three months after we'd first met. Later, there would be a family lunch at Emma's new house in Oxfordshire, roast lamb and an egg hunt with Jimmy and

Dolly clutching coloured-foil chocolate eggs they'd found among the daffodils, but before then I wanted to feel only Pete.

Beside the road leading down from the Ridgeway there's a stone engraved with words from the nineteenth-century mystic and writer Richard Jeffries, about the power of happiness that exists here in the present moment, rather than in reaching for the past or chasing the future: 'It is eternity now/I am in the midst of it/It is about me in the sunshine.'

And, at that moment, only Pete was there. He was about me in the sunshine and something that was happening between us was absolutely right.

I told Candida everything about Pete. I sat in her garden, blue hyacinth in the grass leading to the field where Candida's dappled-grey mare Lily grazed, and talked. She wanted to know about him, about how the children were, about how work was going. We'd usually meet every few months to gossip and smoke cigarettes; or because she was in Oxford and wanted to see the children.

Almost always, she would arrive with a funny present she'd bought for them: a red-and-white-spotted enamel tea set for Dolly, or a clock inside a tin can she'd found for Jimmy. She'd want to know how Dolly's reading was coming on, or whether I'd managed to persuade Jimmy to keep riding. 'Darlings!' she collectively called them when she saw them – and that's maybe what Mum would have called them, if she'd been able to speak. Candida was a writer and journalist so loved trading stories about the gossipy world of newspapers, but what she was really doing, of course, was consciously keeping a sense of Mum alive for me. She believed in the rituals that hold a whole life together and championed continuance as the essence of life. 'We pass it on, from one to another, and we live our lives more fully because of the people before us who've informed what we do today,' she told me. I'd never had the big, essential conversations with Mum about marriage, home, children . . . those conversations that only come at certain moments in life when a woman looks to her mother for guidance, but when Mum's voice was silenced, Candida spoke the words to me for her.

Naturally enough, Candida was the first person I told, two years later, that I was pregnant with Evangeline. And two months after that, she was the one I asked to help do the flowers for our wedding.

'Your mum was the person who taught me you never have to buy cut flowers but should always use greenery from the hedges,' she reminded me; and Pete and I organised all the details of our wedding in the same spirit. We wrote simple postcards to invite about thirty friends, and decided we'd walk to the service at the town hall in Oxford with the children. We arranged that the same pub where we'd had our first drink together would do some food, but agreed we'd leave by teatime for a weekend by the sea with Jimmy and Dolly.

It was simple, but Dolly was perplexed by what I'd wear. A year before, in 2011, we'd taken her to Hyde Park to watch the royal wedding. Pete had instinctively picked Dolly up and carried her on his shoulders when the crowds intimidated her, but the image of Kate Middleton, a perfect princess in lace and diamonds, had left a strong impression. Now her mother was the bride so, in her eyes, I must wear white, and ideally a dress as big and frothy as possible.

I have a natural resistance to the white dress. Nevertheless, I tried to appease Dolly, going to Bicester Village to tug my body into a perfect, beaded wedding gown. I felt ridiculous, flushed and sweating beneath bright changing-cubicle lights, as if I was dressed up in fancy dress or borrowed clothes. Back at home, I raked desperately through everything I owned, until I found one of my favourite dresses. It was mid-thigh-length and black, a Versace print covered with hundreds of hot-pink, orange and purple butterflies and pansies. It tied at the back and had a scoop neck and in it I felt far from the blushing bride, but instead the woman I wanted to be.

On our wedding day, Pete and I got up at dawn, stealing out to the playing field near the house to cut down green boughs from a hedge which we took to the pub to dot between bunches of tulips and daffodils. Afterwards we walked through Oxford to the town hall together, Pete and the children and I, already a sort of family. Later, walking out of the town hall into a rain of rice and petals, I've never felt happier, nor more utterly myself.

And Candida was there too, like a mother, the day after Evangeline was born. Evangeline arrived quickly, with the same certainty and confidence with which she now moves through life. She is a very exact little girl who likes nothing more than standing up to her brother Jimmy, twelve years her senior. She was absolutely perfect and as Pete lay on the hospital bed with her, I felt flooded with love for them both, like warm bliss. Candida arrived after I came out of hospital, sitting on the sofa to kiss this newest tiny person.

'My bubba,' she purred at Evangeline, rubbing her cheek against the baby's soft hair.

It was that same afternoon that I felt a sharp, new feeling of loss which arrived when I was expecting it least, since our new life and the baby had felt so happy. That afternoon, Dolly and I walked to the park with Evangeline wrapped up tightly in the pram. As Dolly pushed her sister carefully across the grass in the pram, a strange new feeling caught in me, of happiness mixed with a special sort of poignancy for the passing of time. I don't remember feeling the same thing after Jimmy and Dolly were born, but so much time had passed since Dolly was the same age as the new little baby in the pram. It made me dizzy, and I thought this was just because I was tired.

I hardly recognised the familiar anxiety about Mum wordlessly moving inside me, like a bird caught inside a house with its wings beating against the glass of a window. Yet the intense, absolute happiness Pete and I had found in each other was cracked open by new motherhood. And feeling the strong emotions of becoming a mother for the third time brought my own mum back into my life, after so many years of trying to push her away. All of a sudden, Mum came rushing back to my mind, to my heart, my soul, and I was longing for her.

★

I was in the kitchen, having fed Evangeline and put her back to bed for a rest. She was eight months old. Pete was working on his laptop in a bedroom, but I was starving and had made a poached egg. I'd enjoyed watching the ghostly fingers of egg white as they fell through the bubbling water, turning from see-through to solid. Two slices of brown bread popped up in the toaster. The kettle boiled.

I had been feeling better. The sadness and violent thoughts that had lapped around as postnatal depression hadn't gone away, but they were now like a tide that went in and out. Over the winter I'd had regular sessions with a cognitive behavioural therapist who had helped me calm the panic in my head which had threatened to suffocate me after Evangeline was born. I still fought with a special sort of poignancy which flooded through me almost every time I looked at Evangeline's tiny face, and there were still mornings when I had to hide the tears that sprung to my eyes, as if from nowhere, when I heard Dolly singing a song to herself that Mum had taught me. My longing for Mum was still everywhere around me, but CBT helped me calm that longing, at least a little, so that it was no longer a wild storm, raging and terrifying like it might drown me. Sometimes I felt almost normal, and the gaps between the waves got longer.

I took a slotted spoon and lifted the egg out onto the buttered toast, setting it down beside a cup of tea at the kitchen table. I ground some black pepper and salt onto the egg, then flecked the gleaming yolk with flaked chilli. I'd seen a cowboy do the same in El Paso when I was living in Texas and since then have never eaten eggs without chilli.

As I sat down, Mum's doctor's number came up on my phone. I knew the number by heart and that each call usually brought news of some new medical issue she was facing, like complex eczema or another epileptic fit. I looked down at the egg on the plate, the glossy yellow yolk deliciously swollen, but put my fork down and answered the phone.

'Your mother has a tumour,' he said, his soothing voice suddenly right inside my head. 'The tumour is pressing on her kidneys which is causing their function to fail. We hope we can stabilise her so that she experiences no discomfort. But we don't feel that a general anaesthetic and invasive surgery would be appropriate. Do you feel that you and your family would agree?'

I paused, breathing deeply through my nose as his voice rang in my ears, then nodded wordlessly, forgetting he could not see me, asking him if he would explain it again.

'Clover, we cannot categorically say how your mother will respond over the next few weeks, but the size and severity of her tumour, combined with the failure of her kidney function, means that there's a very high probability she will die.'

I looked out at the weeping willow beyond the kitchen as he spoke, its fingers of green leaves lifted by a breeze. The long, delicate branches of the tree drifted sideways, sending a handful of thin leaves shaped like minnows swirling onto the ground. There was a small patch of purple crocus growing under the tree; flowers Mum had loved. I remembered being eight or nine, and telling her that crocuses looked like cows' hooves because they were cleft. After that, we always called them cows' hooves and I still thought of that every time I saw crocuses.

'I am so sorry to bring you this news,' the doctor continued. 'I know what your family has been through over the years and we know that minimising your mother's suffering has always been a priority for you all. But the tumour is serious. She is dying.'

After he'd rung off I pushed my chair backwards, knocking the edge of the table so that the cold poached egg quivered on the plate. I thought of Mum's tumour, growing silently inside her. I threw the toast and egg straight into the bin, as something like the extended grief of twenty-two years started pressing inside me, urgent and painful and wanting to get out. Then I went upstairs, because what I needed was to be beside Pete.

CHAPTER 9

Summer in Baulking is over, the ground crackled into spiky white frost again. Mist hangs on the field beyond the house when I get up early to make the children's breakfast, and leaves litter the drive. Since we arrived in Baulking the previous December, seasons have rolled into one another and now we're approaching a year. When we moved from Oxford, every part of me had been straining to believe in Baulking as our new home, even if there were moments when I felt like I was acting and I still really wasn't clear where home was. In those moments, I'd always turn back to the White Horse, because catching a glimpse of it galloping across the hill as I turned off the A420, or walking on the hill with its outline branded into the chalk below me, always felt timeless and consoling.

It is a Tuesday in late autumn on White Horse Hill when suddenly I feel like I really do belong and that none of this has been an act. I am there with Dash and Evangeline. Dash can walk now, his steps smaller than Evangeline's, who is like a shot of bright-blonde adrenalin darting ahead of us as we cross the sheep field closest to the horse. The children shriek as they run ahead,

their voices echoing down to the glacial folds of the Manger as
we cross the concrete track before the climb up the last steep hill
of Uffington Castle. Evangeline runs ahead of Dash to the cattle
grid and I can see her mentally daring herself to try to walk over
the metal rungs. A thick black hedge skirts along the edge of the
field below Uffington Castle, and suddenly, as if from nowhere,
there's a blurred kinetic sense of wild movement beside us so that
both children stop, automatically slipping their hands into mine.
In a ping-pong movement, five deer spring out in front of us, then
plant themselves on spindle legs in the field. Their soft eyes are
unblinking, pricked ears cocked but completely still as they stare
at the children, who are stilled into uncharacteristic, astonished
silence at this vision before them. The deer watch us for one
moment until a wood pigeon disturbs that completely still scene,
flapping in the blackthorn hedge so that the deer glance round,
then back to the children, before springing away into the dark-
green morning towards the Ridgeway.

'Bambi!' Evangeline suddenly shrieks, jumping up and down in
her red Wellington boots as she grips my hand, and I laugh at her
as Dash joins in as well. A clutch of sheep stop grazing to stare at
us, bleating stupidly before dropping their heads to the grass again,
and the children run forward into the space where the deer had
stood, who are now just vanishing spots in the distance.

I turn my face back towards the chalk horse and follow the
children up the wet grass slopes, a path I've taken many times with
them both, or with Jimmy and Dolly, or alone, since we moved to
Baulking. I've seen the hill change from winter to spring and
summer into autumn and back to winter again, like it's taking long
deep breaths across time, a bigger and older thing than I can ever
understand.

I just need to keep walking up the field behind the children,
following the sounds of their voices and their laughter, to pick them
up when they slide over on the wet ground, or stuff a small damp-
socked foot back into a Wellington boot. That's all I need to do for
them here on the hill, and as I follow them up towards the White

Horse, with the valley cosy like a blanket lying towards Baulking in the distance, I feel, suddenly, as if I truly belong here.

Pete and I drove to Purton to see Mum that same afternoon her doctor called. The M4 slid by like a metallic sea, vehicles moving as if without sound. Inside the car, Pete's voice made me feel safe and distracted, and that it was only out there, in the concrete distance, that the idea of a death existed at all.

'Are you alright, sweetheart?' said her nurse, Kim, when we arrived. Kim never sat still, always moving around the home, chatting to relatives, cheering patients, checking drug charts, making cups of tea. She always had time to talk, however busy she was, and on more than one occasion I'd stood in her office, unravelling with tears, her kindness surrounding me. I had jokes with her too, and after Evangeline was born she had sent me a silver charm shaped like a baby's shoe. This time, I looked up at her and smiled weakly. I said I'd spoken to the doctor and she nodded gently.

'We'll look after her, you know, you don't have to worry about that,' she said, reaching across to squeeze my hand. 'But Mum's waiting. Go to her.'

Kim was right. Mum was waiting, as she had been for so many years, in a chair in front of the French windows looking out to a small garden and beyond that the car park. She cast her eyes up at me as I sat down, allowing me to take her hand before she withdrew it. I leant forward and kissed her cheek, enveloped by a sense of her that smelt like warm milk and diluted disinfectant and a slight smell of something sharper, like a mild infection, mingled together.

We'd rushed to get to her that afternoon, hastily concocting plans for a friend to look after Evangeline and make supper for Jimmy and Dolly, as if the phone call from her doctor had brought a new urgency to a situation that was unchanged across two decades. The doctor had said she was dying, and in my mind I'd imagined she might be in bed or look weaker or somehow have a sense of death close to her.

She didn't, and looked just as she had done all the way through my twenties and thirties. She looked very sweet, her wiry hair a fuzz of peppery grey, her skin still smooth and pale, unmarked by the outside air. As she'd got older, her eyes had become more closed, tugging downwards at the sides, but although she looked a bit thinner, she was the same as ever.

She stared around the room, then looked back at me, tugging on a frayed thread of cotton on my jersey, as if she was doing an imitation of looking after me. Something of Mum was there, but so far away it felt like the deepest echo of a real life. As Kim rattled towards us with a tray of tea and biscuits, Mum looked up, animated.

'There you go, my love, a nice cup of tea,' Kim said, balancing the tray on the sliding table Mum kept pulled in front of her knees most of the time, as if she wanted to create another barrier between herself and the rest of the room, a layer of protection in her vulnerable state. 'Clover, will you do the honours and then can I get you to put the tray back in the kitchen, please, just to be on the safe side? Charlotte does like to take everything off it, don't you, my love?'

Kim reached over to stroke Mum's cheek and Mum looked up at her, patting her hand and connecting with her, since Kim now was like her daughter. Kim was the person who knew her best and made her feel safe. I'd gone far beyond feeling envious of Mum's nurses, as I had in the past when I'd realised that they were the ones Mum turned to, if she turned to another human at all. They were the ones who could read anxiety or discomfort into her movements, and who knew how to connect with the fractured parts of her personality. I was an onlooker and an afternoon visitor.

I showed her a picture of Evangeline on my phone, holding out the screen while she stared at it then pushed it back to me, and I told her about Dolly's new school. We drank milky tea, Mum wiping the inside of the cup with her thumb when she had finished, all the time gently tapping her feet on the ground, until I ran out of things to say, my voice losing momentum as I sat back in the chair and closed my eyes.

Bright sunlight and rain greeted us as we left a little later. The sky was blue and cold like the best April day as raindrops glittered through the light. Pete put his arm over my shoulder, pulling me tight to him and kissing the side of my face.

'I love you, Clover, I love you,' he said, holding me as drops sparkled around us. After the gentle heat and slow movement in one direction of being in the nursing home, the light of the afternoon was absolute and sharp.

Emotions collided inside me like the hard crash of multi-coloured snooker balls scattering across green baize. The accident had been the moment when life and death had twisted around each other and then around my mum, and the idea of them disentangling themselves from one another made my mind shudder in many different directions. I did not know how to arrange my thoughts as shock, relief and something new, perhaps grief or perhaps something indeterminate, bumped off one another, failing to find a place to settle inside me. My palms pricked and even though the afternoon was cool I felt sweat under my arms.

It was almost impossible to think of the journey ending. In my head the words galloped backwards and forwards like thoroughbreds let out to grass for the first time in ages. *Mum is dying.* Hooves thundered on hard ground in my head as my breath quickened and I said it again in my brain, *Mum is dying*, so that my eye sockets throbbed.

Until 25 November 1991 I'd been a child and the thought of Mum dying was the most terrible thing I could possibly imagine. Now that thought was knotted and frayed and not so clear, as guilt I'd ever had a thought so wicked as to dream of her death gripped me. The truth was that at that moment none of my emotions had any clarity but instead they all shattered into one another.

I had been poised for death for two decades and had sat at her bedside while she hovered on the brink of death many times. There had been days immediately after the accident when Mum was strapped to machines in intensive care when death had seemed very close. Then her surgeon and the nurses around her had always had grave faces as if priming us for the end of her life. We were told, many times, during those first weeks that the chances of her making it through the next operation were very slim. And we had prayed and hoped that she would, and it had worked.

The years since her accident had been dotted with the presence of her possible death. At least once a year, one of us had taken a call from the staff at the nursing home she was in or from her doctor, with the speaker afraid that the latest bout of winter flu, or an infection of some sort, would be Mum's last. But across the years the doctors had always been wrong and Mum had held on, sitting in a nursing home, inches away from death yet holding firmly onto life.

Her GP said it was different this time. He called again when I was with Dolly a week later, walking down a back lane near the house with her pony Bliss. The pony stopped when I answered the phone, putting her head down to work her way hungrily through the spring grass along the verge. Dolly raised her voice to object, but I put my hand up and turned away from her.

Beside me, I could hear the slow sound of Bliss munching grass as Mum's doctor told me more about her tumour. It was pressing against her kidneys, he confirmed, and although he didn't feel she was in pain, her recent blood counts suggested that, this time, she really would die.

'Of course we cannot say clearly how long your mother might survive in this condition,' he said, pausing slightly across the phone line. He picked his way around the words delicately, like he was sketching the finest lines across a plain piece of paper without wanting to leave dark marks. 'Your mother . . . Charlotte . . . she has a tremendous strength and will, as I'm sure you know. She has defied our expectations so many times in the past, but I do want you to be clear that this time it is very different.'

He was kind, his voice calm and measured, and although he vaguely groped into the future, he didn't want to put any sort of timescale on this. 'Normally, based on your mother's blood results and general health, a patient would pass away within about two weeks, but we cannot know now. Perhaps a few weeks; perhaps as long as a few months.'

It was terrible and tantalising at the same time, but the thought of living with another long future of uncertainty seemed unbearable, so I pressed him again.

'Do you think it might be as long as a year, or do you have any clearer idea of the timescale? Are we looking at months, or years?'

'Certainly not years,' he said quietly. 'A month or two, at the very most.'

In the end, her death overlapped with new life. I found out I was pregnant with my fourth child, Dash, just a week after that first call in the early spring from her doctor telling me she would soon die. The thought of the ball of life rolling onwards with another child made me feel happy, blurring the growing sense I had of grief approaching, even though Mum at first seemed to defy everything the doctors said about her, as she always had done. For a while, after the diagnosis, she held even harder onto life than ever before. She started putting on weight and was brighter than she had been in months. When I visited, she'd sometimes look at me and hold my gaze as I spoke to her, for several minutes at a time, rather than looking away or pulling her hand out of mine almost immediately.

But each time I drove to see her, I felt bewildered. The doctors had been wrong about her so many times in the past that perhaps this would be no exception. Perhaps she'd be one of those miracle cases of people who defy a terminal diagnosis. Perhaps the monologue really was supposed to go on for another ten, even twenty, years. Each time I left the home, I felt I had to tell her, more emphatically than ever, how much I loved her, but I also felt like a rubber band stretched tight by the effort of living on her deathbed. Remaining poised, constantly ready for death, was exhausting, and

I felt confused by the tension between how I thought I should be feeling, and how I really was feeling.

I wanted to smash through the glass wall of grief I'd been living pressed up against for the past twenty-two years and allow it to flood over me. I remembered watching the sheep being sacrificed in the mountains in Ossetia, and the quiet, faraway look on its face as its throat was cut. Blood pooled around its little hooves like a crimson apron, and I imagined this might be what the real pain of grief would feel like, a possession of the body and mind which I could finally give myself over to as something bigger than me. I'd wrestled and tussled with grief in a relentless rugby scrum for all my adult life, resisting it, loathing it, yet craving it, but never, ever being able to realise it, since my mother was alive and I could not grieve a person who was not dead.

The strength that Mum demonstrated in the first couple of months after her diagnosis, when I was newly pregnant, subsided as the summer moved forwards. I went for my twenty-week scan, Pete sitting beside me on a plastic chair as the shapeless form of life appeared and vanished on the ultrasound. There was the skull, the backbone, two folded legs; and could we make out those little fingers? The baby moved in and out of focus, its heartbeat like galloping hooves, tantalising with its presence before it vanished again into the darkness of the screen.

I felt the first butterfly movements of new life inside me that summer, flutterings that grew more insistent until I could feel small fingertips scratching inside me or the poke of an elbow or heel. A few days later, when I went to see Mum, she looked different. The only part of her that was unchanged across the years after the accident were her forearms and fingers. Her brain damage had ripped through her body, changing her face and outline so much, but her arms were still strong, her fingers dextrous, topped with her thick blunt nails. Suddenly, though, her arms looked like those of a very old lady and her grip, which had been strong enough to make me wince if she squeezed my hand, was weak. The skin on her forearms was crepey and she could not move her fingers – to pick up a cup or fiddle with a button on the front of my coat – with the insistence she usually did.

We were still living in Oxford then, so I was relieved when summer slid into autumn. I'd known, as soon as Evangeline had started toddling that summer, that we were outgrowing the townhouse with the upstairs kitchen and living area, which had felt so much like home when I'd bought it, six years before. Now the heat of summer trapped me upstairs with Evangeline and I fantasised about being able to spill out of the house, straight from a kitchen onto a lawn.

I tried to compensate by spending longer periods at the yard where we kept Bliss. Dolly and I took Evangeline in her buggy there almost every day after school, tying the pony up on the cracked concrete yard to brush her soft white mane and pick the stones from her hooves. In the late summer the fields were mowed for hay, and sometimes Pete would come and meet us there in the early evening as we walked through the blunt, newly cut grass with the sound of Oxford so close.

I had a gathering uncertainty about living in the city, since it was when I was down at the yard with the children and Bliss that I felt calm and enjoyed being a mother the most. Seeing my own daughters enveloped in their relationship with the grey pony disturbed old memories so that I felt a growing urgency to leave the city. But that would also mean rearranging all our lives. Doing that now, with a new baby on the way, as Mum lay dying, felt like an impossible task.

In March, the doctors had said 'a couple of months', but in the end Mum proved them all wrong. She held on, very tightly, until midwinter, when she changed again as death stepped closer. We'd been poised for so many years, but the end, when it came, shocked all of us.

Pete and I visited her on the first Sunday in December, greeted by the cheer of Christmas songs playing in the nursing home. The nurses had spent an afternoon making paper chains with the residents which were strung across the ceiling in spidery loops. Jimmy and Dolly were not too old to exclaim with excitement when they saw a fuzzy metallic-green Christmas tree in one corner strung with red baubles and shiny silver tinsel, a string of coloured lights flashing on and off around it. Evangeline, in Pete's arms, leant forward to grab the glimmering tree, and as we approached Mum, she slowly turned her face towards us and it was clear that some more dramatic change was coming. She was very thin, her skin grey and translucent. Her eyes were narrowed but she still looked towards the children, pointing to Evangeline who stumbled towards the tree again as Pete grabbed the back of her jersey to stop her pulling it forward.

We sat and talked to Mum, telling her about Christmas plans, until my talk ran out. Jimmy had found a puzzle with oversize pieces on a sideboard and he and Dolly sat on the carpet at Mum's feet, fitting it together until they'd formed an image of a rabbit sitting up on its hind legs. Pete sat Evangeline on the table in front of Mum, who reached over and gently squeezed one of her feet as if she recognised her.

There were mince pies on the tea tray that afternoon, and we sat with Mum, simply being together as a family. Quietly, I felt a longing I'd carried for so many years seep away from me. I'd spent so much of my life in fantasy, thinking about what my relationship with Mum would have been like without the accident. I had spent hours and hours running through a film in my head of arriving at Mum's house as an adult, with my own children, to spend the afternoon with her. I knew she'd have a beautiful garden and a messier house, and that somewhere there would be a pony in a paddock she'd tack up for one of my children to ride. I knew that all these things would happen and in my mind and my dreams I'd lived through them, so many times, like a film I could rewind and pause and play again and again, over and over, and it never bored me.

But as I sat beside Mum in a nursing-home chair, surrounded by the flat smell of weak tea and cooked food, as Mum silently moved her eyes over my children playing at her feet before looking away, I let the fantasy go. The yearning inside me for that version of my mother shifted, becoming less distinct with each in-and-out breath I took.

For a while that afternoon, I saw my relationship with her in that moment alone, not overshadowed by the past, but instead quite still in the moment. It was a million miles from the life I imagined I'd have with Mum and the children, and was utterly damaged, but it was still a real moment together and, in some way, that was infinitely precious.

Mum's nurses has promised to call me immediately if she changed at all, but she'd seemed peaceful when we'd left that evening so I wasn't expecting the call that came the next morning, at 5am, telling me to come quickly.

'Her breathing has changed, we think it's close now.'

I pulled on my clothes, calling my brother and sisters so that I had a sense of them too dressing in the darkness and starting the journey towards Mum. I was lucky, my drive was easiest as I lived closest, and it was still inky dark as I drove from Oxford towards Purton. As I got further west the black sky streaked into dawn and at 6 a.m., as I ran from the car park into Mum's room, I heard the sound of a blackbird in the thick hedge along the edge of the garden.

Mum's breath was shallow and her eyes were closed as she lay flat in the bed. I took her hand, which felt cooler, stroking her cheeks, telling her again and again I loved her. And I remembered being a child, when Mum would read to Nell and me before we went to bed, and how, when we begged her to stay just a little longer, she'd say, 'Look, girls, look at the angels. They're standing around your bed and they're watching you and keeping you safe even when it is dark.'

Quiet morning light slipped into the room as the spaces between her breaths grew longer.

'Look, Mum, the angels are waiting for you. They are waiting for you, with their soft golden wings outstretched, go to them,' I whispered to her, trying to hide the cracks in my voice. 'I love you, Mum. Look at the angels. I love you.'

And then, just minutes after I'd arrived, it was like Heaven breathed a huge sigh of relief, because at last she was on her way. And suddenly Mum's spirit was soaring, free, surrounded by nothing but the brightest light and the purest, strongest love.

Just moments afterwards, Emma, Tom and Nell arrived and for a while we sat, stunned, silent, united, around Mum's body. It was like the end of a very, very long journey. Like a big sheet of ice on a pond that creaks and slowly starts to crack before it smashes completely, I could feel grief straining inside me.

Outside in the corridor the nursing home was waking, with nurses making visits from room to room with medicine or tea trolleys, the home alive with the strange noises of confusion and pain that some of the elderly patients made. I've almost never felt as close to any other human beings as I did to my brother and sisters as we sat together in Mum's room beside her body as that new day began. I felt they were the only other people in the world.

Mum looked very dead very quickly. It was like her spirit had darted away from her body, free, so that her skin soon settled into a waxy pallor.

In labour, with each of my children, I've touched the gaps in between life and death, moving into a completely alien dimension that I've only ever glimpsed while giving birth. Now, I imagined that was the place Mum had gone through to. My grief was fresh, but for Mum there was relief.

Later that morning, the vicar from the church in Purton came and read Mum the last rites and said some prayers beside her body as Nell, Emma, Tom and I stood around her bed. Sophy was on her way, and arrived a little later. Mum's skin was quite pale by then, and the nurses had slipped a rose between her hands. Her soul was far away and suddenly I wanted to grasp it back, to make her stay a little longer. All those years, I'd thought I'd lost her soul and searching for it had sent me out so far from her, but now I realised, with a sudden jolt of guilt and sadness, that it had been there, though unreachable, all the time. Now it really was gone and all that was left was the vessel of her body.

Later the undertaker arrived and took her body away. Emma went back to her house and Tom was with our sister Sophy, so Nell and I cleared out Mum's cupboards in the home. There was a terrible poignancy in the fact her whole life could be contained in one small bedroom. When she'd moved to the home, Nell had decorated her room with black-and-white photographs of Mum as a little girl with her father or as a young woman with her sister, and then pictures of her with all of us, first as a new mother in the sixties with Emma and on into the eighties when I was very small. I stacked the photographs into a cardboard box but I felt too sad to look at them.

Rick arrived later and we sat in Mum's room, sorting through old photographs and postcards in Mum's drawers. The room seemed to throb with the empty space between us all and for a while Nell and I just sat on the edge of the bed surrounded by black bin bags.

'I feel like we've just got to the end of watching a very, very long film,' said Nell, rubbing her eyes. 'Like I'm watching all this from a distance.'

Afterwards, reaching for some kind of ritual to hang our hearts on, we drove to the church in Purton, Rick, Nell and I together, and walked around the churchyard. Mum's accident had been in late November, and she died on 3 December 2013, twenty-two years later, in almost identical, cold, hard weather. Smoke from a bonfire drifted across the graveyard, but the white shock of being outside in the translucent daylight felt good. I don't think that any of us really knew what to say or what to think, apart from sharing a growing sense it really was all over.

Nell then had to go back to her house for a few hours, but she would return later that afternoon. The official process of registering Mum's death meant I had to stay close to Purton that day to see her doctor, so Rick and I went to the nearest town, Wootton Bassett, to find a café for lunch. I felt like I was walking across an unknown planet as the unreality of what was happening surrounded me like dense mist. The ground beneath my feet no longer felt flat, but uneven, as if rushing up to meet me before falling away again, my feet flopping heavily, like I was concussed or drunk. Rick and I went to a café, but as I slipped into the wooden booth to order a plate of scrambled eggs, I felt my breathing was amplified in my eardrums, as it sounds when you lie in the bath with your head underwater. A teacup in my hand suddenly appeared fuzzy and indistinct, like it would just vanish if I squeezed it hard enough.

Across the table, I could see Rick's mouth moving as he spoke to me, but it was as if there was an invisible film separating me from him.

'Clover? Bug? Are you alright, Bug?' he repeated, and I blinked, trying to relocate something important I'd lost, as grief came down and struck me.

I felt stiflingly hot, my mind dancing and prickly, unable to focus. I thought that practical activity might steady me, so I told Rick I needed to go and buy some food for the children's supper. Outside, I stumbled up and down the high street, pavements flopping beneath my feet, with no clear idea of what I was doing at all. I stopped at an old-fashioned greengrocers where boxes of cabbages and oranges were propped up on counters beneath mirrored benches, and bought some apples and a head of broccoli. In a charity shop, my eyes skimmed, glassy, over a row of paperbacks, fixing on a copy of *The Little Wooden Horse* Dolly might like. At the till I fumbled with my purse, struggling to identify the strange pieces of silver in my purse which I knew should be a twenty- and a five-pence piece, but which now looked completely alien.

A few doors along was an embroidery shop selling balls of wool in electric colours. Hanging behind the counter were some small hand-knitted jerseys. A tiny blue tank top jumped out at me, but it wouldn't fit Evangeline, who was over a year old. There was a red knitted cardigan decorated with a slightly garish outline of Father Christmas, his nose a little too large and his eyes a little too small. Behind it, I spotted a pale-pink jersey with Babar the Elephant knitted onto the front and pointed towards it. Mum had sometimes read us Babar stories when we were very young, although I think she found them too long, as she'd always start yawning halfway through. But the jersey was the right size for Evangeline. I handed the lady behind the counter a £10 note as she wrapped the jersey in a plastic bag.

'My daughter will love it, thank you,' I said, then paused so that silence hung between us. I didn't want to leave the shop and go back out there, but the lady had started sorting balls of wool into different-coloured piles.

At the door, I turned back to her and, without thinking, said, 'My mother died. She died. This morning.'

She looked up at me as if startled, then smiled, her eyes slicing downwards as she nodded her head slowly at me.

'I'm sorry to hear that, dear. I'm sorry to hear that.'

Much later that afternoon, after Rick had gone, Nell came back to Purton to go through the last of Mum's things. There was nothing to keep us there, it really was over, but leaving the nursing home was hard. Her nurses had been our friends for years, and finally saying goodbye to them felt wrong, although, in my heart, I knew I wouldn't come back.

But, like a pigeon circling round looking for its nest, I didn't really know how to leave Purton or the area around Mum's home, as being there made me feel closer to Mum. I knew I'd have to go back to Oxford at some point, where Pete would be making supper for the children and where I was needed now, as their mother. I was five months pregnant with Dash then but felt fragile, as if I had absolutely nothing to give to the children.

So, instead, Nell and I drove back to Wootton Bassett where we sat in a pub and drank Coke. There was a broken jukebox in the corner and a fruit machine along from a bar, where a line of men made quiet jokes with one another. There was no food, or tasteful colours, just a dark bar covered with pints and beermats and a dark-red carpet decorated with yellow lines. It was the sort of pub

Nell and I had driven our pony and cart to when we were teen-agers, deeply familiar and completely unchanged by time. We sat together and talked about Mum. I felt like a very young child and I fervently didn't want to leave Nell's side although, when it got dark, we hugged each other and drove home to our families.

I lay beside Pete the following morning as he held me, our bodies tangled together in the darkness as I pressed my heart closer against his. After he had got up I sat on the edge of the bed, the blinds pulled shut, because dark was easier than facing daylight. I felt flung out into a new world, barely capable of leaning forward to pull on my maternity jeans, which anyway felt far too casual. I was divorced from the sounds of Jimmy and Dolly arguing over who should have the last of the cereal, and of Evangeline banging her spoon against her bowl as she sat in her high chair.

'Mum is dead,' I said into the half-light of my bedroom. It sounded like someone was sitting beside me, talking to me, so I tried it again. 'My mother is dead. She is dead. Mum is dead.'

*

The days straight after Mum died were not like those after the accident, which had been shrill with hospital life. Now there was the quiet work of organising a funeral, which was a relief from the idea of even attempting to engage with domestic life or my children, since their little clawing hands and endless demands felt impossible. Instead, I wanted to experience epic ritual to match the feelings inside me, but I had no idea where to find it.

This new feeling of fresh, raw grief was lonely. I craved escape from the kitchen and the children, but didn't know what on earth I was supposed to *do* once I left my house. I wanted to go to some ancient, austere, mystical place to wail and chant Latin hymns. I wanted to drape myself in black, drown my cries in solemn classical music, escape my world and myself by burning incense and candles while offering incantations to Mum. I wanted to wrap myself in her. If I could, I would have sent a burning ship into the middle of an ocean then buried myself alive with her body.

Instead, two days after her death, I found myself driving to Minety, parking near the churchyard which was separated from the house by a tall limestone wall. Since we'd left, when I was eighteen, I'd never been up the drive, let alone inside the house, because I didn't want to undo my special secret fantasy that we were all still living there in a place in the past where I remained seven years old. Now, with the tall garden wall separating me from the house, I was close enough to feel its old familiar presence around me.

I could still see the bathroom Mum had painted palest pink, from where I'd once watched swallows sweeping under the eaves. I could see the room that had been Tom's, with a tangled rosebush under the window, and on the far side of the garden I could see the big yew tree and the top of the stable block. Picking through the mud in my trainers, I opened the gate at the back of the churchyard which opened onto the paddock Mum and Rick called the church field. It was where Nell and I had made jumps out of hay bales in the summer after the hay had been cut.

The Minety clay Mum complained about was holding big pools of water as I stepped out into the field, wet grass drenching through my shoes and soaking the ends of my jeans. Three crows rose from the hedge, spattering the grey sky with dots of black as I crossed the field. Behind me, I could feel the throbbing presence of the house, my house, my home, that was all absolutely gone, long gone, and at the same time still so present. I walked to the far side of the field, heart hammering, making the field separate us before I turned around and allowed the house to see me.

And inside my head, inside the house, I saw our lives there in the past. There was the bathroom which had been part of Mum and Rick's bedroom where I'd often sat at Mum's dressing table, playing with the strings of wooden beads she had slung across a mirror and opening the lid on the white-and-gold box of Chanel powder she liked. There was a mirror covering one wall, over red Laura Ashley wallpaper decorated with flowers and butterflies, and a line of black-and-white French prints Mum had hung there. There was the back of my bedroom too, and under that window would be the small mahogany writing desk Mum had moved from another bedroom for me to do my homework at. For a while I'd kept a pair of pink-collared doves in a cage in my room, until their noise and mess annoyed everyone too much, but now I caught a glimpse of the movement of their wings in my head. Standing in the wet field, I could feel the scratch of the red rush matting on the floor and the cool, solid heaviness of an ink pen in my hand that Mum had given to help me improve my terrible handwriting. I was right there in the room and I saw cowboy boots slung across the floor and green-and-white curtains at the windows, and I could hear the sound of some of the tapes of country music Mum and Rick's friend Ken would make for me. I could feel myself slipping back through time into that bedroom while I was thirteen, fourteen, fifteen . . . but then it stopped. I looked away across the field, my breath very shallow, so that the horizon across the field and the black hedges spun, because when I got to sixteen all that stopped and I could only hear the sound of a girl crying.

We had horses at Mum's funeral. Two of Nell's friends from the circus rode my sister's big grey cob and a black-and-white half-breed through Oxford so that they were waiting outside the church when we arrived. Mum's body had been cremated the day before with just my siblings and Mum's brother and one of her oldest friends present. The service today was to be a celebration of her life, and soon the church was full of hundreds of people, many of whom had not seen her since the immediate aftermath of the accident.

I wanted to do a eulogy about Mum because she was an easy person to eulogise. Earlier in the week, Pete and I had gone to the church so that I could practise it, as I didn't want to read it from notes, but to know it by heart. Pete sat in a pew as I stumbled through it, then grew more confident, until he told me that we should stop because I was starting to sound like Margaret Thatcher.

Emma's husband Matthew spoke about Mum as well, and Nell read from *The Waste Land* and Rick from *Pilgrim's Progress*. Sophy and Emma read a psalm together and Tom read from the bible. Mark Palmer wore his hair as spiky as Mum would have liked it, his gold teeth glinting as he read from *The Merchant of Venice*. Ken read a sonnet while Candida swooped up in a long leopardskin coat, reading Louis MacNeice's 'Snow', her voice pure and clear until she got to the last line, when a sob suddenly grasped her throat. We sang 'How Great Thou Art', and afterwards the horses rode ahead as we walked from the church across the big meadow nearby, where a flock of geese rose up from the winter flooding and a herd of ponies in the distance raised their heads, suddenly startled by the crowd converging near them.

We stood on the bridge by the river, watching as the vicar said final prayers for Mum while her body was still with us, before Tom knelt down, quickly lifting the lid from the urn that contained Mum's ashes. I know I was there, standing on the wooden bridge, feeling the rain on my face, with the dark, wet smell of winter around me, but I did not feel present, and when Tom gently tipped the urn into the water, and the river swirled with a great pool of grey that rushed onwards, I had to look away because I did not want to see the grey dissolving. She was gone, she was gone.

EPILOGUE

I am on the Ridgeway when I see the horses approaching. A bay and a chestnut, moving with long, straight paces so that they seem to own the field around them even though they're just walking. Even at a walk, the horses are like tight arrows moving through the grass. The horses appear to arrive first, but they're ridden by two men who talk quietly to one another as they approach, their stirrups pulled up short so their knees are pressed under their thighs, goggles pulled on top of crash hats covered with faded silks. They don't see me but I watch them as I walk along the hedge line, following the white snake of track.

As the horses move closer, it's as if the men become a part of the shapes of the animals. The horses move a little faster and the men tighten their reins, standing up in their saddles to trot and then lope forward into a rolling canter.

Suddenly the horses are not just an idea in the distance but a gallop of hooves and manes and flowing tails, so fast and close that I clench and unclench my palms as I watch them tracking the fence line, holding my breath. The men are galloping so close to one another that I know they must be rubbing calves as the horses pound onwards, around the edge of the field and along the low-lying fence line before it suddenly switches uphill. The horses turn: long, lean lines with tails streaming as they gallop towards me and past me, pressure rising as their hooves beat the ground.

In the past, while Mum was still alive, there would have been sadness inside me for something that had been lost, but now the feeling is just pure desire. I cannot pretend it's not there any longer, or that it's something I can get rid of, even if I wanted to. It's that feeling that makes me know I'm alive and makes my heart thump faster and my soul realise itself, like being high, or scared with adrenalin, or being hurt and fucked and loved at the same time. It's the darkness that becomes goodness when it floods through me and which I always want inside me, whatever happens. The horses gallop past as the hill swallows them up like a throat and I feel desire for them again, like a trapped nerve snagging inside me.

Pete brought everything I love most back into my life, so it's not surprising he was the one who made me ride again. I'd ridden friends' horses, very occasionally, in the years I'd been a single mother, when I was concentrating on my work and my children and keeping that wagon moving forward towards the horizon. The last time I'd really ridden a horse was in the mountains with Zour, but after that they'd fallen out of my life. The children's little ponies that I'd kept over the years – Bliss and Dash in Oxford, and then my driving pony, Trigger, and the miniature Shetland, Holly – didn't really count since they were more like toys.

I told myself I didn't miss riding. Small children and big, exciting, dangerous horses don't mix together very well. A large horse close to a small child is not a good thing and, just like a baby, a horse needs constant, daily attention. Tough little ponies, however, like Holly and Trigger, don't mind being left out in the field. They don't need to be rugged up at night, and they're easier to manage within family life than horses. Holly is the size of a large dog, so if she stands on Dash's foot when he's waving a currycomb at her, or skits forward so Evangeline falls off, no one is going to get hurt.

But while I could play with the ponies for the children, I couldn't ignore the vast, magnificent White Horse, carved onto the hill near our house, reminding me exactly what it was I was missing, every single day.

Pete knew it. He saw it in me every time we drove through Lambourne, and I'd press my face to the window to get a better view of a skittering string of racehorses as they clattered down the road, or drove past White Horse Hill and I'd breathe, 'Look at the horse, look how powerful it is.'

Once, walking down the green at Baulking with Pete, as I led Evangeline on Holly and pushed Dash in his buggy, we saw a girl riding a black-and-white pony. It had a long mane and big hooves and cantered easily across the grass.

'Beautiful, isn't it?' I'd said, shielding my eyes from the sun with one hand to watch the girl as she moved seamlessly forward with her horse.

'You should do that. We could buy a horse so you could ride again. Isn't that why we're here, anyway?' Pete had said, turning round to face me, his hand on my shoulder so I felt his fingers on my shoulder blade. I'd looked down, pulling at Holly's mane to draw the knots from it. In the saddle, Evangeline's tiny legs were barely long enough to reach the stirrups and blonde curls escaped from the side of her crash hat. I'd shaken my head.

'It's too difficult to keep a horse. I can't do it with the children and work. I'd never be here and would always be mucking out or something. It's too expensive, too demanding, too annoying for everyone else around me who might not want to do it,' I'd said, aware my voice sounded a bit hollow. 'I'd rather just enjoy the ponies with the children and you.'

This was partly true, although the idea of being able to ride on the miles and miles of tracks along the Ridgeway was seductive.

But there was something else stopping me from buying a horse of my own. I didn't want to just hack out alone on a fat cob. The jolt of envy I felt for the girl on the black-and-white horse riding across the green had passed quickly. I didn't want that, not really.

If I was going to ride again – really ride, in the way I liked – I still wanted thunder and fear.

In the decades between Mum's accident and her death, I thought I'd known grief, since I was constantly mourning the loss of the person and all the life she had been. But after she died I realised more clearly that although I had glimpsed grief, it had never really been present in my life. I'd just mistaken it for trauma, which is very different. Trauma is electric and dynamic, intensely painful but sometimes strangely exciting too. Trauma had whipped me awake in the night to shout words I couldn't hear as I was shaken out of sleep from another dream about finding my mother then losing her again, or being violently dispossessed from a childhood home I didn't recognise.

Trauma had sometimes made me angry and strange among my peers, but it was energetic too. I understand when I look back on it all now that trauma made me really grip life and feel it with every part of my body. Something had propelled me out among the gypsies in Ireland, or onto a ranch in west Texas, or into a recovering warzone in the Caucasus and that thing was trauma. It terrified me, but it also gave me some of the best moments in my life. I am grateful to trauma.

Grief, though, did not feel electric like that. Grief was very different and I felt it all around me after Mum died, growing thicker and heavier in the months that followed, because of what happened to Candida. After Mum died, Candida wrote all of us a letter which described exactly what it was about Mum that her friends had loved so much. She wrote about Rupert introducing her to Mum at a dance in 1963. Candida remembered that Mum was wearing a three quarter length white dress but wrote in her letter that she had forgotten everything else about the evening except the meeting.

I felt an instant affinity, she was so bright and beautiful – shiny, really. But it was her strength of spirit which mesmerised me in those first moments. It was almost tangible. Now this is the truth. I have seen that spirit come into all of you lot over the last two decades. Now that she has gone completely, that spirit will burn even stronger in you all. It only happens when someone who is as good and great as she was dies.

Your mother is only supposed to die once. Mum's accident took her away as if she'd died, and then her real death was like she died a second time. And just after Mum's death, Candida told me she had inoperable pancreatic cancer, and that soon she was going to die too. It was like standing in an unstoppable wave of grief, crashing around me like a storm.

Sometimes I think of grief and trauma as two beautiful, dangerous big cats – trauma is a leopard, flashy and dazzling, which wants to prowl and pounce and refuses to keep still. My grief was a different creature. It was a black panther, slinking around in the shadows, watching me and purring deep inside my head after Mum died and then Candida followed her, the panther staring at me with eyes that shone like golden glass marbles, unforgiving, unblinking. It stayed with me every day for over a year, and then it retreated, occasionally pausing to look back at me before it slunk silently away, and now it has left me.

I feel more possessive of my trauma. When the time I spent in Russia became a thing of the past, but I was still on my own with Jimmy and Dolly, I'd sometimes look back at what I'd done with guilt, berating myself for leaving them to go to a dangerous place where I didn't need to be with a man I barely knew, to do things I shouldn't really have done. I beat myself, internally, that I'd neglected every duty I had to Jimmy and Dolly by taking these risks. *How could I have done that as a mother?* I asked myself afterwards, furious and ashamed. Why hadn't I been a better mother, and sacrificed my own pathetic desires, however strong they'd felt at the time?

But then, a few years later, when I'd embarked on motherhood again and Dash and Evangeline were very small, I felt that familiar,

almost terrifying, tug of the wild. As the babies clawed at my legs
and kept me trapped indoors, I remembered exactly why I had left
Jimmy and Dolly when they were the same age and gone to the
Caucasus. This doesn't reflect my feelings for my children. My soul
is bound around and through theirs and I love them with all parts
of me, but I also can't give up the part of me that needs to be
separate from them and to touch the wild other.

A similar desire to escape was what took us to the Ridgeway
and to our home in Baulking. We found the white house where
we live now entirely because of Candida. Although she never knew
we had moved there, she had a hand in it, I'm sure, and she showed
us the way.

I last saw Candida three weeks before she died, in the summer
following Mum's death, when Dash was a newborn baby. Candida
was very ill by then, but had texted me, saying she wanted a glimpse
of Dash, since she didn't know him as well as the rest of my children. I knew she was saying goodbye. She was lying in her bedroom,
with the Ridgeway and the White Horse just outside. Dense green
July throbbed beyond the window, and the roses outside her room
smelt almost hypnotic. She was sitting up in bed in a white night-
dress and white turban, reaching out to cuddle Dash as soon as I
walked into the room. He lay on her stomach, staring at her as she
held his tiny hands, and I lay in the bed beside her, feeling wetness
on my cheeks as a breeze shifted the white curtains hanging at her
window and the world revolved.

'How do I keep going? How do I go on?' I asked, stifling the
wobble in my voice, because neither of us needed to say that this
would be the last time I saw her. It felt selfish to cry when she was
being so brave but the pain was big. Mum was gone; Candida
couldn't leave as well. I needed her to show me the way. I needed
her to be there for the next bit of life.

'You have to be a grown-up now,' she said, her tone tough, but
calm and simple too. 'After my mother died, I thought I wouldn't
cope, but you do; you will.' She looked away from Dash and back
at me, her hand on my shoulder. 'I kept her in my head. It was a

cosy feeling, and it was as if I wore her like a coat. She is so close to me now and so much a part of me that sometimes I think we are one and the same person. She was always there, in everything I did.' We lay on her bed together and talked for two hours about the secrets of being women, laughing as life flooded around us. When I kissed her goodbye she reached up and wiped my tears away.

'Be brave,' she murmured, and then laughed. 'Go on, go out smiling. You'll thank me for that.'

Later, after she'd gone, her daughters, my childhood friends Lucy, Imo and Delli, called me back from Wales, asking me to help them decorate the horse-drawn cart that was to be their mother's hearse. We stood in the rain looping pieces of mayflower and beech leaves onto the cart. When the girls went to decorate the church with more flowers, I was left at the house winding the boughs into Candida's funeral cart, wet rain on my cheeks and rain drenching my hair as time seemed to flood into me and out of me. Behind the house, there was the Ridgeway.

When the hoops were finished, Lucy and Delli took me to the church to look at the enamel jugs of roses, peonies and lavender they'd picked for her mother. The church wasn't in Uffington, but next door in a village I'd never noticed before, called Baulking . . . and in front of the church was the white house with the black barn that became the home Pete and I made together. It was as if she'd made it happen. Candida never knew that our children would run along the Ridgeway she'd lived her life beside, or that I'd drive my pony Trigger up onto White Horse Hill as she had shown me how to do with so many ponies before in my childhood. Mum and Candida never saw any of that, but they are inside me in every part of what I do, like bells ringing in distant rooms, the ties that bind me to them and to my own children, and into the future, onwards, re-assuring, through time and space.

No one knows why the White Horse is there on the hill above Uffington. It's a mystery that belongs to ancient man, and we can speculate but we are only ever guessing. When I look at that chalk horse's strange, almost geometric outline, I'm reminded of ancient cave paintings in France and the outline of a horse I first saw there in my late twenties on holiday with Emma. The mystery of those cave horses had remained imprinted in my head, and when Pete and I had been together for a year we took Jimmy and Dolly on holiday to the Dordogne, to find the paintings again.

Miles deep in an underground cave in Rouffignac, Cro-Magnon man crawled into the thick darkness to lie on his back and draw an outline of a horse on the roof of a cave so low it was just a foot or two above his face. We'd ridden a little, open-topped train deep into the flood-lit cave as a guide pointed out scratch marks on the walls where bears were living at the time the paintings were created. The guide reminded us that although we could walk through the caves, since they'd been cut out to make it easier for tourists to admire the paintings, ancient man would have had to crawl into a deep, dark slit in the ground. He would have scraped along on his knees and belly for several kilometres, a dirty, flickering flame torch lighting his way, before he found the expanse of flat wall where he drew mammoth, bison, rhinoceros, mountain goats, and fifteen extraordinary horses.

The animals are not drawn as smudgy outlines, but in bold, single strokes, as if the artist had created the shapes in one go, making no mistakes as his hand moved across the cave wall. They are startling and look utterly modern, some of the images of the animals overlapping one another as if their outlines echoed across time and space to a distant but always present past.

All the drawings are beautiful and strange, the mammoth particularly so since it feels a bit like looking at contemporary sketches of dinosaurs, but I was most haunted by the humanity and presence of the horses. One drawing stands out among the outlines: a line figure of a pony, its tail outstretched and mane standing up, eyes wide, staring forwards, but also aware of all that's going on around it. Cro-Magnon man lived and breathed and dreamed the emotion of that horse. He had looked deep into its eyes, reproducing in the inky darkness of the cave a love that he must have felt for this animal to honour it in this way.

Returning with my children and Pete, a decade after the holiday with Emma, the power of the drawings remained just as intoxicating, even as Jimmy shivered in the darkness, whispering to me questions about when we could go back out into the sunlight. I cannot forget the cave horses and the unanswerable question of why those men crawled so far into the dark to draw them. Their rituals and rites of passage will always be unknown to us, just as we'll never know who their gods were and where they searched for them. Archaeologists do, however, think the Rouffignac caves were created roughly 14,000 years ago; about 10,000 years later, another man drew a white horse into the chalk on a bright-green hillside in England.

It is impossible to know why these images of horses exist, and whether their creation was a way of marking territory, or celebrating manhood, or worshipping an ancient god or even the *feeling* that god, and horses, and landscape, gave these men. I like to think that ancient man saw the deep, dark inside of the cave, and the bold green curve of the hillside, as a film between this life and another, equally unknowable world. Best of all, ancient man did not draw an image of himself onto the walls of the Rouffignac cave, nor reproduce himself on the hillside in England. Instead, he drew horses.

He knew there's no power or energy comparable to the ancient thunder of a horse's hooves galloping across the earth.

After living through the years of Mum's life following the accident, which were marked by a sense of unending loss that simply moved forward with time as I grew up, the White Horse is my own full stop. I see it from our house in Baulking and it's the lodestar I look to when I want to go home. When Mum sent Nell and I out on our ponies along the Ridgeway she wanted to teach us to be brave, although she didn't know how brave we'd have to be after we lost her. And horses sent me out into the world, later, when I lost her after the accident. Wherever I was, and however far I rode, I was always looking for her. When I met Pete I realised I could stop looking, because she was here, with me and part of me, all along. Until then, those warriors on their horses had been an army riding with me. The gypsy ponies moving on their tethers in the dark, or the cowboys way out there in the canyon on their bucking horses, and the wild Alani with their knives and guns, were never really there to scare me. I went out to look for them because I needed them to ride with me across the battlefield. I needed them to survive. In the weeks after Mum died I kept being confronted in my brain by an image of a warrior stepping off the battlefield, clutching a battered shield and splintered sword, skin torn, bleeding, badly damaged, certainly, but not broken. It was like a distant image of Alfred or Arthur, or even battle-weary Wela-nandaz, the Proto-German translation of Wayland, the ancient blacksmith. Mum's death brought the battle to an end. I'd left home to ride dangerous horses not because I wanted to wreck myself but to be my chargers across that battlefield and to be my brothers in arms.

It's still dark in Baulking as I leave the house, driving up onto the Downs for five miles to the village of Letcombe Regis. The village clings to the hill with the crest of the Downs looming above it, and white fingers of light are beginning to crack through the night as the sky starts to flood blood red with the dawn. I switch off the radio, shivering as I think of the Iron Age hill fort above the village. There's nothing but sheep and maybushes there now, but local legends say that Letcombe got its name after a battle between the Danes and Saxons, when the enemy's blood ran down the Ridgeway into the valley and the villagers shouted, 'Let it come! Let it come!'

The first string of horses has already left the yard by the time I arrive, clattering up the narrow road that leads to the Ridgeway, the lads riding them crouched over their necks, stirrups pulled up short. I buckle the leather chaps Pete gave me onto my calves, pulling tight the straps that fasten with little brass studs. I pull my crash hat on, zipping my jacket right up to my chin because it's cold this morning and will be freezing up on the hill, stretching my hands into a pair of black nylon riding gloves covered with little rubber grooves running across the palms, which help me keep a tighter grip on the reins.

My riding trousers are tight, more so than they were a month ago when I first came to the racing stables, to bring horses back into my life again. They don't sit so comfortably on my waist now because I am pregnant again. My fifth and final baby will arrive in the summer. He will be a strong, beautiful son called Lester. Now, though, he's the size of a kidney bean, a secret for just Pete and me for another few weeks.

The stable is dark and smells of clean straw and warm horse. I slip the snaffle into Bally's mouth. He's a dark-bay gelding I've been riding all autumn and he opens his mouth easily as I pull the browband over his ears and fasten the buckle of the cheek piece. Under his rugs, his short brown hair feels warm and soft. I throw a saddle pad over him, tightening the girth as he stamps, his hard metal shoe smashing against the concrete stable floor. I run my hand over his big neck, breathing him in as he watches from the deep pools of his big brown eyes where I see myself reflected.

Up above the yard, the Ridgeway runs east to the Devil's Punchbowl, with the all-weather gallops where the racehorses are exercised lying parallel to the track, separated by two strands of barbed wire. I kick Bally on as he splashes through the greasy puddles dotting the track, then shorten my reins when he skitters forward as a crow suddenly flies from a clump of hedge beside us.

In the distance, as the hillside curves east, I see the outline of two more horses working their way, fast, along the gallops until they suddenly vanish over the far horizon. Bally spots them too, dropping his head and snorting as we pass through the gateway separating the Ridgeway from the field. I bridge my reins, crossing them onto Bally's neck as he trots onto the springy grass, then stand up in my short stirrups as he lopes into a bouncy canter and we hack down to the bottom of the gallops. As we approach the bottom of the hill, I shorten my reins again because Bally is moving faster now, his hooves pounding as he anticipates the work he will do on the gallops.

He wants to eat the ground up. He wants to go. His breathing changes and he pushes his head forward, grasping the bit as he moves faster towards the line of white markers that indicate the furlongs of the gallops.

It's daylight on the Ridgeway as we approach the hill. Darkness has gone. And now I feel all of this powerful horse like a spring beneath me, so I stand up in my stirrups to lean over his neck. Bally jumps forward at the bottom of the gallop and new life is flickering inside me before the ground rushes forward and we're galloping, we're flying, we're going home.

ACKNOWLEDGEMENTS

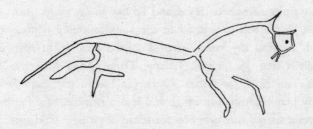

My memories of Mum and the strange circumstances of what happened to her in the accident were the reason I wanted to write this book. I am infinitely grateful to my brother Tom and sisters Emma, Sophy and Nell, for the time and the love we have shared, both before all this happened and since then. We travelled this journey together, but our paths were all different and this book is only my interpretation of what happened during that time.

Mum was looked after by some extraordinary nurses and I am forever grateful for the love and care they gave her, especially Kim, Mark and Hilary in Purton, and Sarah Farmer-Wright and Kate Reid in Norfolk.

I am really grateful to my agent Kirsty McLachlan who had the first sense of what my grief looked like and encouraged me to write about it. Her encouragement took me up onto the Ridgeway and helped me find a way back home too.

I'm also indebted to my editor Maddy Price, a source of ceaseless encouragement and support, and I am especially grateful for her early enthusiasm for the idea that was to become this book, and her careful editing throughout. Thank you so much. I'd also like to express my gratitude to the team at Hodder who have worked on the book, but especially Kerry Hood, Caitriona Horne and Auriol Bishop. Thank you to Sarah Young and Sara Marafini for the beautiful artwork on the cover.

While writing *The Wild Other* I've returned to my notebooks and diaries, but I'm indebted to Gillian Stern, who is a wise editor and great friend. Joanna Frank helped me a long time ago, when I was writing first about Texas, and I'd like to say thank you.

As a journalist I'm grateful to the commissioning editors who helped me find my voice when I started writing, in particular Geordie Grieg, Jo Craven, Tiffanie Darke, Anna Murphy, Tim Jepson, Tim Auld, Jon Stock, Catherine Fairweather, Sam Baker, Lindsay Frankel, Anna van Pragh and Jessica Brinton. Julia Perowne deserves a special mention too, for some inspiringly wild times.

I will always be grateful to Gareth Stone, Jessica Balkwill, Nicky Johnston and Lucy Rose Singh, who all played distinct and vital roles in helping Pete and I realise our sense of home in Baulking.

I would especially like to thank a handful of close friends who read early chapters and versions of my manuscript, in particular Antonia Quirke, Kirsten Foster, Toby Glanville, Mary Wakefield, Lorraine Hart, Tiffany Roy, Irene Molodtsov and especially Imogen Lycett Green and Clem Cecil. Thank you, too, to David Barabas, Brent Cauble, Vikki Bond, Paule Cifuentes Lopez and Arturo Blanco Alonso for wrangling the children when I was writing the pages.

I want to thank Ninia Ritchie for Texan Dreams, Etain McDaid for that night at Gaz's, to Abi Strevens, for so many wise words, to Mark and Sarah Bradstock, for the gallops, Isabel and Julian Bannerman for their wayward inspiration, and to Mark and Catherine Palmer, for many, many of the best times of my life.

I'm really grateful to Rupert Lycett Green. You and Candida have given Pete and me and our children so much.

I talk to my father, Rick Stroud, almost every day. I don't know if he knows how much these conversations mean to me, but they are vital. I'd like to thank him and my stepmother, Alexandra Pringle, for their infinite love and wisdom, and for the time we spend laughing.

Most of all, I want to tell Jimmy, Dolly, Evangeline, Dash and Lester that I love them all very much. You are my dreams.

And to Pete, for you, all that I am, always.

TEXT ACKNOWLEDGEMENTS

When a Knight Won His Spurs by Jan Struther is reproduced with permission of Curtis Brown Group Ltd, London on behalf of the beneficiaries of the Estate of Jan Struther. Copyright © Jane Struther 1940.

ABOUT THE AUTHOR

Clover Stroud is a writer and journalist writing for the *Daily Mail*, *Sunday Times*, *Daily Telegraph*, and *Conde Nast Traveller*, among others. She lives in Oxfordshire with her husband and five children.